19 - CUISINE DU TERROI

DIX-NEUF

CUISINE DU TERROIR CORRÉZIENNE

Malcolm Alder-Smith

ISBN
1 901253 43 0
First published November 2004

British Library Cataloguing in Publication Data.
A catalogue record for this book is
available from the British Library.

Published by
Leonie Press
13 Vale Road, Hartford
Northwich, Cheshire CW8 1PL
Great Britain
Tel: 01606 75660; fax 01606 77609
email: anne@leoniepress.com
websites: www.leoniepress.com

Printed by Anne Loader Publications
Illustrations by Patricia Kelsall
Collating and binding by Valley Binders, West Bollington
Cover lamination by The Finishing Touch, St Helens

*Author Malcolm Alder-Smith pictured on the steps of the family
chambres / table d'hôte, La Maison aux Quat'Saisons*

Dedicated to

My darling wife Twink and my brilliant kids:
Ash, Chris and Larnie.

Special Thanks to

The hotel and restaurant proprietors and chefs
of La Corrèze for sharing with me their secrets,
knowledge and culinary expertise.

and to

The Comité Départemental du Tourism de la Corrèze,
Comité Régional du Tourisme (Limoges),
Logis de France du Limousin and
Promenades Gourmandes.

and finally to

Anne and Jack Loader, for giving me the encouragement
to have sufficient belief in myself to write '19'.

INTRODUCTION
Une petite histoire

My very first experience of France was when I was just 13 years old. I had arrived home from school one dark December evening, when Mum and Dad announced that we were going on holiday for a month to spend Christmas in the Canary Islands. This was way back in 1963, so you don't have to be a rocket scientist to work out how old I am now! We were going to travel through France and Spain in Dad's smart two-tone grey Wolseley 6/99, catch a boat from Cadiz to Gran Canaria and spend Christmas in the sunshine; what a fantastic bunk off school !!!

I vaguely remember the family killing time in Dover on a wet, miserable and incredibly cold December night before catching, what looked like a very small car ferry to Dunkerque. When we got off on the other side of La Manche, we had to travel through thick, freezing fog for what seemed like ages; Dad had to drive with his head stuck out of the window to enable him to see where he was going. I am sure he had icicles hanging from his eyebrows when he eventually got his head back inside the car. Eventually the fog cleared and we headed south at a pace, passing through endless villages and towns that I had never heard of before and after only one brief night's stop in France we crossed into Spain via Perpignon. We stopped in Barcelona for one night, where Mum and Dad booked our passage to Gran Canaria, traveling with the very grand-sounding Trans Mediterranean Line.

The above journey was typical of every drive I ever took to Denia, Javea, Fuengirola or Miraflores over the next 30 years or so. "Get your boot on the floor, son, and get through France as quickly as you can – the food's bloody awful, everything is far too expensive and the French don't like us Brits at all". Well, Mum and my dearly departed Dad, how wrong you both were – on all counts!

In the late Eighties, just after 'Twink', my darling wife Diane, and I were married, we booked a short Easter vacation *en France*, staying at a delightful old stud farm called the Haras de la Potardière, a small *château* near La Flèche, not far from Saumur, and that was it folks -- we were totally hooked.

In the early Nineties we paid our first visit to Argentat in the Corrèze (Limousin), South West France, to stay with my old buddy Jim at his

1

newly acquired B+B, Le Pont de L'Hospital. Jim had been divorced recently, as had I, and he had decided to 'up-sticks' and go to live in a part of France which he had visited with his parents since his childhood. We were captivated by the scenery and greenery, the food, architecture, history, hospitality and most of all the people. We found the French, Dutch and Brits alike to be so kind, generous and helpful in every way and the food in the local hotels and restaurants was always fantastic. That first summer, Jim had to return to the UK for his daughter Charlie's birthday, and he asked us if we would run the 'Le Pont' for him for a few days while he was back in "dear old Blighty". I guess that we sort of decided there and then that this would eventually be the life for us.

I don't think a single year has gone by since when we haven't visited La Corrèze at least once (occasionally three times), and in 2001 we took what we then considered to be a calculated risk and purchased a fairly large *maison*, which we are (at the time of writing) converting into a *chambres d'hôte / table d'hôte*, which should be open by late Autumn 2004.

Malcolm Alder-Smith
April 2004

ABOUT THE BOOK

Several of my good 'catering buddies' have said that I would be shooting myself in the foot by writing a cook book based on just one French Department, instead of one on the whole region of Limousin. I have argued the point with them that the cooking of Corrèze, like the nearby Perigord, is steeped in hundreds of years of history and is totally unique in the Limousin Department and France itself. I have received a great deal of support from Corrézienne hotel and restaurant owners and chefs who were unbelievably happy that someone from outside France (especially a Brit), recognizes the uniqueness of what the Department has to offer in terms of culinary expertise.

There are many French people who have voiced their concerns that the old traditional cooking of the Department will die out over time, but I feel that this just will not happen. The Corréziennes are an intensely proud people and the old recipes hold pride of place at the table, be it at home, in a hotel or restaurant or in the local Salles de Fêtes for a wedding. Tradition *en Corrèze* will still hold true for tens, if not hundreds of years to come.

If you haven't guessed yet, the title of this book, '19', is taken from the French Department number for the Corrèze, where we live. We have always been more than inspired by the quality of the cuisine *en Corrèze*. As we have always said, the Department is unbelievably rural and full of character, and so is the food which is as unique as the local architecture and topography. The big thing with La Corrèze is that the land produces so many natural ingredients and the Department is famous for it (in France). This fact is maybe not so well known in the UK; it's a secret that has been well kept for generations. Our garden in Laborie, Monceaux-sur-Dordogne, which has about three acres of woodland, has 15 or more large and bountiful chestnut trees – and under the strict supervision of my dear friend and neighbour, Georges Fruitiere, we can pick four or five different varieties of edible mushrooms, including the locally prized *cèpes*.

This is also the kingdom of the *foie gras*, of *magrets de canard* and *confit* of goose or duck preserved in their own fat and of course the locally prized Blason Prestige veal. This part of the upper Dordogne Valley is undoubtedly one of the few remaining rural areas which has some of the best preserved culinary traditions. You will still find the older folk wearing berets and walking with canes; as the winter evenings draw in they sit in their armchairs beside the fire and shell walnuts and chestnuts – very prestigious crops in these parts. Traditional ingredients abound which end up in dishes that bring the aroma and taste of the whole Department to the table.

Veau elevé sous la mère, foie gras, confits, miel, the unique Moutarde Violette de Brive, *confiture,* deep purple red *cerises* for *Clafoutis, myrtilles, noix* such as walnuts, *châtaignes* and hazelnuts plus strawberries and *fraises du bois, champignons* such as *girolles (chanterelles), cèpes,* river fish and fabulous *fromages de chèvre...* These are but a few of the Corrézienne delights available to the band of creative chefs and their brigades who work their magic in hotel and restaurant kitchens across 'our' Department. We are so proud to live here and try, in our own kitchen, to emulate as best we can the culinary skills of generations – and personalities – past and present.

There are so many local specialities such as *Clafoutis aux cerises, La Flognarde, La Mique, Omelette aux Cèpes, Paupiettes de Veau, Cassoulet, Tourtous Corrézienne,* I could go on and on and on. The list is inexhaustible, but there is little to compare with the vision which will appear on your plate in local hotels and restaurants, which is only matched by the depth and range of textures, flavours and aromas produced by skilled hands from recipes passed down through numerous generations.

Somebody once said that "a dinner plate is a canvas" (was it Gary Rhodes?) and the chefs of La Corrèze certainly do know how to paint the most creative pictures. All this can be enjoyed in the many hotels and restaurants in the Department, from the inexpensive *fermes auberges'* offering simple local country cooking from *produits du terroir* often grown on site, to haute cuisine in some of the excellent hotels. You will not need a Michelin Guide here, and if you think that "I just have to eat somewhere with at least two Michelin stars" just to get a good meal, then you will be more than pleasantly surprised at the high quality of the food to be found at many of the excellent establishments in the department.

The wines available here tend to be, in the main, 'local'. Vin de Glanes, Cahors, Gaillac and Bergerac are prevalent on most wine lists, plus of course a good selection of Bordeaux. The more up-market hotel/restaurants stock some of the better quality Bordeaux. What you won't find is any evidence of New World Wines: Australia, New Zealand, America,

South Africa, and Chile etc., which are frowned on big time and are not deemed as being suitable to accompany the local food produced in this unique area of rural France. The French are certainly patriotic in the extreme and have every right to be so, just look at the cars they drive (mainly French), and if they can sell their own home-grown produce over and above that from another country, then so be it.

When I decided to write this book, I knew that I was fulfilling an ambition that I had held for about the last 15 years. I wanted to combine my own extensive knowledge of cooking from my life's work in the hospitality and catering industry along with that of the outstanding chefs and the owners of restaurants and hotels in the Corrèze, to produce a cookbook which I hope is somewhat different from others currently available in the UK.

The aim of this book is to inspire you to try some of these prized dishes in your own kitchen and even more so, to encourage you to visit the historic Corrèze – *bon courage, mes amis*.

How to find us
at
La Maison aux Quat'Saisons

Driving south from the beautiful city of Chartres (which has one of the best cathedrals in France) to Orléans, take the new ring-road around Châteauroux. Continue on down to Limoges and on to La Corrèze heading south, then drift away from the A20 after you have passed the Porte de Corrèze services and head for Tulle at Junction 45 or Brive-la-Gaillard at Junction 50 or 51. If you prefer to indulge in a little shopping in an historic big town environment, there are some fabulous hotels, restaurants and shops to be found in Brive, or if you prefer a more rural setting, maybe one of the numerous *chambres d'hôte, tables d'hôte* or *fermes auberges* would best suit your pocket. Take the N120 south towards Argentat-sur-Dordogne and make La Maison your base to investigate the gastronomic treasures of the Department which is blessed with some outstanding eateries.

There are numerous internationally celebrated visitor attractions within easy driving distance of Argentat: Collonges la Rouge, Le Gouffre de Padirac (fantastic!) and Rocamadour to name but a few. But whatever you do, when you visit, don't forget that it is compulsory for you to take at least two hours for your lunch break !!!

Our *chambres / table d'hôte*, La Maison aux Quat'Saisons, is located in the beautiful picturesque commune of Monceaux-sur-Dordogne in the tiny hamlet of Laborie.

Driving north, south, east or west, Argentat (the main town) is ideally situated, so why not stop over for a week or more and take in the Dordogne air and fabulous scenery. The historic Quai, market and unique architecture are a must and compliment the established attractions previously mentioned.

This part of the Dordogne Valley is not as hectic as you may find further to the west, it is for the people who love the peace and tranquility of rural France. The scenery is stunning and everyone here will give you such a warm and friendly welcome.

If sporting and leisure activities are more your thing, the area offers canoeing down the Dordogne, mountain biking, horse riding, indoor and outdoor tennis, an outdoor swimming pool and more, plus of course some fabulous restaurants.

The bedrooms at La Maison are named and decorated to reflect the four seasons of the year – Printemps, Été, Automne and Hiver – hence **La Maison aux Quat'Saisons!!!**

LA MAISON AUX QUAT'SAISONS

LABORIE
19400 MONCEAUX-SUR-DORDOGNE
CORRÈZE

ABOUT ME

I was born in Overwallop, near Salisbury, in 1949 and trained as a chef and hotel manager at Highbury College in the mid-Sixties.

I can only ever remember cooking and catering when I was growing up. My mum and dad bought a guest house on the Isle of Wight when I was three and moved to a much bigger house two years later, which they developed into a 40-bedroom three-star hotel and ran for more than 30 years.

Because my big sister and I (she's only five foot nothing, but a year older than me) were pretty well left to our own devices as kids, as Mum and Dad were far too busy with the hotel to spend much time with us, I used to dabble in the kitchen as often as I could.

I was never the brightest button in the box at my private school and left at the tender age of 15 to do a pre-catering course at our local second-ary modern school. At that time, there was no catering department at the local college on the Isle of Wight, where we lived, so catering students had to go to Highbury College, Portsmouth to study. My only way to study there was by doing this preliminary course, which I thoroughly enjoyed.

Lecturers crossed the Solent coming over from the UK mainland one day per week to guide us along our way and introduce us to dishes with mys-terious names and ingredients, which were an exciting challenge for us to prepare and cook. One such lecturer was Eddie Burnett, a massive man who amused us all by taking maybe more sugar in his cup than tea. Eddie was a larder chef and taught me a great deal when we all eventu-ally got over to the big college on the mainland.

I spent three happy years at Highbury and although I was prone to mess about a bit, I still learnt an awful lot in the time I was there which has stood me in good stead into my fifties. We were taught by what we, as 16- year-olds, considered to be very, very strict lecturers, mostly French, Swiss and Italian. The very mention of names like Len Nice, Harry Ferrioli and Bill Land brought fear and trepidation to each and every one of us. There were of course the 'nice' lecturers such as Alan Williamson, Jeff

Hall and Freddie Watts who were 'the young ones' in those days, but nevertheless, very talented and they taught us some fantastic skills.

I was employed in hotel management until 1978, when I bought my own restaurant, before taking up employment as a college lecturer in hospitality and catering in 1983.

My wife, Twink, and I have worked for a number of well-known catering companies and have memorable experiences of working in hospitality management during the late Eighties and Nineties for Ring & Brymer and Forte in the City of London. We also worked in corporate hospitality management for Gardner Merchant and Sodexho at the Open Golf, Wimbledon, Chelsea Flower Show and the Farnborough Air Show.

We also had the honour of working at various royal palaces. However, I guess that our most memorable and enjoyable experiences were spent as part of the corporate hospitality management team for Rolls-Royce at the Paris International Air Show at Le Bourget in 1991 and 1993.

Working at numerous prestigious events over the years, we have looked after the most senior members of the British Royal Family, heads of British Government and Foreign Heads of State.

I spent a number of years teaching Wine & Spirit Education courses at the Isle of Wight College on behalf of the Wine & Spirit Education Trust, hence the inclusion of, I hope, some helpful wine suggestions with many of the recipes.

Twink and I both love cooking and also experimenting with different types of food and recipes in our kitchens in England and France. We enjoy creating new dishes and I have included a number of these in this book. Although some are not strictly Corrézienne by definition, the prime ingredients are, so I feel that there is sufficient justification to include them, plus the fact that it may encourage you to come and stay at La Maison aux Quat'Saisons and try some of the dishes in this book for yourself.

When in France, our French friends and neighbours are rather amused by the fact that I do tend to do quite a bit of the cooking in our house. Traditionally the women of the Department reign over the kitchen, the men decided many years ago that this was an art best left to the women folk. However, many of the recipes in this book have been passed on to us by hotel/restaurant owners and chefs, men and women alike, who just want to see the age-old traditions of Corrézienne cuisine kept alive. I hope that I can make a small contribution to their wishes by raising the profile of what the Department of Corrèze has to offer.

VEGETARIANS

The country folk of La Corrèze, in general, find the idea of vegetarianism quite amusing – however, our good friend Susie Scott who has lived in the Department for over 25 years kindly sent me a copy of "Promenades Gourmandes – Corrèze 2003" and I was more than a little surprised to see that the Auberge de St-Julien-aux-Bois, run by a German couple Doris Coppenrath and Roland Pilger, actually have a vegetarian menu priced at 15 euros (at the time of writing). As they are only about half an hour from *chez-nous*, we will definitely be heading in their direction in the near future to sample their 'normal' menus which range from 13 euros up to 39, plus of course 'la carte'.

INGREDIENTS

It would be really difficult to give you a definitive list of ingredients which you could keep in your kitchen as a number of them would definitely be difficult to get hold of in the UK. There are, no doubt, quite a number which you already have to hand, but to produce the authentic flavours you may need to expand your larder – just a little! You will be able to get most ingredients from your local supermarket – however, some of the truly authentic ones can only be purchased in the Corrèze and so you will either have to visit or find an alternative substitute.

What you will need to do is to find yourself a good butcher and fishmonger, both of which are becoming increasingly difficult – but not impossible – to locate in these supermarket days. I will try to guide you down the right road for ingredients for your larder, but the big secret about many of the recipes is that you need to use the freshest ingredients you can get your hands on and you will have to select these yourself.

The rural French, in general, do not 'do' spicy food. What you will be cooking will give you clean, fresh, natural flavours, brought out by using the freshest of ingredients. They do not have to cost an arm and a leg, but the fresher the better to get a true authentic flavour to your dishes.

In the UK, we are, I guess, fairly lucky that we can pop down to our local Tesco or Sainsburys and buy most anything food-wise that we want. Unfortunately, we Brits are generally denied the accessibility (or in some cases availability) in these stores to the guidance, expertise and knowledge that was traditionally offered to us by our high street butcher and fishmonger. We live inland in South West France, about one hundred and forty miles or so from Bordeaux, yet we tend to be spoilt by the wondrous selection of fresh fish and crustacea from our supermarkets and the bi-weekly open market when a massive refrigerated trailer arrives to fight off the queues of kindly country folk. If I want to buy some beef to make Boeuf Bourguignonne, I am guided by the knowledge and expertise of one of the butchers behind the counter, who will not only tell me which is the right cut and the best quality, but will also guide me on the quantity I should be buying for the amount of people we are entertaining.

The local outdoor market (every first and third Thursday) has that extra buzz in the summer, when the Dutch, Belgian and British tourists have arrived. The market stalls filter off down side streets meandering away from the Place de Marché in the general direction of the River Dordogne. We could literally stock our fridge for a week or more if we wanted, with local cheeses, poultry, fish, shellfish, fruit, vegetables, fabulous pink bulbs of garlic and much, much more. The market is a meeting place for the old and young alike, where the town and its surrounding villages and hamlets join together every couple of weeks, to chat, socialise and maybe do a little business.

ABOUT LA CORRÈZE AND GASTRONOMY

La Corrèze has to be one of the most beautiful and unspoiled Departments in France. It is generally referred to as being situated in Central France because it is a department of the Limousin region, but personally I like to think that we are located more in South West France. Ask anyone who lives there and many will proudly announce that they live in *"le sud-ouest"*, and quite rightly so!

The Department is split down into six different areas or regions:

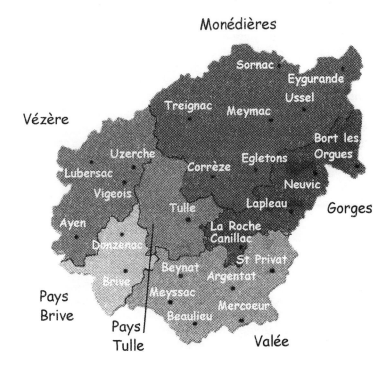

Monédières

Vézère

Sornac

Eygurande

Ussel

Treignac   Meymac

Bort les Orgues

Uzerche   Egletons

Corrèze

Lubersac

Neuvic

Vigeois

Tulle   Lapleau   Gorges

Ayen   La Roche Canillac

Donzenac

St Privat

Beynat   Argentat

Brive

Meyssac

Pays Brive   Mercoeur

Beaulieu

Pays Tulle   Valée

Le Pays de Tulle

It has to be said that Tulle itself is not the prettiest Department capital in France, but the old town which is divided down the middle by the river Corrèze can be very interesting if you are prepared to tread a little shoe leather. There is a good range of shops there, including some of the usual hypermarkets and of course a McDonalds. In the early days, when driving down to Argentat, we always said that once we had reached Tulle and turned off onto the N120 heading south towards Argentat itself, that everything would be green, no matter what time of year we were visiting. The very hot, dry summer of 2003 has been the only time that I have remotely changed this image in my mind. This is farming country, with fields criss-crossed by numerous hedges, trees and thousands of fence posts; it is deeply verdant with some beautiful waterfalls and thousands of trees producing kilo upon kilo of cherries, chestnuts and walnuts.

Le Pays de Brive

The old town of Brive is very pretty. Our good friend Jim always describes it, geographically, as a cart-wheel and for good reason. Slap-dab in the centre of the old town is the church, the hub, with a road running all of the way around it. From this miniature ring-road, there are numerous other roads (spokes) heading off in different directions towards the 'proper' ring road (of the old town) and each of these 'spokes' is a delight to explore, as there are many interesting shops and of course lots of café-bars and restaurants waiting to be visited. Brive does have some outstanding eateries such as La Cremaillere, to name but one, at 53, avenue de Paris.

La Vallée de la Dordogne

What can I say folks – this is us, this is where we have set our hats and if I were to die here I guess I will be quite happy to do so. Since we brought our *maison*, I have always said to my darling Twink that when I 'pop my clogs' she must scatter my ashes from the Brievzac Bridge, because as the Dordogne meanders down towards Bordeaux and the west coast, I guess that I would get my final chance to visit nearly every vineyard of high global repute that I have ever dreamed of visiting, and sample the very best Cabernet Sauvignon and Merlot on this, our planet Earth.

Le Pays de la Vézère

This is an area which we have not visited a great deal. In the 'old days' before the A20 autoroute cut a swathe through central and southern France, the route south or north took us through the old town of Uzerche, which has the most beautiful bridge, totally bedecked with flowers for the majority of the summer months. The town, I think, has had to take a step backwards since the autoroute opened, but it is definitely worth a visit as it is an area of contrast and colours.

Les Monédières

We have yet to spend any leisure time in this area which offers vast granite plateaux, extensive forests and moors, fishing, rambling, hiking and walking, so if you are into the outdoor life, this is somewhere which you will find interesting.

Les Gorges de la Dordogne

If we want to take a picnic lunch, we pack the car and head off into the hills of this picturesque area of high plateaux, massive hydro-electric dams, fauna and flora, fishing and boat trips in replica *gabares* (river barges)

LES QUAT'SAISONS

We have named our maison in France La Maison aux Quat'Saisons, partly because each and every season *en Corrèze* offers its own exciting recipes and I will try to give you a flavour of each season and what you might expect to eat during *les quat'saisons en Corrèze.*

L'automne: the wet leaves fall in resplendent colour making the roads slippery under the treads of your tyres and the winds blow gently up through the Dordogne valley from the west. When we return home from the open air market to the warmth of our *pôele* (wood-burning stove), burning mighty lengths of ash or oak to keep us warm, we sit and eat steaming bowls of peasant soup accompanied by chunks of *pain: la soupe à l'oignon, potée* or my own cabbage soup braised slowly in home-made chicken stock with onion, garlic and lardons of smoked bacon.

L'hiver: the first flakes of snow often arrive around Christmas time, and the nearest skiing is only an hour or so away by car at Aurillac, but we haven't braved it yet. Our son Ashley, has played in the snow with his friends, apparently oblivious to the cold. *"À table!"* we shout from the kitchen steps, "It's time to come back in and eat some good hot food." Soup again, but more substantial now. *Potage aux legumes*, or our version of the classic *Cassoulet*, which we enhance with huge chunks of potato and carrot to produce a one-pot dish 'with style', which has to be our ultimate anti-freeze. My own version of *Boeuf Bourguignonne* which often takes well over a day to prepare and cook (if time allows), is another dish which suits the time of year, and the end result brings gastronomic delight beyond the reach of the most critical gourmand.

Le printemps: spring arrives early in our part of France, the flowers are in bud and life is reborn. It is not unusual to get nice warm days of sunshine even in mid-February and by March the daffodils bordering each side of our driveway will be in full bloom, along with the tulips by the front steps, both competing for the most vibrant colour in the garden. It's time to change our daily life and our recipes. Pigeons with peas, roasted veal, kidneys cooked with the distinctive Moutarde Violet de Brive and Cahors red wine dished up with some steamed turned potatoes and braised leeks.

L'été: summer is here and we welcome the return of the intense aromas and scents of fruit on the trees in our garden. In June the large juicy black cherries are abundant on our trees and will finish up in the Corréziene classic *Clafoutis*, along with a good dash of *l'eau-de-vie* given to me by my neighbour Georges.

Enhanced by the scorching heat, which can turn the fields a golden brown, there is a slightly pungent smell, almost oppressive on the air, because laden with dust, haymaking has started. The locals help each other out and even the smallest patch of hay is cut, turned and baled in no time to avoid the thunderous storms and heavy rain which can appear from nowhere and with little notice in this part of la Belle France.

We sometimes cook *Paupiettes de Veau* if we are partying, or we eat voluminous salads at lunchtime, dressed with our favorite raspberry vinaigrette with home made *pâté*, cured ham and *saucissons*, followed by some local cheese such as Cantal Entre-Deux and Auvergne Bleu, finishing our meal with *fraises du bois* from Beaulieu-sur-Dordogne.

No, my dear friends, none of the above is an indulgence in any shape or form, just everyday life *en Corrèze* and I am happy to have the opportunity to share some of its delights with you.

LE PONT DE L'HOSPITAL

Jim and Fi's beautifully located riverside hotel, just outside Argentat.

BIG BIG THANKS

I couldn't possibly have written this book without saying some special "thank yous" to some exceptional friends.

Our move to France would never have happened, and therefore our love affair with La Corrèze would not have evolved, if it weren't for two of our best buddies: Jim Mallows and his wife Fiona. They have done so much to help us during the last few years and have been a constant source of knowledge, inspiration and support in all that we have done. When we brought La Maison and used to visit frequently. Jim pointed us in the right direction, but often refused to pull the trigger, telling us to muddle through ourselves "the French way" and sent me off to sort out my own problems. *"Good on you, Jimbo."*

Jim's wife Fi has sewn curtains for us (how she found the time I don't know), given us endless good advice, told us where to shop for this and that and has cooked us some wonderful meals - *"You're a darlin', Fi Bob!"*

Susie, Jim's sister, has lived *en Corrèze* for nearly thirty years with her amazing husband Gillie (famous locally for his jazz band). She is the linguist, organizer and trusted friend and has to be the most knowledgeable 'Brit' in town. She has put me straight on my use of accents (I think!) and other scripted cock-ups! *"Thanks a million, Susie."*

Our dear friends Roger Déjammes and Edwige Laage used to run Chez Roger at 2, Place Josephe Faure, Argentat, which was one of our favourite watering holes in our 'early days' visits to Argentat. Edwige and Roger's mother, Pierrette Déjammes, have donated a number of *recettes du terroir* to this book for which I thank them. Roger and Edwige sold their business early in 2003 and now live in a beautifully renovated house on the historic Quai de Lestourgie in Argentat sur Dordogne, while the flamboyant Roger carries on his trade as a *négociant du vin* (wine merchant). *"À la tienne, mes amis."*

I could not possibly mention Roger and Edwige without also saying a big, big thank you to our good friends Michel and Isabelle Roussanne who, at the time of writing, own and run the Auberge des Gabariers at 15 Quai de Lestourgie. Their beautiful restaurant is situated only metres away from the River Dordogne and was, I guess, a big part of the inspiration for me writing this book. Isabelle, who worked in the States for a while, answered my plea for traditional Corrézienne recipes by sending me so many it was difficult to decide which ones to use. *"Big, big hugs and kisses to you both!"*

I thank you all, my dear friends, from the bottom of my heart.

Merci bien, mes amis.

CONTENTS

SOUPES - soups - p24

MIQUES - dumplings - p46

ENTRÉES - starters - p51

POISSONS – fish – p81

Cassoulette de Saumon aux Giroles en Surprise	83	Individual Salmon Cassolettes
Escalope de Sandre Rôti au Lard	85	Roast Escalope of Perch with Bacon
Filet de Saumon aux Fines Herbes	87	Fillet of Salmon with a Herb Cream
Filet de Saumon aux Poireaux	89	Fillet of Salmon on a Bed of Shredded Leek
Filet de Truite Citron Verte et Câpre	91	Trout Fillet with a Lime and Caper Sauce
Filet de Truite Saumonée Sauce Safran	92	Fillet of Salmon Trout with a Saffron Sauce
Sandre aux Poireaux	95	Perch on a Bed of Leeks
Tourte au Saumon et aux Champignons	97	Salmon and Mushroom Tart
Truite aux Girolles, Beurre Citronné	99	Trout with Girolles and Lemon Butter
Truite Farcis aux Miel	102	Trout Stuffed with Mushrooms and Honey
Truite Saumonée Poché	104	Poached Salmon Trout with a Lime & Dill Mayonnaise

VIANDES – meat – p106

Blanquette de Veau Fermier à l'Ancienne	109	Veal Stew in the traditional Limousin Style
Boeuf à la Bourguignonne	111	Beef Bourguignonne
Carré de Porc à la Limousine	114	Loin of Pork – Limousin Style
Cassoulet # 1	116	Pork and Sausage Casserole
Cassoulet # 2	119	Casserole with Pork, Duck and Sausages
Chou Farci	121	Stuffed Cabbage
Côtelette de Porc aux Moutardes	123	Pork chops with a Grain Mustard Cream Sauce
Échine de Porc en Marinade	125	Marinaded Loin of Pork
Épaule d'Agneau Confite à l'Ail	127	Shoulder of Lamb with a Garlic Compote
Farcidure	128	Potato Cake
Farce	129	Stuffing
Gigot d'Agneau Fermier	130	Leg of Lamb – Farmer's Style
Navarin d'Agneau au Printanier	132	Brown Lamb Stew – Spring Style
Poêlée de Ris de Veau de Lait Fermier aux Cèpes de la Région	134	Veal Sweetbreads with local Cèpes
Pot-au-Feu Corrézienne ou "Farcun"	136	Slow Cooked Beef Stew
Queue de Boeuf à la Moelle	138	Oxtail with its Beef Marrow
Queue de Boeuf Braisée	140	Braised Oxtail
Ris de Veau Limousine	142	Calves Sweet-bread – Limousin Style
Rognons Sautés aux Moutarde de Violette de Brive	145	Lamb's Kidneys in a Moutarde de Violette de Brive Sauce
Rôti de Porc à la Boulangère	149	Roast Leg of Pork – Baker's Style

21

DESSERTS - desserts - p225

SOUPES
soups

Just take a look at the shelves at your local supermarket in the UK; they are stacked high with all sorts of soups, broths, purées, consommés, tinned, packet, dried, powdered, cup-a-soup etc, etc – we Brits just love the stuff. Be it thick or thin, winter or summer, we indulge ourselves in cups and bowls of tasty Heinz, Campbell's, Knorr or whatever takes our fancy. In the UK, I guess we are blessed with having some very well produced manufactured soups which cut out all the hard work for your average punter. There are a number of companies out there in 'business land', i.e. The New Covent Garden Soup Company or The Soup Ladle, which make 'fresh' or 'home made' soups, and all you have to do is bang a tub into the microwave, 'nuke' it for a couple of minutes and hey-presto – gastro' delight. The thing is, and what really bugs me, is that soups have to be one of the easiest dishes to make in the whole wide world, yet we Brits always go for the soft option and it really is a 'lose – lose' situation, because at the end of the day, *mes amis,* there really is no substitute for the real thing.

If you are making fresh soup here in the UK, I guess that you will usually use one or two stock cubes to give the dish added flavour. I am sure that you will note that with one or two of the recipes that I have included I use milk or water – both natural ingredients, with the wonderful subtle flavours coming from the freshest of vegetables used as the base for the soup. I see one of the problems in the UK being that the majority of our vegetables are grown to supermarket specification and you really do have to go out hunting to find the real thing. This is fine if you live in the country, but as we know, the majority of the population lives in towns and cities and maybe cannot access what I would call the tastiest of products that easily.

En Corrèze we are fortunate to have a diverse selection of quality local produce – we can buy half a dozen different types of onion, and massive pink garlic bulbs from Lautrec further south between Albi and Castres in the Tarn. The leeks and celery have the most intense aroma and they smell as though they have just been picked – I am truly in seventh heaven just walking around the 'veggie' stalls of our local outdoor market or supermarkets, be it Super U or Inter Marché, which are just a five minute drive from *chez nous*. As a small boy my dad often told me about the peat-grown celery which his mum used to buy from the market stalls of Oldham or Rochdale in Lancashire. I was lucky enough to watch my grandmother prepare soups and stews using this type of celery and I remember that it had the same sort of intense aroma as that which we now buy in France.

The soups (and stews) of Corrèze were, and still are, often made from a variety of fresh vegetables, especially with beans, potatoes, cabbage and leeks. In the old days soups were often cooked for two or three hours in a large pot *(marmite)* suspended on a rack or chain from a hook over the open flames of the fire from the traditional *cantou* fireplace. These are usually constructed in granite and are about 8-10 feet wide, with a massive oak beam over the top.

Soups of the other two Departments of Limousin (Creuse, Department 23 and Haute-Vienne, Department 87) will be a tad different; you may find that vegetables and onions are browned in goose or duck fat in a deep frying pan, the water or stock is then added and after cooking the ingredients, they are made *la bréjaude,* which means that the veggies are crushed with a fork. I guess that the easiest way to get a similar result is to semi-whizz them with your domestic hand blitzer, which will alter the consistency of the soup to a semi-*purée* but leaves some 'lumpy' vegetables to give an alternative texture.

Another local tradition for anyone who can manage 'seconds', is basically adding a glass of red wine to the remainder of the soup in the pan and leaving it on the stove to simmer gently for a few minutes – this is known as *chabrol* or *faire chabrol.*

LA POTÉE LIMOUSINE
thin soup with pork, ham and vegetables

In the old days an enormous traditional *cantou* fireplace was, and still tends to be, the dominating feature in the household during the cold winter months *en Corrèze*. The traditional design of Corrézienne houses often incorporated one large room, which included a corner kitchen, dining area and seating area near the *cantou*, which was naturally used for heat and more importantly for cooking. You will still occasionally find, in antique shops or a *dépôt vente*, *banquettes*, wooden seats which were placed inside the *cantou* on either side of the fire. Husband would sit one side and wife the other, to keep out the winter chill.

Black cauldron-style pots would be suspended by hooks and chains from vast oak beams, allowing soups and stews alike to cook slowly over glowing embers.

Potée is a classic dish of the Limousin region, and people tend to use up their dried bread by putting slices into their soup bowls and pouring the hot broth over the top.

Recipe idea provided by Michel Fouillade
11, place Gambetta – 19400 Argentat

Preparation time: 30 minutes
Cooking time: 160 minutes

Ingredients for 6 people

- *500 g joint of pork (demi-sel)*
- *500 g breast bacon (petit salé)*
- *6 Toulouse sausages (or andouille de viande)*
- *1 calf's foot*
- *2 medium onions – thinly sliced*
- *4 carrots*
- *3 turnips*
- *6 waxy potatoes*
- *1 Savoy cabbage*
- *1 onion stuck with 2 cloves*
- *6 cloves of garlic*
- *4 bay leaves*

- *1 sprig of thyme and rosemary*
- *1 bouquet garni*
- *chicken broth (stock)*

Peel the root vegetables, cut them into approximately 6 cm lengths and turn them into barrel shapes.

Place the joints of meat into a large container, cover with cold water and soak for at least 2 hours or more, depending on how salty the meat is. Prick the sausages and place them into a *faitout* (a large stew pot), with a little duck fat. Place the pan over a medium flame and cook for around 10 minutes, colouring on all sides. Remove the sausages and set them to one side. Pour off any excess fat from the bottom of the pan.

Return the cooking pot to the stove, add the joints of pork and bacon, the calf's foot, sausages, onion and garlic then cover well with cold water and slowly bring to the boil. Using a ladle, skim off any deposits which rise to the surface, reduce the heat to low and allow to simmer very slowly.

After about an hour and a half, add the turned carrots, turnips, *bouquet garni*, a dozen pepper corns, the onion and the cabbage (previously blanched in boiling water for 5 minutes). Continue to simmer for a further 30 minutes, and then add the turned potatoes. Complete the cooking for another 45 minutes or until the potatoes are just cooked.

Arrange the cooked meat and vegetables on a large oval meat plate and keep hot in a pre-heated oven, ready for the main course.

Pour the *bouillon* into a large soup tureen over thick slices of *pain bis* (a fairly dry, flat, round country bread, not available in UK, so use slices of baguette).

My secret: The soup has to be served piping hot. The meat and veg' just has to be served after the soup, accompanied by a pot of Orélia Moutarde de Dijon - *"forte et onctueuse"*. My neighbours think I'm *fou* (crazy), but the mustard goes a mega treat with the pork and sausages (I guess that much of the Brit in me still remains!).

Wine: Go for a fairly light red or rich white. Try a lightweight Côtes de Marmandais from the South West or why not have a bash at a Côtes de Frontonnais a little further to the East, sometimes called the "Beaujolais of Toulouse"

LA SOUPE DE CHÂTAIGNES
chestnut soup

"If chestnuts were missing, France would be ruined" used to be a popular saying in Limousin in bygone days.

Next time you are in your local supermarket (especially around Christmas time), take a look at the cans of chestnuts or chestnut *purée* on the shelves to see where they came from. I would not be too surprised if you found the word Limousin or Corrèze on the label of origin – the region is famous for them.

Now for a little history lesson – *"Since the middle ages, the chestnut has provided the people of Limousin with a great source of nourishment, up to around the middle of the 19th century when the potato arrived. Chestnuts were considered to be as nutritious as meat and were also dried and ground into flour for bread making. The quarter-master, Turgot, worked hard to introduce the potato as a substitute for chestnuts to combat the frequent food shortages."*

This recipe is a little gem sent to us by our good friend Edwige Laage.

Recipe by Gilles Dudognon

Preparation time: 15 minutes
Cooking time: 60 minutes (approx)

Ingredients for 4 – 6 people

- *500 g of blanched and peeled chestnuts*
- *1 stick of celery cut into four pieces*
- *1 onion stuck with one clove*
- *1½ - 2 litres of milk*
- *1 egg yolk*
- *salt and pepper*

Preparation

Put the blanched and peeled chestnuts in a saucepan (retaining half a dozen), with the celery and *oignon piqué*. Moisten with 1 litre of milk and bring to the boil. Reduce the heat and cook for 30 minutes over a medium flame, stirring from time to time.

Remove the celery and onion and blitz the chestnuts until smooth. Add more cold milk until the mix reaches a velvety texture (*velouté*). Season to taste with salt and pepper and reheat.

Pour one or two ladles of soup into a bowl and thoroughly mix in the egg yolk. Don't be tempted to put the egg straight into the saucepan or you will finish up with scrambled egg!! Whisk this mixture back into the soup to add richness and to slightly thicken. Roughly chop the remaining blanched chestnuts and sprinkle them evenly between the soup bowls. Pour the soup over and serve with your favourite crusty bread. (You may want to finish the soup off with a little cream.)

Le secret de Gilles Dudognon: Accompany the soup with some freshly cooked croutons fried in butter.

MINESTRONE D'ÉTÉ
summer minestrone

Don't tell me – I know already – Minestrone is Italian, but 'Minestrone' is the best way I could possibly describe this dish, not having found another name more suitable for it.

Back home, in dear old Blighty, go out and buy almost any brand of pre-prepared Minestrone soup and you will generally finish up with a semi-thickened tomato soup with chopped vegetables and some spaghetti in your bowl. Usually quite tasty, I guess, but to my taste, sometimes with a bit of a question mark hanging over it.

I think that this recipe takes Minestrone to a new level and I hope that you will find that the end result is better than any that you have tasted before. It is intended to be fairly lightweight with bags of flavour. I know it's called Summer Minestrone, but naturally it is great at any time of year and I never have much difficulty in ploughing through more than one bowl full with some crisp country bread, heavily spread with some French Président butter.

Recipe by Malcolm Alder-Smith
La Maison aux Quat'Saisons, Laborie, 19400 Monceaux-sur-Dordogne

Preparation time: 30 minutes
Cooking time: 60 minutes

Ingredients for 4-6 people

- *250 g onions – peeled and chopped*
- *250 g carrots – peeled and finely chopped*
- *3 good sticks of celery – finely chopped*
- *1 medium sized leek – finely chopped*
- *¼ savoy cabbage – shredded*
- *2 large cloves of garlic*
- *1 tin of cannelli beans*
- *25 g spaghetti*
- *1 x 400 g tin of chopped tomatoes*
- *2 soup spoons of tomato purée*
- *125 ml medium dry white wine*
- *1.5 lt vegetable bouillon*

- *bouquet garni*
- *unsalted butter, olive oil*
- *a good handful of chopped flat leaf parsley*
- *salt and black pepper*
- *small baguette*
- *grated Gruyère cheese*

Preparation

Take a large heavy-bottomed saucepan and place over a medium flame. Add a couple of slugs of good olive oil and around 25 g of butter. Once the butter has melted and the bubbles start to subside, slightly reduce the heat and add the chopped onion, carrot, celery and leek, cover with a lid and cook for around 5 minutes without colour. Remove the lid and add the tomato *purée* and stir well; cook for a further 2 minutes, then add the tin of chopped tomatoes. Add 1 lt of the hot vegetable stock, stir well, add the *bouquet garni*, cover with a lid and simmer for around 45 minutes.

Make a *persillade*. Take the garlic and flat leaf parsley and place them onto a chopping board. Sprinkle with a little salt and finely chop until the mixture starts to resemble a paste.

Remove the lid and take out the *bouquet garni*. Add the cannelli beans (with the juice), dry white wine, spaghetti and the shredded cabbage. Add the *persillade* little by little, stirring all the time, this will give the broth lots of fresh herb and garlic flavour. Simmer for around another 15 minutes.

While the soup finishes off cooking, cut the baguette on an angle into 5 mm thick slices. Allow a couple of slices per person. Place onto a metal tray, brush with melted butter and toast one side under a medium grill so they turn a light golden brown, remove the tray, turn the slices over and sprinkle with the grated cheese. Pop the tray back under the grill and while the cheese is melting, ladle the broth into some heated soup bowls. Float a couple of the 'toasties' on the top of each bowl of soup, sprinkle with the chopped parsley and serve piping hot. The cheese can become quite runny, so warn any unsuspecting guests.

My secret: The soup has to be served piping hot and I do prefer to use fresh tomatoes rather than tinned. Take around six good red tomatoes and they just need to be blanched, skinned, de-seeded and chopped.

MOURTAIROL
chicken and saffron soup

This is a soup which you would expect to find to the south of the Corrèze and even more so in the Quercy Department of the Lot. It is one of the dishes with which you may find *fars* or *miques* (types of dumplings) from the Corrèze, served as an accompaniment to the meat and vegetables for the main course.

Mourtairol is a chicken soup which is coloured and perfumed with saffron and is typical of the 'waste nothing' approach of the country folk of the Department. There are many French 'soup' classics which involve drinking the liquid from a bowl as the soup course and then producing a hearty meal with the meat or fish and vegetable ingredients to follow.

Preparation time: 30 minutes
Cooking time: 180 minutes

Ingredients for 4 – 6 people

- *1 good sized chicken*
- *1 piece of blade beef (300 g)*
- *6 medium sized carrots*
- *6 nice small turnips*
- *3 leeks*
- *3 large potatoes*
- *3 sticks of celery*
- *1 bouquet garni (leek, thyme, bay leaf and parsley stalks)*
- *1 onion*
- *1 good pinch of saffron*
- *salt and black pepper*
- *12 thin slices of flat round country bread*

Preparation

Truss the chicken with butcher's string and place in a large saucepan along with the blade of beef and cover with cold water. Peel all the vegetables and chop them into good-sized chunks. Trim and split the leeks down the middle, leaving the stalk intact, then wash them thoroughly, fold over and tie up, by folding each in half lengthways and tying with some kitchen string. Add the vegetables with the onion and *bouquet garni* to the saucepan, and bring to the boil. Reduce to a simmer and add enough saffron to colour the liquid and to give the dish its unique flavour. Cook very slowly over a low heat for around three hours.

Place the slices of bread in a large soup tureen and pour over the stock. Place the tureen into a low oven for around 30 minutes and top up with a little stock if needed.

The steaming hot soup is ready to serve, so place the tureen in the middle of the table and let everyone help themselves.

The soup is followed by eating the chicken and beef, surrounded by the vegetables, served on a large platter as the main course.

SOUPE À L'OSEILLE À LA CRÈME
creamy sorrel soup

Sorrel is something that you will not easily find in your average super-market here in the UK, so you will have to do some local research to find a supplier.

The first time I used sorrel in a soup was back in the early Nineties, after Twink and I had first visited our friend Jim in Argentat. We took a day out and drove south to Cahors (famous for that twin turreted bridge and its wine – of course!). On the way back, we stopped at a large commercial *cave* to have a little *dégustation*, and while we were there, we purchased a book called 'Recipes from Quercy', by Claudine Duluat and Jeanine Pouget.

The book had a fabulous recipe for Soupe aux Haricots Frais et Oseille, a fresh bean and sorrel soup, which we liked the look of, tried, and were totally impressed with. I would have loved to have included that recipe in my book, but unfortunately, the publishers refused to allow me to repro-duce any of their recipes. Ah well, *c'est la vie!*

Recipe by Malcolm Alder-Smith
La Maison aux Quat'Saisons, Laborie, 19400 Monceaux-sur-Dordogne

Preparation time:	20 minutes
Cooking time:	60 minutes

Ingredients for 6 people

- *300 g sorrel leaves*
- *500 g potatoes*
- *1 medium onion*
- *2 shallots*
- *2 small cloves of garlic*
- *50 g duck fat*
- *50 g unsalted butter*
- *1 lt milk*

- *bouquet garni*
- *2 free range eggs*
- *150 ml cream*
- *salt & black pepper*
- *2 cloves of garlic*
- *4 slices of bread*
- *half a bunch of flat leaf parsley*

Preparation

Thoroughly wash the sorrel leaves in some lightly salted water and drain in a colander for a few minutes. Wash, peel and chop the potatoes into 1.5 cm dice. Place in a pan of boiling salted water and blanch until they start to become tender, refresh under cold water and put to one side.

Skin the shallots and garlic and chop finely. Place a large saucepan over a medium flame, add half of the butter and half of the duck fat. Once the butter has melted, add the sorrel, chopped shallots and one chopped clove of garlic, stirring constantly, then add the milk, *bouquet garni* and lightly season. Reduce the flame to low and gently simmer for around 30 minutes or so, until the sorrel is quite tender, then remove the *bouquet garni*. Drain the potatoes and add to the soup.

While the soup is simmering on the hob, you can use the time to prepare some crispy garlic croutons. Cut the crusts off the bread and then cut each slice into approximately 1.5 cm dice. Place the garlic onto your chopping board, sprinkle with a little salt, and roughly chop the garlic, then add the parsley leaves and chop the two ingredients together. Once chopped, place the parsley mixture into a tea towel and squeeze out any excess moisture, and yes, your tea towel is now useless for anything else except a 40°C wash in your appliance of science! Pop the mixture into a bowl with the diced bread and mix thoroughly together.

Take a heavy-bottomed frying pan and place over a medium to high flame. Add the remaining butter and duck fat. When the bubbles subside, add the croutons and cook quickly and evenly, to a golden brown on all sides. Remove the croutons and place onto some kitchen paper.

Break the egg yolks into a bowl, add the cream and mix well. Take a ladle and little by little add two or three ladles of hot soup to the mixture, whisking briskly as you go, so you don't finish up with scrambled egg.

Remove the soup form the heat and pour the mixture (*sabayon*) back into the bulk of the soup, whisking constantly to blend in the egg and cream mixture. Return to a low flame and stir continuously until the soup thickens a little. Check for seasoning and consistency.

Pour ladles of the steaming soup into hot soup bowls, add a little swirl of liquid cream, a little chopped parsley and a few garlic croutons.

My secret: Pop the remaining garlic croutons into a small bowl or ramekin and place into the middle of the table so everyone can top up on that crunchy texture as the level of soup reduces in their bowls.

SOUPE AUX CÉLERI-RAVE
lightly spiced celeriac and apple soup

This dish is derived from one of our favourite 'quick knock-up soups' which we throw together now and again as a toe-warmer at lunch time in the middle of the winter. We have always used parsnips, apples, potatoes and onions as the base for this dish, but unfortunately, you do not tend to see many parsnips on the shelves of our local French supermarkets or on the open market stalls in our Department, so we had to think of a suitable alternative.

Numerous trips down to La Maison over the last two or three years, to close the house up for the winter months, saw us heading south from the beautiful cathedral city of Chartres towards Orléans. The N154 runs parallel with the A10-E5 autoroute for a short while and just before we join the motorway at either junction 12 or 13, we would pass huge, field-side mountains of recently harvested celeriac, just sitting there waiting to be collected and sent off to a factory to be processed.

I guess that celeriac is not that popular in the UK; I appreciate that in its raw state it really does not look too inviting and many people just do not know what the heck to do with it. In La Belle France, however, it is used for a variety of wonderful dishes, such as pheasant casserole with celeriac and apple or as an accompaniment such as *purée de celeri-rave gratiné.* You will usually find pre-prepared celeriac salad available at the local supermarkets during the summer months and we just love to keep some of this in the fridge ready for our pre-requisite lunch break, before we start preparing the evening meal for our guests.

Recipe by Diane Alder-Smith
La Maison aux Quat'Saisons, Laborie, 19400 Monceaux-sur-Dordogne

Preparation time:	20 minutes
Cooking time:	60 minutes

Ingredients for 6 people

- *1 large celeriac*
- *1 medium onion*
- *2 sticks of celery*
- *50 g unsalted butter*

- *1 lt good chicken stock*
- *2 sweet eating apples*
- *300 g potatoes*
- *150 ml double cream*
- *2 coffee spoons ground coriander and 2 of ground cumin*
- *flat leaf parsley, salt and black pepper*

Preparation

Peel and roughly chop the onion, celery and potatoes and place to one side for a few minutes while you prepare the celeriac. Trim away the root and the skin from the celeriac then cut into 2.5 cm dice and add to the other vegetables.

Peel and de-core the apples, cut into a rough dice and place in a bowl of cold water with a little lemon juice to stop them from discolouring.

Melt the butter in the bottom of a heavy-based saucepan over a medium flame. Once the bubbles start to subside, add the vegetables, apples and spices, reduce to a low flame, stir well and cover with a lid and sweat for around 5 – 8 minutes without colour, stirring from time to time.

Add the stock to the vegetable mixture and cook for a further 30 – 40 minutes, or until the vegetables are tender.

Remove the broth from the hob and whiz the whole lot up with your hand blender. Add nearly all of the cream and return to a low flame on your hob. Check for seasoning and consistency, adding a little salt and black pepper or even a little more spice if it is to your taste. The soup should have the consistency of a fairly thick *purée*, but this is down to individual preference.

Di's secret: Ladle the soup into hot, deep white soup bowls. Drizzle a little liquid cream over the soup in each bowl and sprinkle with a some chopped flat leaf parsley. Serve some freshly cooked garlic croutons separately.

SOUPE AUX CHOUX
cabbage soup

Reminds you of your old school dinners, doesn't it – and sounds just as awful, I hear you saying to yourself. Well, my friends, we first discovered something like this dish on my 44th birthday at the Hotel Central at Pleaux in the Auvergne, served as an accompaniment for a braised *boudin blanc*. In fact, I think that the *boudin* were actually cooked in the braising liquid with the cabbage.

A few years later Twink played around with a Gary Rhodes recipe which we think included smoked bacon and garlic, so the recipe below is rather an amalgam of the two with the addition of one or two twists of our own. We think the end product is very rustic and can make a wonderful meal served with huge chunks of granary bread or local *pain bis* thickly spread with butter.

Twink wanted to keep this recipe as rustic as possible and therefore she has not altered her "Corrézienne version". In the UK, you may need to buy some lightly smoked lardons of bacon or go and have a chat with the friendly butcher, that I was talking about at the beginning of the book, to get hold of a joint of smoked breast bacon (the bit used for streaky).

Recipe by Diane Alder-Smith
La Maison aux Quat'Saisons, Laborie, 19400 Monceaux-sur-Dordogne

Preparation time: 20 minutes
Cooking time: 60 minutes

Ingredients for 6 people

- *1 small savoy cabbage*
- *1 medium onion – sliced*
- *200 g smoked joint of breast bacon (or lardons)*
- *250 g potatoes*
- *50 g unsalted butter*
- *olive oil*
- *1 lt. chicken stock*
- *garlic*
- *dry baguette*
- *salt and pepper*

Preparation

Place the joint of bacon into a large heavy-bottomed pan, cover with cold water and bring slowly to the boil. Reduce the heat and simmer for one hour.

During this time, take another pan to cook the cabbage. Cut the cabbage into four quarters and remove the stalk from each, then cut into narrow strips, wash in cold water and drain. Melt the butter with a good splash of olive oil in a heavy-bottomed pan over a medium to low flame and then add the sliced onion, garlic and cabbage. Cover with a tight-fitting lid and 'sweat' for five to ten minutes.

While the cabbage is cooking, peel the potatoes then cut them into 6mm discs and blanch in the cooking pot with the bacon joint.

Add one litre of chicken stock to the onion, garlic and cabbage mix and add the blanched potatoes to the *mélange*.

Strain off the cooking liquid from the bacon joint and add about a quarter of a litre to the other pan – this will help to give the soup a slightly salty and smoky flavour.

Cut the joint of bacon into 6mm thick slices, cut each slice into strips and add to the cabbage soup. Check the soup for consistency and add a little more of the bacon stock if need be, taste and check for seasoning. Cut six slices of *baguette* into 6mm thick discs for each soup bowl.

The soup is now ready to serve, so get yourself six large soup bowls and ladle in the steaming mixture, add a *baguette* disc to each bowl, making sure each disc is pushed below the surface, and sprinkle a good amount of chopped flat leaf parsley over the top of the broth to serve.

SOUPE AUX HARICOTS FRAIS et SAUCISSES
bean soup with toulouse sausages

I have eaten this soup on a number of occasions and it makes an especially hearty meal on a cold winter's evening served with huge crusty chunks of rustic rye bread. However, I have really struggled to find a recipe to do it justice, so I have played around with some basic Corrézienne ingredients and come up with a recipe that I hope you will enjoy.

It is important that you soak the beans thoroughly overnight, or you can cheat just a tad if you like and use a couple of large tins of canelli, or white *flageolets* beans.

Recipe by Malcolm Alder-Smith
La Maison aux Quat'Saisons, Laborie, 19400 Monceaux-sur-Dordogne

Preparation time: 25 minutes
Cooking time: 120 minutes

Ingredients for 6 people

- *1 kg dried flageolets*
- *2 lt water*
- *1 lt chicken stock*
- *2 medium onions sliced*
- *1 clove of garlic*
- *2 sticks of celery cut into 1 cm dice*
- *6 x Toulouse sausages (10's)*
- *4 soup spoons duck or goose fat*
- *2 soup spoons flour*
- *salt and black pepper*
- *6 slices round country bread*

Preparation

For the beans, I like to use the real thing, so soak them overnight in cold water and drain them in a colander the following day. The Toulouse sausages (10 to the lb) are larger than the traditional chipolatas which we use in the UK (16 to the lb); they are full of wonderful flavours and packed with herbs.

Put a large saucepan over a medium heat, add two soup spoons of the fat and cook the flavoursome Toulouse sausages until they are golden brown, remove and keep to one side. Cook the sliced onions gently over a low heat in the same saucepan with the chopped celery and garlic until the onions go soft and translucent. Add the flour and mix well before gradually adding the hot chicken stock a little at time, once thoroughly blended top up with the water and stir well. Bring to the boil, add the beans and sausages, reduce the heat and simmer for 90 minutes. Do not season, as the sausages should provide enough flavour at this stage.

When the soup is ready, check the seasoning and add a little salt and pepper if necessary. Remove the sausages, distribute them and the slices of bread between six large soup bowls and pour the simmering soup and bean mixture over the top until the bread is well soaked.

My secret: For anyone who can manage seconds, the local tradition is to add a glass of red wine to the remainder of the soup in the pan and leave it on the stove to simmer gently – as I said before, this is known as *chabrol* or *faire chabrol*.

SOUPE À L'OIGNON
onion soup

The first thing that comes to mind when writing this recipe is that I should point out that I have never really tasted an onion soup in France that tastes much like those which were so popular in UK restaurants back in the Seventies and Eighties. I am really not too sure where the classic 'British French Onion Soup Experience' originated from, because it is seldom like the real thing. However, I guess that like anything else, recipes are very much open to regional and national variations.

The basics of this recipe below are Corrézienne, although I have adapted it from an old recipe from Quercy, just a little further south (Lot and the Tarn-et-Garonne), which involves slightly thickening the stock with golden egg yolks which give the soup quite a rich flavour.

These thin, sometimes watery, soups are celebrated throughout the Department and the content is usually dependent on the seasons and what is available growing in the garden.

Recipe by Malcolm Alder-Smith
La Maison aux Quat'Saisons, Laborie, 19400 Monceaux-sur-Dordogne

Preparation time: 10 minutes
Cooking time: 60 minutes

Ingredients for 4 people

* *500 g onions*
* *2 cloves of garlic*
* *2 free range egg yolks*
* *50 g unsalted butter*
* *2 soup spoons sunflower oil*
* *5 cl dry sherry*
* *5 cl Armagnac*

* *25 cl red wine*
* *1 lt veal or chicken stock*
* *olive oil*
* *1 baguette*
* *50 g grated Gruyère*
* *50 g grated Parmesan*
* *salt and pepper*

Preparation

Peel the onions and garlic and thinly slice. Place a heavy-bottomed saucepan over a medium to high flame, add the sunflower oil and melt the butter until the bubbles start to subside, then add the onions. Stir constantly all the while, so that none of the onion catches on the bottom of the pan. It is vitally important that none of the onion burns, as it will give the soup a bitter flavour and ruin the appearance of the end product.

After five minutes, reduce the heat to a medium flame, add the garlic and cook for a further five minutes or so, until the ingredients turn soft and golden brown.

Add the Armagnac and flambé for a few moments. Once the flames have died down, add the wine. Cook for another five minutes or so to reduce the liquid by around 50%. Keep stirring all the time, to avoid any ingredients getting stuck on the bottom of the pan.

Pour the hot stock over the onion and wine mixture, reduce the heat and allow to simmer for 45 minutes.

While the soup is simmering, cut a few slices of baguette on an angle at about 1 cm thick allowing one slice per person. Place the slices onto a baking sheet, sprinkle with some olive oil and pop them under a hot grill. Once the first side turns golden brown, turn them over and do the same with the other side.

Put the egg yolks into a bowl, add the dry sherry and mix well. Pour this mixture into the simmering liquid and stir well. Check the soup for seasoning and consistency.

Sprinkle each crouton with some grated Gruyère and Parmesan and flash under the grill for a minute or so, until the cheese melts and colours slightly. Place a crouton into the bottom of each soup bowl, cover with the onion *bouillon* then sprinkle more Gruyère and serve immediately.

My secret: I tend to use the classical white French soup bowls, which are much smaller and taller than the ones which we use in the UK. I pop these onto a baking sheet and put them into a very hot oven for a minute or so before I serve them, so the cheese melts and the whole mass is bubbling when I serve it at the table. A verbal health warning is always appropriate for your guests with this one, as the soup can be lethally hot and the cheese melts and becomes very runny.

Place a bowl of grated Gruyère and more croutons on the table so that people can sprinkle more on if they wish.

VELOUTÉ DE CÈPES DE CORRÈZE
CROÛTONS À LA GRAISSE DE CANARD
cèpes velouté with croutons cooked in duck fat

This recipe comes from La Crémaillère, one of the two restaurants in Brive which Twink and I are just dying to try out (the other being La Truffe Noire); they both have a great reputation and we are hoping to give them both a bash later in the year when things quieten down a bit. Many folks consider La Crémaillère to be one of the best restaurants in the Department, but I will reserve judgment until we have tried it for ourselves.

The word *'velouté'* means velvety or creamy and this is just what you must aim for with the texture of the end product. Some people will add one or two egg yolks and some cream to a ladle or two of the *purée* which has been allowed to cool a little (otherwise you will get scrambled egg), whisk well and then return to the pan of soup, stirring well. The egg yolks and cream will give the soup a wonderful shiny glaze.

This is a very simple recipe and one that is packed with oodles of flavour. If you can't access *cèpes*, then go for any other type of 'smoky' woodland mushroom.

Recipe by La Crémaillère
53, avenue de Paris, 19100 Brive-la-Gaillarde

Preparation time: 30 minutes
Cooking time: 45 minutes

Ingredients for 6 people

- *250 g leeks*
- *250 g cèpes*
- *200 g potatoes*
- *200 g celery*
- *25 cl crème fraîche*

- *salt and pepper*
- *duck fat*
- *1 lt chicken bouillon*
- *100 g butter*
- *1 x 20 g truffle*

Preparation

Finely chop the vegetables, place them into a saucepan and sweat them off, without colour, in the butter (with a lid on) for between five and ten minutes. Moisten with the hot chicken stock and cook for a further 45 minutes.

While the soup is ticking over on your hob, use this time to make the croutons. I normally cut mine at around 1 cm thick.

Place a heavy-bottomed frying pan over a medium heat and allow it to get hot. Add the duck fat, get this nice and hot, and then add the croutons. If the fat is not hot enough, it will absorb straight into the croutons making them very greasy instead of nice and crisp.

Allow the croutons to cook for a few seconds then toss them quickly to get an even brown colour all around. If you find it difficult to toss the croutons, as they do on telly, then turn them quickly and often with a large spoon. Once evenly coloured, remove them from the frying pan with a slotted spoon, straight onto some kitchen paper which will absorb any excess fat.

After this time, whiz up the soup to a fine *purée* with your hand bender, add the cream, check for seasoning and consistency and add a little seasoning if necessary.

To serve, pour the soup into individual soup bowls, divide the croutons between the bowls and sprinkle in the centre of the soup. Over the top of this, grate some fresh truffle.

Le secret de La Crémaillère: Just before serving, whizz up the soup once more in the pan with your hand blender.

WINE: To enjoy this *velouté* try a lightly chilled dry white Bergerac or Montravel

Recipe supplied by Comité Départemental du Tourisme de la Corrèze

MIQUES
types of dumplings

This is definitely going to be the briefest chapter in the book. Miques appear to be a little short on documentation but rather long on tradition and history. These days they are more likely to be found on the domestic table than in hotels and restaurants of the Department, although some are still known to indulge their customers on the odd occasion.

There has been endless discussion over the centuries as to what constitutes a *mique* and to add to the confusion, there is also a *'mique farcie'*! They are a form of dumpling, but generally not the same type as you know them in the UK and are often cooked and served with chunks of boiled salted pork with whole vegetables, cabbage and chitterling sausages – sounds excellent!

As well as *miques,* there are also *fars* and *pouls* and a good friend advises that when it comes to typically Corrézienne recipes, *pouls* are "spot on". She advises that there are several forms of *'pouls'* or *'poule'* (apparently the spelling is very much a matter of personal preference). They were the most basic form of survival food for peasants. Some of these 'dreadful' *pouls* (she quotes) are made of grated potatoes mixed up into a sort of dumpling. They originally kept the peasants from starving through the winter in particular. Once the piece of pig had been cooked (probably boiled) for Sunday lunch, the remaining juice and any fat would be used to flavour up or even fry up the *pouls* for the rest of the week, until another piece of pork came upon the menu.

It's currently becoming rather fashionable, she says, to dole them up in some of the smart restaurants in the department. Michel, the head chef at the exceptional Hôtel Fouillade, Place Gambetta in Argentat has been known to serve up a slice of something 'poulish', with the addition of herbs etc and I understand that they are very nice indeed.

These dumplings (*miques*) date back to pre-potato days and were used to bulk up a meal, much the same as bread used to, and still does! Each village or hamlet had its own bread-oven, a small stone-built construction where folks took their home-made bread to be baked.

We have looked at a couple of old houses over the years (with a view to purchase), which had an individually constructed bread oven in the garden with the distinctive local *lauze* slate roof. One such house which we viewed in the early Nineties had a bread oven in the grounds which been converted into a rather smart, compact and bijou studio apartment.

The flour which was used for making the bread and dumplings was, in these parts, usually produced at a local *minoterie* (water-mill). As the Department has its fair share of rivers and *cascades* (waterfalls), there was no shortage of power to turn the grind-stones. There is currently a renaissance of traditional *terroir* methods right across the Department and there still remains an authentic mill just north of Tulle, the Department capital, where they produce about seven different types of flour. The Minoterie Daniel Farges can be found at Vimbelle, 19800 Bar on the D23 road, and en-route to the village of Corrèze.

Farine de blé	wheat
Farine de blé moulue à la meule	millstone ground wheat
Farine de sarrasin	buckwheat
Farine de seigle	rye
Farine de mais	maize
Farine complète	full/complete
Farine de châtaigne	chestnut

We have noticed recently that the products of a company called La Cuisine Corrézienne are to be found on the shelves of local supermarkets. They produce a fine selection of local specialities and we were pleasantly surprised to find some whopping great big *miques* on display.

LA MIQUE
Dumpling

Preparation time: 10 minutes
Cooking time: 60 minutes

- *500 g flour*
- *½ cube of baker's yeast*
- *3 large eggs*
- *200 g butter*
- *1 pinch of salt*
- *25 cl warm milk*

Preparation

Warm the milk and add the salt and butter, which you have cut into small dice.

Pour 250 g of the flour into a bowl, make a 'well' in the centre and add the warm milk with the yeast, which you have dissolved in half a glass of warm water.

Mix the ingredients to a clear paste, knead well, make a ball shape with your hands and add, little by little, the rest of the flour.

Lightly flour a clean tea towel, put the dumpling inside and place into a bowl. Keep the bowl in a warm place and wait for two hours while the dumpling rises (proves). Take a *faitout* (large saucepan), filling it with sufficient water to contain *'la mique',* and bring to the boil.

Put the dumpling in the boiling water with the tea towel. Jam any loose edges of the tea towel under the lid of the saucepan.

Cook *'la mique'* for around 1 hour.

You can eat this type of dumpling with stewed game, *petits salés* (salted pork), or sliced cold and smothered in jam !

MIQUE AUX PETITS SALÉS
Dumpling with salt pork

Preparation time: 25 minutes
Cooking time: 180 minutes

Ingredients for 6 people

- *500 g flour*
- *20 g fresh yeast*
- *3 eggs*
- *25 cl warm milk*
- *salt*
- *80 g melted butter*
- *2 kilo salted loin of pork (large bacon joint would be OK)*
- *1 chitterling sausage*
- *500 g carrots*
- *3 leeks*
- *small green cabbage*
- *onions*
- *garlic*

Preparation

Mix the fresh yeast with the warm milk, then mix in the eggs, salt and the melted butter. Little by little add the flour, kneading by hand, and work it well into a clear dough on a lightly floured work surface, in order that it becomes supple and elastic, dusting with more flour if necessary.

You have the choice of making individual dumplings or one large dumpling. Once prepared, cover with a floured clean tea towel and leave to raise for two hours in a warm place.

Peel the carrots and cut into big chunks. Peel the onions and cut into quarters, leaving the stalk in place which will help to hold them together. Split the leeks down the middle, wash thoroughly, fold in half and tie with some kitchen string. Dispose of any damaged outside leaves of the cabbage and cut into four or six wedges through the stalk.

While the dumpling(s) are proving, rinse the salt pork in cold water and dry well to remove any excess salt. Take a very large saucepan and fill three quarters full with cold unsalted water. Add the pork, the chitterling sausage, prepared carrots, cabbage, leek, onion and garlic. Place the pan over a high flame and bring to the boil, reduce the heat and allow to simmer for half an hour, skimming off any residue which may float to the surface from the pork.

Add the dumpling(s) and cook for 1 hour if whole, or around 20-30 minutes if you are using individual dumplings, according to their size. Turn the dumpling(s) over half-way through the cooking time, by using a couple of large spoons.

Get hold of one of those massive serving plates that your great-grandmother used to use, alternatively buy a large white platter from Habitat. Warm the serving dish through in the oven, place the dumpling(s) in the centre and surround with the steaming hot vegetables and meat.

According to tradition, the dumpling is divided into portions using two forks.

WINE: This dish gives you an opportunity to try some wines which you maybe have not considered buying before. This dish will comfortably accommodate either red or white.

My advice for a red would be to take a look at Chinon or Bourgueil, both reds from the Loire, which up to recently were very much *en vogue* in Paris. Bourgueil, a fruity Touraine red with deep flavours, can age well. Chinon from the south bank is a rich Cabernet Franc and can be drunk cool and young.

If you prefer to go for a white wine – it just has to be Chablis!

Recipe supplied by Promenades Gourmandes
EDIL Communication BP 23, 34370 Maraussan, France
www.promenades-gourmandes.com

ENTRÉES
starters

Cèpes, foie gras and *cabecous* are all synonymous with the Corrèze in the same way that they are with the Quercy region farther to the south. Yesterday's staple, part of today's vast choice of *produits du terroir,* are now the luxury products that make the Corrèze one of the most outstanding gastronomic Departments in France.

Mushrooms such as *cèpes* and *morilles* and of course *la Truffe* (the truffle) are at the heart of Corrézienne cooking and are to be found in a range of dishes which make up the 'entrées' section of most hotel menus. I mustn't forget to include some of the more basic ingredients which we tend to take for granted, such as potatoes and the fabulous local, golden, free range eggs which are available everywhere.

I was surprised to learn that the small town of Chartrier-Ferrière (just south west of Brive) hosted the first ever Fête Nationale de la Truffe on

6th February 2003. Quercy and more so, Perigord are synonymous with the 'black diamond', yet this town on the cross-roads of the two areas was the base chosen for what I hope will become an annual event.

The Corrèze was formerly a hot-spot for truffle 'production' and over twenty years ago the commune (Chartrier-Ferrière) decided to structure its development around the truffle.

It is always difficult to pin down which dishes should contribute towards the 'starters' section on a menu. Certainly in recent years, since we brought our *maison*, we have become far more adventurous when eating out. We now tend to venture towards dishes which we have never tried before, just for the sake of experiencing classic country food. Fortunately the ubiquitous Prawn Cocktail is unlikely to be served in this part of France, and you are far more likely to find dishes containing some of the ingredients noted above.

Recently we were fortunate enough to experience a wonderful Sunday lunch at Les Voyageurs at St-Martin-la Méanne, cooked by Jean-Françoise Chaumiel, when Twink and her dad ate an amazing kidney dish cooked with the unique Moutarde de Violette de Brive as their starter. You will find my version of this dish later in the book, on page 145.

CÈPES FARCIS ET GRATINÉS
stuffed cèpes gratinés

Recipe by Gilles Dudognon

Preparation time: 30 minutes
Cooking time: 20 minutes

Ingredients for 6 people

- *12 large cèpes*
- *3 slices of cured ham*
- *5 shallots finely chopped*
- *1 clove of garlic crushed*
- *small mixture of herbs – chives, parsley, chervil*

- *1 knob of butter*
- *2 soup spoons of olive oil*
- *4 soup spoons of fresh bread crumbs*
- *Salt and pepper*

Preparation

Wash and pat dry the *cèpes*, remove and retain the stalks and lightly season the mushrooms with salt. Heat some olive oil in a frying pan and lightly brown them. Remove the *cèpes* and place into an oven-proof dish.

Finely chop the stalks and the cured ham. In the same pan that you used to cook the *cèpes*, melt the butter over a medium to low heat and add the ham, stalks, shallots and crushed garlic. Take care not to get the pan too hot; cook the ingredients gently for 10 to 15 minutes and then stuff each *cèpe* with the mixture.

Season with salt and pepper and sprinkle the top of each generously with the breadcrumbs. Cook in a pre-heated oven at 200°C for 20 minutes.

Remove from the oven and sprinkle with the mixture of chopped herbs then serve the dish up at the table so your guests can help themselves.

You will find that this is a very flexible recipe and you can play around with the ingredients if you wish. We quite often use some finely chopped smoked bacon instead of the ham and sprinkle a little freshly grated parmesan over the top. This can be an impressive starter or garnish to a main course.

WINE: A nicely chilled Sancerre would suit a lot of people, but if you want to push the boat out, then a good quality red Bordeaux or a good Burgundy.

CREVETTES FLAMBÉES
prawns flamed in brandy

This is a dish which Twink often has when we eat at the Auberge des Gabariers on the quay in Argentat and although our good friends Michel and Isabelle did not send me this recipe, I have decided to include the dish anyway, so I hope that I do it justice.

You will need to allow between four and six nice large prawns per person, depending on the size that you can get hold of.

Recipe by Malcolm Alder-Smith
La Maison aux Quat'Saisons, Laborie, 19400 Monceaux-sur-Dordogne

Preparation time: 5 minutes
Cooking time: 5 minutes

Ingredients for 4 people

- *24 large prawns (uncooked –*
  ask at your fish counter)
- *1 small onion – finely chopped*
- *2 shallots – finely chopped*
- *1 clove of garlic – crushed*
- *4 cl Armagnac*
- *50 g unsalted butter*
- *olive oil*
- *3 lemons*
- *salad leaves*

Preparation

Garnish four plates with a few salad leaves of your choice. Cut two of the lemons into eight wedges and place two onto each plate. Cut the third lemon in half and squeeze the juice through a sieve into a bowl or jug.

Take a large heavy-based frying pan and place over a medium to high flame. Add a slug of olive oil and the unsalted butter. When the butter bubbles, add the finely chopped onion, shallots and crushed garlic, reduce the flame to medium and cook these for two or three minutes. Add the prawns, and toss or turn them gently for around five minutes.

Tweak the heat up again, add the Armagnac and flame the prawns. Reduce the heat again, and when the flame starts to subside, sprinkle a little lemon juice over the prawns and serve onto the plates immediately.

GALETTES DE TARTOUFLES
goat's cheese potato cakes

If you see the word *'galette'* on a menu in France, it likely to be in a *crêperie* and will usually indicate a savoury pancake filled with cheese, ham, egg etc, and they are usually very nice indeed. I could never understand why the French went out for a meal and ate just pancakes, but now I have definitely seen the light.

The batter for these pancakes is often made from buckwheat flour, which gives them a much darker appearance than the sort of pancake that you or I would usually make at home.

I have spent many a happy hour over the years sitting at tables outside street café bars in France, eating a savoury *galette* and slurping some ice cold *pression* (draught beer), just watching the world roll by.

La Galette des Rois (Galette of Kings) is a cake which is traditionally eaten on the Twelfth Night.

However, just to totally confuse you, my dear readers, this recipe has absolutely nothing to do with *crêpes* or pancakes at all!

The cooking of the potatoes in their skins for this recipe is really important, because the potatoes do not take on any moisture as they would if you peeled and boiled them in water.

Recipe by Diane Alder-Smith
La Maison aux Quat'Saisons, Laborie, 19400 Monceaux-sur-Dordogne

Preparation time: 50 minutes
Cooking time: 20 minutes

Ingredients for 6 people

- *4 large potatoes*
- *40 g butter*
- *4 soup spoons of fresh goat's cheese*
- *2 egg yolks (free range)*
- *150 g four*
- *chives*
- *sunflower oil*
- *salt and pepper*

Preparation

Score each potato around its circumference, place into a pre-heated oven set at 200°C and bake until cooked through. Remove the potatoes from the oven and cut each in two, then remove the pulp into a bowl with the goat's cheese and the butter. Mix together with 1 egg yolk and gradually drizzle in the flour and blend well. Season with the salt and pepper and add a handful of chopped chives. Set aside and allow to rest for one hour.

Lightly dust your work surface with some flour and divide up the potato and cheese mixture into equal-sized pieces. Form the pieces into a disc shapes, so that you end up with potato cakes around 10 cm in diameter and 1.5 cm thick. You can either form these by hand or with the aid of a palette knife.

There are a number of ways of cooking these, the main ones being either in the oven or in a frying pan. I tend to go for a mix of the two and start cooking them for about three to four minutes on either side in a heavy-bottomed frying pan over a medium heat until the underside starts to turn a golden brown. Turn them over for another three minutes or so before transferring them onto a baking tray and finishing them off in a pre-heated oven at 200°C for about another ten minutes.

Alternately, you can put the *galettes* straight onto a baking sheet, egg-wash with the remaining egg yolk and a little milk and put straight into the pre-heated oven for around 20 minutes.

MELON AU VIN DE NOIX
melon with walnut wine

One of my favourite apéritifs from the Corrèze is Quinqui Noix which is produced by a company called DENOIX in Brive-la-Gaillard (they also produce the distinctive Moutarde Violette de Brive). The *apéritif*, which to my mind has to be served nicely chilled, has the most unique flavour which I guess would not be to everyone's taste. However, I love the stuff and usually have a glass or three whenever we visit our good friends Michel and Isabelle at L'Auberge des Gabariers on the Quai de Lestourgie in Argentat.

This is a really simple recipe and can only be enhanced by the quality of the melon which you use.

Recipe supplied by Promenades Gourmandes

Preparation time: 5 minutes

Ingredients for 4 people

- *2 Gallia melons*
- *5 cl Quinqui Noix*

Lightly chill the melons before use. Trim around one centimetre off the ends of each melon, so that the halves will not roll around on the plates or bowls. Holding firmly with one hand, take a sharp knife and cut down through the melon from side to side (not end to end). Take the four half melons and de-seed carefully with a spoon, discarding the seeds.

Place half a melon onto each plate or bowl, pour in the chilled Vin de Noix and serve immediately.

You can purchase Quinqui Noix from most Corrézienne supermarkets or directly from:

DENOIX (see *Vins, aperitifs et liqueurs traditionnels* at the end of the book)

Recipe supplied by Promenades Gourmandes
EDIL Communication BP 23, 34370 Maraussan, France
www.promenades-gourmandes.com

MILHASSOU À LA CORRÉZIENNE
potato cake

I guess that the nearest I can get to describing this dish is by comparing it with the style of the Spanish Tortilla (omelette) which my old mate Jon Dyer used to make back in the mid-Seventies when we holidayed together on the Costa del Sol at Fuengirola. I have never before, nor since, met anyone of non-Iberian origin (especially a bloke!) who can make that dish better than him.

There is of course quite some distance, in terms of miles at least, between the two dishes but the above description will give you some idea of where I am coming from with this recipe. You are more likely to find Milhassou in one of the more northern areas of the Corrèze, such as the Monédières, just south of the Department of Creuse. You can prepare this recipe in the form of one large potato cake and cut it into wedges (à la Spanish Omelette) or prepare smaller individual cakes which are called Milhassous. You are going to need quite a large heavy-bottomed frying pan to make this dish, if you are going for the bigger option.

Recipe by Malcolm Alder-Smith
La Maison aux Quat'Saisons, Laborie, 19400 Monceaux-sur-Dordogne

Preparation time: 20 minutes
Cooking time: 50 minutes

Ingredients for 4 to 6 people

- *1 kg potatoes*
- *200 g breast bacon*
- *1 good sized Brive onion*
- *white of one leek*
- *1 small bunch of chives – chopped*
- *1 small bunch of flat leaf parsley – finely chopped*
- *2 large free range eggs*
- *2 soup spoons of goose fat*
- *salt and black pepper*
- *freshly grated nutmeg*

Preparation

Peel and wash the potatoes, pat them dry and coarsely grate them into a bowl of cold water. Rinse thoroughly, drain well in a colander, pat dry and wrap in clean tea towel to prevent them from going brown (equally you can leave them in the water with a slice of bread until ready to use).

Peel and finely chop the onions, garlic and leek and mix these ingredients together well.

Put the grated potatoes in a large bowl with the chives and flat leaf parsley and season with salt and pepper. At this stage, you may want to add a little freshly grated nutmeg, according to taste, then add the eggs and blend well into the mixture.

Place a heavy-bottomed frying pan over a medium flame, add the goose fat and when hot add the onion mixture. Cook for 2 to 3 minutes until the vegetables just start to colour. Add the potato, herbs and egg mixture to your pan, blend well with the onion mixture, spread it out flat and cook like a pancake – only a lot longer. Reduce the heat right down and cook the first side for about 20 – 25 minutes, mixing and turning the ingredients for the first five minutes only. Once you have stopped stirring, a golden brown skin will form on the bottom of the potato cake as the ingredients start to caramelise. Check regularly to ensure that the mixture isn't colouring too much.

Now here comes the tricky bit, folks. Once the base is nicely browned, you need to turn the potato cake over. Remove the frying pan from the heat and place a large plate over the top of the pan, holding the 'lid' (plate) and pan firmly together, then briskly rotate through 180 degrees so that the golden brown side is now at the top. Add a little more goose fat if needed and slide the potato cake back into your frying pan, raw side down. You are now ready to continue cooking the other side for about another 20 minutes until the bottom is also golden brown, but making sure that the ingredients are cooked in the middle.

When the dish is ready, simply slide it onto a large serving plate, cut it into wedges and serve it with some crisp green salad.

My secret: This dish can be served with meat dishes cooked in a sauce or it goes equally well served at lunchtime on its own as snack or with some salad leaves of your choice.

WINE: Local red is good. Go for a Vin du Pays or Le Mille et une Pierre.

OMELETTE AUX CÈPES
cèpe omelette

People think omelettes are easy to make, but to do them properly is a tad more difficult. The ultimate knack is to cook off the eggs, add the ingredient of your choice and finish off cooking with little or no colour when you present the omelette on the plate – not always easy! Cooking time varies depending on whether you want the omelette well cooked or *baveuse* (runny). When I was a student at college, we used to cook for the public restaurant as second year students and would sometimes prepare an omelette for up to six people – yes, that was one big omelette – and woe betide us if we didn't get it perfect every time.

Recipe by Malcolm Alder-Smith
La Maison aux Quat'Saisons, Laborie, 19400 Monceaux-sur-Dordogne

Preparation time: 5 minutes
Cooking time: 3-4 minutes

Ingredients for 1 person

- *2 free-range eggs*
- *1 cèpe*
- *10 g butter*
- *1 soup spoon sunflower oil*
- *chopped parsley*
- *salt and pepper*

Preparation

Remove the stalks from the *cèpe*, wipe the mushroom carefully and cut into thin slices. Place a heavy-bottomed frying pan over a medium flame and melt half of the butter along with a little oil. Once the butter has melted and the bubbles start to subside, add the prepared mushrooms and fry them to a golden brown. Season the mushrooms with the salt and ground black pepper and sprinkle with the chopped parsley then place to one side to keep warm.

Beat the eggs thoroughly in a bowl and add a little salt and pepper.

Melt the remaining butter in an omelette pan over a medium/hot flame.

When the bubbles subside, pour in the beaten eggs and using the back of a fork push the mixture from the sides into the centre. When the omelette starts to set, reduce the heat and add the fried *cèpe* slices, distributing them evenly over the egg mixture.

Fold over the omelette, present it in the middle of a plate and serve immediately. You may want to retain of few of the cooked *cèpes* and put a spoonful over the top of the omelette.

OMELETTE AUX POINTES D'ASPERGES
asparagus tip omelette

Many people think that there is some sort of mysticism in preparing and cooking asparagus, which I think is totally untrue. However, you can easily damage your asparagus unless you are very careful. Select smaller asparagus, not the chunky fibrous ones which tend to be rather woody. Use only the 'best' part of the asparagus. This is easy to find, simply by bending the asparagus gently from the bottom end, and the point where it snaps in two is the point between good eating and bad. Rather than having to do this with every piece of asparagus, test one only – this should give you a guideline to the right point to cut the others. Dispose of the unwanted stalks. You can use some of the edible stalks as well as the tips in the omelette.

Recipe by Diane Alder-Smith
La Maison aux Quat'Saisons, Laborie, 19400 Monceaux-sur-Dordogne

Preparation time: 10 minutes
Cooking time: 5–7 minutes

Ingredients for 1 person

- *2 free-range eggs*
- *small pack of asparagus*
- *10 g butter*
- *salt and pepper*

Preparation

Take a *sauteuse* (shallow pan) and half fill with water. Place over a medium flame until the water boils, reduce the heat to simmering point and add a little salt. Add the asparagus and cook for around 5 minutes, depending on how you like your asparagus. I am inclined to only cook them for a short period of time, which leaves them a little crunchy and they retain their lovely green colour. When cooked, drain and refresh under cold water then cut into 2.5 cm pieces and keep to one side.

Beat the eggs thoroughly in a bowl and add a little salt and freshly ground pepper. Gently stir in the asparagus tips and mix delicately.

Melt the butter in an omelette pan over a medium/hot flame. When the bubbles subside, pour in the egg and asparagus mix and using the back of a wooden fork, push the mixture from the sides into the centre. When the omelette has set, fold in half and allow to cook for a few seconds more. Present the omelette in the middle of a plate and serve immediately.

RAVIOLIS DE CHAMPIGNONS DE NOS BOIS COULIS DE MARRONS
raviolis of mushrooms from our woods with a coulis of chestnuts

This recipe was kindly sent to me by the Bidault family who run the Hôtel Le Beau Site, a 3 Star and 2 Fireplace rated Logis de France to the east of Tulle, the Department capital.

The Logis de France classification (between 1 and 3 Fireplaces) is established according to a very strict checklist of more than 200 criteria; warmth of welcome, authenticity, comfort, safety, equipment, surroundings... nothing is overlooked! And, more importantly, nothing is final – the classification of a Logis can be reviewed at any given moment.

This recipe caught my eye straight away, firstly because the raviolis is deep fried rather than being cooked by the more traditional method and secondly because almost all of the critical ingredients, such as the various mushrooms and chestnuts, are all to be found in the woods behind our house *en France*. Unfortunately they are less frequently available in this country, unless maybe you live in London, so get creative, utilise a range of mushrooms and make sure you include at least one with a real earthy flavour.

Recipe by Monsieur Bidault
Hôtel Le Beau Site
Le Bourg, 19320 St-Pardoux-la-Croisille

Preparation time: 30 minutes
Cooking time: 10 minutes

Ingredients for 4 persons

- *20 g trompettes*
- *20 g girolles*
- *20 g cèpes*
- *70 g butter*
- *10 cl chicken stock*
- *20 cl cream*
- *1 clove of garlic*

- *2 shallots*
- *50 g finely chopped fresh mixed herbs*
- *100 g cooked chestnuts*
- *1 litre of oil for frying*
- *butter*

For the raviolis

- *160 g flour*
- *2 soup spoons of olive oil*
- *1 free range egg*

- *yolk of one free range egg*
- *1 flat coffee spoon of salt*

Preparation

To make the pasta, put the flour in a bowl and make a bay. Pour in the olive oil, the egg and egg yolk, 2 soup spoons of water and the salt. Work the ingredients well to obtain a clear paste. Reserve in your fridge for 4 hours.

Peel and finely chop the shallots and garlic and chop the mushrooms well.

Place a frying pan over a medium flame, add 1 soup spoon of olive oil and 10 grams of butter. When the bubbles from the butter subside, *sauté* the mushrooms until they are lightly coloured. Add the shallots and the garlic, then the finely chopped fresh herbs and cook together for another 5 minutes. Remove the pan from the heat, place the contents into a clean bowl and allow the stuffing to cool.

Lightly flour your work surface and role out the ravioli paste about 1mm thick. If you have a pasta machine, all the better. With the aid of an 8 cm diameter serrated cutter, cut yourself 12 discs of the pasta. Place a coffee spoon full of stuffing into the centre of each disc. With the aid of a pastry brush paint around the edge of each disc with a little water, then fold over into half-moon shapes and crimp around the edges. You must make sure there is a good seal all around, otherwise you will lose the stuffing when you cook the pasta.

Take a saucepan and sweat one finely chopped shallot in a little butter, roughly chop the chestnuts and add them to the shallots, followed by the chicken stock. Mix together and add the cream, then reduce the sauce for around 3 minutes. Blitz for a few moments with your hand blender to produce the coulis. Season to taste.

Plunge the raviolis into a pan of hot oil at around 180ºC. Cook them for approximately 3 minutes, then drain well on kitchen paper. Divide up the sauce and raviolis between four traditional soup bowls and decorate with some chervil.

ROGNONS SAUTÉS
À LA MOUTARDE FINS GOURMETS
sautéed kidneys in a wholegrain mustard cream

I have taken a small liberty including this recipe in my book, and I crave your understanding because it really does come off so very well.

I worked with the creator of this recipe for many years at the Isle of Wight College and our past professional lives are spookily very similar. At the end of the day, it turned out that both he (Paul) and I had attended the same catering college as students back in the Sixties, within about three years of each other and we had never met prior to our employment at the college.

It was weird, in a way, that our catering heads were, and I guess still are, so much on the same wavelength. Paul and I would prepare, cook and present dishes in more or less exactly the same way and in a style which our respected college lecturers would, I am sure, have been very proud of. We even dressed in a similar style and would regularly turn up at work for a 'theory' day, dressed in the same suit – no planning, no nothing – even the same ties – just as if we were twins!!!

I am so very proud that Paul was my best man when Twink and I got married, as he, and his wife Gill, were my rock when my previous marriage had fallen apart. However dear friends, I digress. I really could not have written a cook book without including a recipe produced by one of my very best buddies.

Paul and Gill, at the time of writing, run the Windmill Hotel and restaurant at Bembridge on the Isle of Wight and their out-door catering company caters for many 'yachties' at Cowes on the Island during the summer months. I guess their biggest claim to fame is catering for around 2000 'yachties' over four days in September for breakfast and dinner – all under canvas for the Little Britain Cup.

Well, folks, that's enough of me praising my friends, so onward with the recipe.

Recipe by Paul Rogers
The Windmill Restaurant, 1 Steyne Road, Bembridge, Isle of Wight
AA Good Food Rosette

Preparation time: 20 minutes
Cooking time: 15 minutes

Ingredients for 4 people

- *500 g fresh lamb's kidneys*
- *250 g chestnut mushrooms*
- *1 soup spoon Moutarde fins gourmets (course grain mustard)*
- *150 ml double cream*
- *dry white wine*
- *olive oil*
- *bunch of fresh chives*
- *crusty country bread and butter*

Preparation

Go buy some nice fresh lamb's kidneys from your local butcher and either get him/her to prepare them for you, or trim them up yourself at home before cutting them in half from top to bottom. Paul likes to use chestnut mushrooms, as they add that extra little bit of flavour to this dish, alternatively try to get hold of some nice fresh *champignons de Paris*. Which ever you use, remove the stalks, wash under cold water and pat dry before cutting into halves.

Place a medium sized, deep frying pan or *sauteuse* over a medium high flame, getting the pan nice and hot before adding a good slug of olive oil. The oil will reach a high temperature very quickly, so more or less straight away you can add the kidneys. Allow them to lightly brown before turning. If you try to turn them too quickly you can ruin the texture and appearance of the dish. Once lightly browned on all sides, add the mushroom halves and cook for another couple of minutes or so.

Remove the kidney and mushroom mix to another container and keep warm in the oven. Pour off any excess oil from your pan and return it to a medium flame. Add around 6 cl of dry white wine and reduce the liquid by around two thirds before adding the cream.

Return the kidneys and mushrooms to the liquid and heat thoroughly before pouring into a couple of deep soup bowls. Sprinkle with chopped chives (or chopped flat leaf parsley) and serve with some rustic crusty country bread and butter.

Paul's secret: A knife, fork and spoon are a must for eating this dish. You will most likely have loads of sauce left once you have finished the kidneys and mushrooms, even if you have dunked your bread into it, so the spoon will come well in handy!

WINE: Traditionalists would normally advise you to drink a quality red with kidneys, such as St Emillion or Nuits St Georges, I suggest that you try a red Cornas from the northern Rhone. This dish will also go very well with a crisp dry white and I will take a gamble and suggest that you have a go at a bottle of dry white Burgundy, such as Pouilly-Fuissé. Alternatively you can totally indulge yourselves and try to get hold of a bottle of Condrieu, made from the world famous Voignier grape, with its unique peachy aroma, rich feel and warm finish – an absolute delight to drink.

SALADE CORRÉZIENNE 1
Corrézienne salad # 1

I just had to include this 'little baby' in my book, as the period in my life when I first tasted it was one of those important milestones which I will remember for the rest of my days.

It was July 2001, and I spent ten days at our newly-acquired *maison*, all by myself, getting it ready for what we hoped would be one or two summer rental bookings. We had only bought the house six weeks earlier and I had a mountain of work to do on my own, as my wife was busy working back in the UK and we couldn't have taken our son Ash out of school at that time.

I grafted long and hard during the day and set myself specific hours of work, usually from seven to seven, with a target of being down at Bar Chez Roger in good time for my meal. I very quickly got told off by my new neighbours Georges and Paulette if I didn't stop for lunch and take the obligatory two-hour break.

I ate at Chez Roger nearly every evening for the duration of my stay and one of my nightly treats was Edwige Laage's classic Salade Corrézienne, followed by a ham, cheese and egg *galette* swilled down by one or three half litres of *pression* (draught beer).

You will find different recipes and interpretations throughout the Department for this dish, but few will match Edwige's for its simplicity, presentation, flavour, texture and sheer culinary delight!

Recipe by Edwige Laage

Preparation time:	15 minutes
Cooking time:	3 – 4 minutes

Ingredients for 1 person

- *salad – oak leaf, lettuce, webb, frisée, endive*
- *pain bis (flat, round country bread)*
- *2 Cabécous (small round goats cheese) or Crottin de Chèvre*
- *vinaigrette*
- *Corrèze honey (acacia is best)*

Preparation

Wash the salad leaves and cut or tear into a very rough chiffonade, then prepare a light vinaigrette of Dijon mustard, salt, pepper, vinegar and a blend of nut oil and sunflower oil.

Cut two slices of *pain bis*, drizzle a little honey over each *Cabécou* and place the two cheeses in your oven, pre-heated to 200°C for 3 – 4 minutes. Arrange the salad leaves onto a suitable sized plate, add the slices of *pain bis* with the discs of cheese set on top and a little vinaigrette.

Serve with a separate ramekin of vinaigrette mixed with some chopped flat leaf parsley.

For extra taste and texture, you can add some pieces of walnut to the salad.

WINE: To be quite honest, the salad dressing can be quite sharp and would not go well with most wines, so I tend to go for a cold glass of *pression*.

Now although Edwige has not said so in the recipe which she sent me, I am going to take the liberty of suggesting an alternative recipe for the vinaigrette. I am sure that the vinaigrette which I have experienced in the past at Chez Roger has been honey-based, although the above recipe does not indicate this, so you could always try Charlie's Vinaigrette overleaf instead.

The recipe overleaf is adapted from ingredients which my good friend Charlie (Charlotte) Mallows taught me some years back when Twink and I were staying with her dad for our summer hols, so I definitely can't take any of the credit for it. This one's for you, Charlie.

Charlie's Miel Vinaigrette

Charlie is the daughter of my buddy Jim and in his early years at Le Pont, Charlie would insist on joining me in the kitchen to help cook dinner. Even in those early days, she had some smashing little recipes tucked up her sleeve and we would have a great laugh getting food ready for family friends and visitors. Unfortunately at the time of writing, Charlie is spending a year in Oz, so I am unable to get hold of her famous salmon recipe to include in this book – never mind, another time, Charlie.

Recipe by Charlotte Mallows
Le Pont de l'Hospital, 19400 Argentat

Preparation time: 5 minutes

Ingredients for two people

- *2 tea spoons of good quality Dijon mustard*
- *small pinch of salt*
- *a little ground black pepper*
- *4 soup spoons of raspberry vinegar*
- *small pinch of caster sugar*
- *huile de noix (olive oil if you prefer)*
- *2 tea spoons of Corrézienne honey (acacia is best)*
- *chopped fresh herbs – flat leaf parsley, chives and a little thyme*

Take a bowl and add the mustard, salt and pepper. Using a fork or whisk, blend in the raspberry vinegar and the Corrézienne honey. Gradually add the nut oil until you reach the consistency of your choice. Add the herbs to finish.

Check for flavour and add more salt, pepper or honey to taste. If the end result is too thick add more vinegar or warm water, if too thin add more oil and whisk well.

SALADE CORRÉZIENNE 2
Corrézienne salad # 2

I guess that this is one of those recipes which will not have the universal approval of most Brits. Gizzards, like tripe, are not at the top of every house-wife's shopping list. However, both of these items are found in most super-markets *en Corrèze*, which tends to reflect the "eat all, waste nothing" approach to life of the Corrézienne forefathers.

Recipe by Malcolm Alder-Smith
La Maison aux Quat'Saisons, Laborie, 19400 Monceaux-sur-Dordogne

Preparation time: 20 minutes
Cooking time: 10 minutes

Ingredients for 4 persons

- *200 g tin of gésiers confits (gizzards)*
- *200 g assorted salad leaves*
- *100 g walnuts*
- *2 slices of country bread*
- *25 g butter*

- *sunflower oil*
- *chopped fresh herbs – flat leaf parsley, coriander and chives*
- *Charlie's Miel Vinaigrette (previous recipe)*

Preparation

Wash the salad leaves and shake dry.

To prepare the croutons, slice the bread and remove the crusts, then cut into 1 cm dice. Place a heavy-bottomed frying pan over a medium to high flame, add a slug of oil and the butter. Once the bubbles start to subside, add the croutons, toss in the butter and colour evenly before removing and placing onto some absorbent kitchen paper.

Wipe out the frying pan and return to a low flame. When warm, add the *gésiers* and their fat and heat through very gently. As soon as they start to take on some colour, turn out the flame and allow to rest in the frying pan for a couple of minutes. Remove the *gésiers* from the pan and place onto some absorbent kitchen paper. When they have cooled a little, thinly slice and keep warm.

Divide the salad leaves between four plates and top with the *gésiers* and wal-nuts. Make the vinaigrette, pour a little over each salad and sprinkle with the chopped fresh herbs.

SALADE DE TRUITE FUMÉ
smoked trout salad

When I started researching this book, this was one of the first recipes which I received and it was sent to me by Roland Pilger and Doris Coppenrath.

Roland and Doris are a German couple who were both teachers in their homeland before they decided to move to France and run their hotel: the Auberge St-Julien-aux-Bois in the village of the same name, which they have now done successfully for eight years.

Their concept of gastronomic cuisine is offering a marriage of the natural ingredients of the Corrèze with the flavours of other regions and above all they love to use the organic products of our local farmers. They are fortunate to have a large organic farm in their commune.

Roland and Doris sent me some interesting recipes, for which I am truly grateful, such as Deer steak with a Xaintrie sauce and Roulades of veal stuffed with apples and chestnuts, all truly and deeply Corrézienne.

This is an unusual dish which offers the traditional combination of smoked trout and horseradish, which is complimented by the addition of apple, crème fraîche and beetroot.

Recipe by Doris Coppenrath
Auberge de Saint-Julien-aux-Bois
19220 Saint-Julien-aux-Bois

Preparation time: 30 minutes

Ingredients for 4 people

- *4 fillets of smoked trout*
- *1 apple "Reine de Reinette"*
- *40 g walnuts*
- *1 cooked beetroot*
- *1 soup spoon mayonnaise*
- *3 soup spoons crème fraîche*
- *2 coffee spoons grated horseradish*
- *salt and pepper*

72

Preparation

Cut the fillets of trout, the peeled apple, the walnuts and the peeled beet-root into small pieces and place into a bowl.

Prepare separately a sauce with the mayonnaise, crème fraîche and horseradish and mix well. Add the sauce to the other ingredients and blend gently with a spoon.

Le secret de Doris Coppenrath: This *entrée* is generally served on a salad of Mache leaves, but you can equally use a mixed green salad of your choice.

TARTARE DE SAUMON
tartare of fresh salmon

The Roche de Vic, a two-star Logis de France, is a fairly well-known hotel in our part of La Corrèze, with a reputation for good quality food. Although we have not yet had the pleasure of eating there, it is high on our 'must eat there' list, as it comes highly recommended by many friends.

Recipe by Alain Paillier
Roche de Vic
Les Quatre Routes – 19380 Albussac

Preparation time: 20 minutes

Ingredients for 4 people

- *200 g fresh salmon fillet*
- *1 shallot*
- *10 g fresh chives*
- *3 soup spoons of mayonnaise*
- *whipping cream (150 ml approx)*
- *juice of half a small lemon*
- *salt and pepper*

Preparation

Cut the salmon into a small dice or fine strips. Take a bowl and mix with the finely chopped shallots and chives. Add the mayonnaise, some cream, salt and pepper and little by little the lemon juice, taking care that the mixture does not become runny.

Take the salmon mixture and lightly press into four ramekins. Turn out the ramekins onto four plates, providing you with a nicely shaped portion of the tartare in the centre of each plate. Decorate the plates in your own style, maybe with slices of cannelé-ed cucumber, some lump fish roe and a tad of crisp fresh salad leaves.

Secret de Alain Paillier: Serve very well chilled.

WINE: A nicely chilled bottle of Muscadet sur Lie will accompany this dish perfectly.

Recipe supplied by Comité Départemental du Tourisme de la Corrèze

ROCHE DE VIC
LES QUATRES ROUTES
19380 ALBUSSAC

TARTE DE CHAVIGNOL
goat's cheese flan

Crottin de Chavignon is a small, round goat's cheese. It has a unique salty sweet flavour and is quite firm in texture. You should be able to find it easily in your local supermarket, but if not then you can use any *crottin de chèvre* or another goat's cheese, so long as it is a firm one.

Recipe by Diane Alder-Smith
La Maison aux Quat'Saisons, Laborie, 19400 Monceaux-sur-Dordogne

Preparation time: 25 minutes
Cooking time: 30-40 minutes

Ingredients for 6 people

- *Shortcrust or puff pastry*
- *2 crottins de chavignol (or chévre)*
- *½ bag of spinach*
- *4 spring onions*
- *½ sweet red pepper*
- *grating of fresh nutmeg*
- *3 large free-range eggs*
- *100-150ml double cream*
- *olive oil*
- *salt and pepper*

Preparation

Roll out the pastry and line a quiche/flan dish with baking parchment or greaseproof paper and baking beans. Bake blind in a preheated oven at 200°C for 10-15 minutes.

Lightly fry the pepper and chopped spring onions in olive oil until softened.

Remove the quiche dish from the oven, allow to cool for 5 – 10 minutes and remove the baking beans and paper.

Spread the cooked pepper and onion mix over the pastry, wilt the spinach in a hot pan and add to the mix with a little freshly grated nutmeg. Slice the goat's cheese carefully into discs and place neatly over the top of the other ingredients.

Whisk the eggs and cream together and lightly season with salt and ground black pepper, pouring the mixture over the other ingredients, and bake in a hot oven at 200°C for approximately 30 – 40 minutes until golden brown.

Serve very hot with a green salad and new potatoes.

WINE: Check out a Sancerre or a Pouilly Fumé; these are two of my favourites and not overly expensive. Alternatively a Provence Rosé will work well with goat's cheese.

TERRINE CAMPAGNARDE
country pâté

This is another recipe sent to me by our good friends Roger Déjammes and Edwige Laage who used to run a wonderful watering hole in Argentat called Chez Roger, a fantastic bar/café and pavement Glacier-Bar which specialised in pizzas, *crêpes*, salads and the most amazing ice cream concoctions, complimented by wondrous pyrotechnics to excite the minds of both children and adults alike.

As Roger spends most of the year running his wine business, they also sold some very nice house wines, such as Petit Chablis – such extravagance! The place used to heave in the summer months, especially on *le jour du marché* (market day), held every first and third Thursday of the month. Although they have now sold Chez Roger, I felt that I had to include some of Roger and Edwige's family recipes as their food was always outstanding.

I experienced the most ferocious Corrézienne thunderstorm early one July evening in 2001, when sitting outside Chez Roger eating my dinner, with Gil Scott's jazz band playing in the background. It was only when the torrential rain and lightning made it too dangerous for the band to play on that we all ventured inside to continue the party until the early hours.

Recipe by Pierrette Déjammes
(Mother of Roger, Giselle, Claudine et Jean-Pierre << Aubech >> 19400)

Preparation time: 20 minutes
Cooking time: 120 minutes

Ingredients for 6 – 8 people

- *3 kg finely minced pork (1/3 throat, 1/3 breast, 1/3 liver)*
- *salt and pepper*
- *half a glass of cognac*
- *300 gr diced foie gras*

Preparation

Mix the minced pork with the salt and pepper and the cognac. Add at the last moment, 300 g foie gras and mix well. Put into a buttered earthenware terrine, cover with a lid or foil and cook in the oven in a *bain marie* on a medium heat.

Le secret de Pierrette Déjammes: "Beaucoup d'Amour"

TIAN DE SAUMON FUMÉ et AVOCAT
tian of smoked salmon and avocado

As usual, I have a story to relate regarding this dish. Our good friends Paul and Gill Rogers were coming around to dinner with their son David and his wife a few years back and we were at a loss as to what to do as a starter. The Rogers family are well-known caterers on the Isle of Wight and, well, entertaining can become a challenge if you are out to impress your old buddies. So in fact, this is another recipe which I can indirectly 'blame' my mate Paul for. Twink had brought some nice smoked salmon and we just happened to have some avocados in the fridge. I didn't want to do a standard smoked salmon, so I thought I would experiment, knowing that we could always blag it a bit if the dish went slightly wrong!!!

Recipe by Malcolm Alder-Smith
La Maison aux Quat'Saisons, Laborie, 19400 Monceaux-sur-Dordogne

Preparation time:	20 minutes
Storage time:	60 minutes

Ingredients for 4-6 people

- *1 pack of smoked salmon*
- *2 avocados (ready to use)*
- *1 clove of garlic*
- *flat leaf parsley*
- *chives*
- *2 lemons*

- *olive oil*
- *salt and black pepper*
- *6 cl mayonnaise de Dijon*
- *6 cl crème fraîche*
- *chives – finely chopped (leave 2 full strands per person for garnish)*

Preparation

The idea of this dish is fairly simple (I hope). Remove the slices of smoked salmon from their pack, place onto a chopping board and cut them with a sharp knife (head to tail) into approximately 2mm wide strips, making a spaghetti of smoked salmon. Place the strips into a good sized bowl.

Finely grate the rind from one lemon and pop it into another bowl. Finely chop the garlic and the parsley and add it to the grated lemon rind.

Cut the rinded lemon in half and squeeze the juice from both halves into the parsley and garlic mixture. Add a little salt and black pepper, stir well and add a couple of slugs of a good quality olive oil, stir well to make a lemon vinaigrette.

Pour the mixture over the 'spaghetti' and stir gently to ensure that all of the salmon is coated with the dressing. Sounds good eh? Cover the ingredients with a clean tea towel or some cling film and place into the fridge for around 1 hour.

While the salmon is taking on board all the wonderful flavours, you can get under way preparing the avocado.

Cut the avocados in half, de-stone and carefully remove the skin. Lay the halves onto a chopping board, flat side down, and slice them (side to side) approximately 2mm thick.

When you are ready, take 4-6 ramekins (7cm) and brush lightly with some olive oil. Place a little of the smoked salmon into the ramekin, making sure that you cover the base. Take a couple of the 'half slices' of avocado and place them on top of the salmon and so on, building layers of salmon and avocado until the ramekin is filled. You will need to apply a little pressure, as you add the layers, if not the tian may disintegrate when you remove it from the ramekin. The last layer should also be smoked salmon.

When completed, wrap the ramekins in cling film and refrigerate for another hour. Remove from the fridge a good 30 minutes before you intend to serve the salmon, as a cold fridge may have an adverse effect on the olive oil.

To serve, take the plate of your choice, remove the cling film, place a plate over the ramekin and holding both firmly, flip them over through 180° and the tian should slide gently from the ramekin onto the plate. If you have major problems removing the salmon, dip the ramekins into some hot water for a few seconds only and then follow the same method for removing the salmon.

Take a bowl and blend together the Moutarde de Dijon, crème fraîche and the chopped chives. Place a dessert spoon sized dollop onto the side of the plate, garnish with a wedge of lemon and two strands of chives.

Secret de Malcolm: Serve with some thin slices of fresh baguette.

WINE: You have just got to go for dry but pungent white wine, my preference would be a Grand Cru Chablis or Pouilly-Fumé

POISSONS
Fish

The rivers of Corrèze are numerous, which makes the Department a target for professional and amateur *pêcheurs* alike. By the way, take care when using the word *pêcheur*, because if you put the wrong accent on the first 'e' (i.e. *pécheur*) this means 'a sinner', which might just about offend every French angler who ever picked up a fishing rod. It may well be true of course, but they do take their sport very, very seriously indeed and we wouldn't want to upset the balance of the old *entente cordiale*.

In our valley alone, we have five main rivers which can be fished between March and November each year – the Doustre, Cère, Maronne,

Souvigne and the picturesque Dordogne. Permits to fish are easily accessible from local sports shops, which sell of an awful lot of kit for huntin', shootin' and fishin'. The thing is, that being totally landlocked, river fish such as salmon, pike, perch and trout, some of them very large indeed, are enthusiastically fished by *pêcheurs* from near and far.

You will still find dried haddock (*eglefin*, which is dried, not salted, and doubles in volume when soaked) available at the open markets and in some of the supermarkets. Some say that its origins are on the shores of the Baltic and it was intoroduced to the Department by Polish miners working in the local coal mines (*les mines du charbon*). This became an important part of local trade thanks to sailors travelling up-river towards the Valée de la Dordogne from Bordeaux or Libourne.

My friend Jim who lives near Argentat tells me that EDF (*Électricité de France*), which controls the dams in the upper Dordogne valley, is only supposed to open the dams for so many days each year and only for so many hours per day, but in recent years they have been doing this on a more regular basis, which makes the rivers run much too fast. When the rivers "are up" it is too dangerous for *les pêcheurs* to take to the water. This in turn has reduced the number of visiting fishermen to the region, however, there is still a healthy interest in the rivers and the owners of local B&Bs have numerous tales to tell of *pêcheurs* arriving back at their accommodation late at night sporting their catch and hoping that somebody has sufficient time to be able to turn it into a delicious and interesting meal.

I am a great lover of Rick Stein's cooking and have followed his success in recent years with a certain amount of envy. The appeal for me is the relative simplicity of his recipes (much the same as Jamie Oliver), and the use of good quality, fresh produce. I have been sent numerous fish recipes from my 'new friends', the chefs and patrons of Corrézienne hotels and restaurants and I have tried to include those which are relatively simple to cook and will impress your dinner guests. I have included my own salmon served on a bed of leeks with acacia honey and mustard sauce, which I like to think of as one of my signature dishes. The sauce masks the salmon fillet with a beautiful sheen, yet you can still see the pink flesh of the fish through the sauce and the flavour is definitely to die for.

CASSOLETTE DE SALMON AUX GIROLES EN SURPRISE
individual salmon cassolettes

This dish, an upmarket fisherman's pie with a difference, can equally make a tasty starter or an interesting main course.

Recipe by Bernard Viallet
Auberge de la Tradition
Avenue de la Gare – 19800 Corrèze

Preparation time: 20 minutes
Cooking time: 35 minutes

Ingredients for 6 people

- *750 g fillet of salmon*
- *1 dl fish stock*
- *500 g girolles or chanterelles mushrooms*
- *2 shallots finely chopped*
- *2 dl crème fraîche*
- *puff pastry*
- *garlic*
- *flat leaf parsley*
- *salt and pepper*

Preparation

Clean the *girolles* without soaking, then cut them into large pieces, two to four pieces per *girolle* depending on the size. Place a heavy-bottomed pan over a moderate heat and add a knob of butter, allow the butter to melt then add the mushrooms and the chopped shallots. Cook over a medium flame until any liquid in the bottom of the pan has evaporated and remove from the heat. Around this time take the fillet of salmon and cut into 1 cm dice.

Take one clove of garlic and four sprigs of parsley and finely chop. Put the cubes of salmon into a heavy-bottomed pan, add the fish stock and bring up to the boil. Remove the cubes of salmon and keep warm. Add the mushrooms, shallots and *crème fraîche* to the stock and reduce down until you obtain a creamy liquid that will lightly coat the back of a wooden spoon. Incorporate the garlic and parsley mix and the cubes of salmon and blend the mixture together gently.

Share out the mixture between individual *cassolettes* (ramekins or pie dishes), making sure that everyone gets an equal amount of salmon and girolles and top up each with the remaining sauce from the pan. Set to one side and allow to cool.

Roll out the puff pastry and with a pastry cutter cut out 6 discs which are slightly bigger than top of the *cassolettes*. Take a pastry brush and paint around the edge of the dishes with some water then crimp the discs into place. Cut a small cross into the centre of each disc of pastry and lightly brush with some egg wash. This will help give the pastry a nice golden glaze.

Put the dishes onto a large baking sheet, place into the centre of a pre-heated oven at 210°C and cook for 20 minutes or until the pastry is golden brown.

WINE: Try a nicely chilled bottle of Chenin Blanc from the Loire. The acidity will help to cut through the garlicy flavour.

Recipe supplied by Comité Départemental du Tourisme de la Corrèze.

ESCALOPE DE SANDRE RÔTI AU LARD
roast escalope of perch with bacon

This recipe was kindly sent to me by the brilliant Bidault family who run the Hôtel Le Beau Site at St-Pardoux-la-Croisille. The recipes which they have sent me use traditional Corrézienne ingredients but have incorporated some modern ideas in their method of preparation. The end products, from the ones which we have tried, have turned out wonderfully and are certainly ones which we will use ourselves in the future.

When you are next in France, pop into a supermarket and buy yourself some little 110 g tubs of Maggi Fonds (stocks). They produce quite a good range of *fonds* such as *de poisson, volaille, veau* etc., but although they're a little pricey, the end result is very authentic and adds fabulous flavours to whatever you are cooking. The fish stock is especially good.

Recipe by Monsieur Bidault – Patron
Hôtel Le Beau Site
Le Bourg, 19320 St-Pardoux-la-Croisille

Preparation time: 15 minutes
Cooking time: 35 minutes

Ingredients for 4 people

- *4 escalopes of perch (around 180 g each)*
- *200 g smoked bacon – thinly sliced*
- *2 soup spoons of groundnut oil*
- *30 g butter*
- *25 g puy lentils*
- *1 carrot*
- *2 shallots and 1 onion*

For the sauce
- *60 g shallots*
- *10 g butter*
- *10 cl balsamic vinegar*
- *20 cl fish stock*
- *20 cl cream*

Preparation

Wash the lentils under cold running water. Place them into a pan of cold water, bring to the boil and drain immediately. Peel, wash and then cut the carrot and onion into small dice. Place a *sauteuse* over a medium heat, add the walnut oil and quickly brown the carrot and onions, reduce the heat and cook without further colour until the vegetables are nicely tender. Add the lentils and stir, then cover the mixture with two times the volume of cold water. Cook for a further 20 minutes at a slow boil.

To prepare the sauce, skin and finely chop the shallots. Place a heavy-bottomed pan over a medium flame, add the shallots and cook until lightly browned, add the balsamic vinegar, then the fish stock. Reduce the liquid by half, season, then add the cream and keep hot over a very low flame.

Wrap each escalope with the slices of smoked bacon. Take a heavy-bottomed frying pan, put on a moderate flame and add a soup spoon of olive oil and 10 g of butter. Once the butter has melted, add the escalopes and cook for about 5 minutes on each side.

Dress some of the lentil mixture in the middle of each plate and position an escalope on top of the lentils. Finish the dish by pouring a little sauce around the side of the plate.

FILET DE SAUMON AUX FINES HERBES
fillet of salmon with a herb cream

We eat fish quite a lot and find that salmon is incredibly versatile. I guess that now you can buy farmed salmon back in the UK, it is relatively cheap when compared with many other fish, whereby it used to be looked upon as being out of reach of most people's pocket. However, if you can get hold of wild salmon, you will certainly notice the difference in quality, texture and flavour.

Salmon is a little like chicken, in so much as you can cook it in so many different ways: fry, poach, grill, roast, etc. We will often cook salmon in the summer months, serving it with a nice crisp salad and some new potatoes.

I know that the current trend is to serve fillets of fish with the skin on, but I prefer to serve this dish without the skin.

This little recipe is so easy to prepare and I am sure you will enjoy it.

Recipe by Malcolm Alder-Smith
La Maison aux Quat'Saisons, Laborie, 19400 Monceaux-sur-Dordogne

Preparation time: 30 minutes
Cooking time: 20 minutes

Ingredients for 4 people

- *4 x 160 g salmon fillets (skin removed)*
- *1 pack baby asparagus*
- *12.5 cl dry white wine*
- *2 soup spoons olive oil*
- *2 shallots*
- *125 ml double cream*
- *100 g unsalted butter*
- *flat leaf parsley*
- *tarragon*
- *chives*
- *chervil*

Preparation

Take a shallow, heavy-bottomed *sauteuse* and half fill with water over a high flame. When the water boils, reduce the heat to a medium to low flame and add a pinch of salt. Carefully place the asparagus into the water and allow to simmer gently for 3 to 4 minutes. Remove the pan from the hob, drain the water and refresh the asparagus. This will help to retain the colour, texture and nutritional value.

Place the salmon fillets onto a chopping board and lightly season them on both sides.

Heat a heavy-bottomed frying pan over a medium flame. Add a slug of olive oil and around 50 g of the butter. Once the butter foams, add the salmon fillets, reduce the flame slightly and cook for around 3 minutes. Take a fish slice or palette knife and carefully turn the fillets over and cook for a further 2 minutes.

While the salmon is cooking, take about half a handful of each of the herbs, chop them finely and put to one side for a moment. Skin the shallots and slice them thinly.

Remove the fillets from the pan, put them onto a dish and place into a pre-heated oven on 175°C to finish cooking, while you finish off the herb cream. The idea is that the salmon is still just slightly 'pink' in the middle, so it's important that you get your timing just right.

Place a knob of butter into the frying pan, add the sliced shallots and cook for a two or three minutes until they start to go soft. Add the wine, increase the flame to medium-high and reduce the liquid by around two-thirds. Add the cream and blend the mixture together before adding the finely chopped herbs. Cook the sauce for a further 2 minutes, check for seasoning and consistency.

Microwave the asparagus, with a little butter, for about 1 minute, being careful not to over cook it. Place the salmon fillets onto four individual plates, mask some of the herb cream over each fillet and top with a criss-cross of asparagus.

My secret: Serve with a mixture of salad leaves of your choice with a sweet lemon vinaigrette.

Wine: Go for a nice white Burgundy, something like a Pouilly Vinzelles or Pouilly Fuissé from the Macon region. At its best, the latter can be quite outstanding, but tends to be a little on the pricey side. You may prefer to go for a Chablis.

FILET DE SAUMON AUX POIREAUX
fillet of salmon on a bed of shredded leek

I was playing around with a recipe a few years back and was struck with the idea of serving salmon on a bed of shredded leek with a chiffonade of sweet prunes. Sounds nice, but I wanted to create a sauce which would compliment all of the ingredients, but not conform to standard food/sauce combinations. We tried the idea out on a few friends at dinner parties and it always went down a real treat, so I thought I would include it for you to enjoy.

Recipe by Malcolm Alder-Smith
La Maison aux Quat'Saisons, Laborie, 19400 Monceaux-sur-Dordogne

Preparation time:20 minutes
Cooking time: 20-30 minutes

Ingredients for 4 people

- *4 150 g salmon fillets (skin off)*
- *2 medium sized leeks*
- *50 g ready to eat prunes*
- *10 cl medium dry white wine*
- *1 soup spoon acacia honey*
- *½ soup spoon Dijon mustard*
- *unsalted butter*
- *1 lime*
- *20 cl cream*
- *Baleine salt and black pepper*

Preparation

Clean the leeks thoroughly, by splitting from the root end all the way down the vegetable. Run under a cold tap and make sure that you clean well between all of the layers. Drain the leeks and shred them quite finely, no bigger than say 3 mm, on your chopping board. If you cut them any larger, it will slow down the cooking process. The leeks can be cooked at the last moment, once the salmon fillets are cooked, or you can always prepare them in advance and re-heat when you are ready.

Place the four salmon fillets onto a chopping board and lightly season with the salt and black pepper. Place a large heavy-bottomed frying pan over a medium flame, add a knob of butter and once the bubbles start to subside, add the four pieces of fish and allow to cook until they start to turn a light golden brown, this should take around 3 – 4 minutes. Turn the fillets over and cook for around another 2 minutes on the other side. Remove the fillets from the pan, place onto a warmed oven tray and pop into a pre-heated oven set on 175°C to keep the fish warm and just finish off the cooking perfectly. I like to cook mine so that the middle of the salmon is just slightly underdone.

Drain off any residual butter in the frying pan and return the pan to the hob over a medium flame. Add the glass of wine, stir well to remove any deposits from the bottom and reduce the liquid by around 50% to concentrate the flavours.

Strain the reduced wine into a clean saucepan and place on the hob over a medium to low flame. Add the acacia honey and the mustard and blend the ingredients thoroughly. Reduce the flame to low, add the cream and bring the sauce up to a slow simmer. Check for seasoning and consistency. The sauce should be fairly translucent, which looks great on the fish, because you can still see the golden pink colour of the fish and get loadsa flavour from the sauce – FABULOUS!

Place a large heavy-bottomed frying pan over a medium to high flame, add a knob of butter and throw in the shredded leeks. Season with salt and black pepper and toss well in the pan, this will help to cook them evenly, for three to four minutes. You don't want to overcook the leeks, otherwise they will lose their shape and start to look rather sad!

Reduce the heat to a medium flame and drizzle in the shredded prunes so that they mix in thoroughly with the leeks. Once the prunes are sufficiently heated through, add a little more butter and the juice of half a fresh lime.

Using a slotted spoon, divide the leek and prune mixture between four warmed plates. Rest a salmon fillet over the top of the leeks and mask each fillet with some of the sauce. Drizzle a little sauce around the plate to serve.

My secret: For the sake of perfect timing and spending lots of time with our guests, I cook the leeks ahead of time and nuke them for a couple of minutes.

WINE: Try a young oaked Condrieu from the northern Rhone. The grape, Voignier, produces quite a fragrant, soft wine of fairly unique character. I love it and jump at the remotest opportunity to have a glass or three.

FILET DE TRUITE CITRON VERTE ET CÂPRE
trout fillet with a lime and caper sauce

Recipe by Diane Alder-Smith
La Maison aux Quat'Saisons, Laborie, 19400 Monceaux-sur-Dordogne

Preparation time: 30 minutes
Cooking time: 5 – 10 minutes

Ingredients for 4 people

- *8 trout fillets*
- *100 g unsalted butter*
- *4 soup spoons of capers, drained and dried*
- *4 soup spoons of fresh chervil*
- *2-3 soup spoons of fresh lime juice*
- *salt and pepper*

Preparation

Place the trout fillets onto a chopping board and lightly season with salt and pepper.

Place a large heavy-bottomed frying pan over a medium flame and add around 25g of butter. When the butter has melted and it starts to bubble, add the trout fillets, reduce the heat and fry them very gently for around 3 minutes. With a palette knife, very gently turn the fillets over and cook them for a further minute or so.

Using your palette knife, transfer the fillets between four pre-heated plates and place them into a pre-heated oven to keep warm.

Place the pan back onto your hob over a medium flame, add the remaining butter and fry the capers for a few moments, then add the chopped chervil and cook for another minute or so. Add the lime juice and season to taste with a little salt and pepper. Spoon the mixture over the fillets and serve.

FILET DE TRUITE SAUMONÉE SAUCE SAFRAN
fillet of salmon trout with a saffron sauce

These days, you can usually get hold of prepared salmon trout fillets from your local supermarket, but you will need to try to buy some which are a reasonable size.

Recipe by Jean Marko
Hôtel du Parc, 1, place de Vieux Lavoir
Arnac-Pompadour, 19230 Pompadour

Preparation time: 15 minutes
Cooking time: 20 minutes

Ingredients for 6 persons

- *6 salmon trout (around 200 g each)*
- *3 soup spoons of olive oil*
- *20 cl dry white wine*
- *juice of 2 lemons*
- *salt and pepper*

For the sauce

- *3 shallots – finely chopped*
- *30 cl fish stock*
- *30 cl of crème fraîche*
- *5 cl Noilly Prat (dry Martini will do)*
- *2 to 3 pinches of powdered saffron*
- *butter*
- *salt, pepper and piment doux (powdered sweet red pepper)*

Preparation

Remove the fillets from the salmon trout, skin them and pop them into a buttered oven tray. Sprinkle with the olive oil, white wine, lemon juice and season with the salt and pepper. Cook in a pre-heated oven at around 200ºC for 15 minutes before you are ready to serve.

Lightly brown the shallots in a little of the butter, add the Noilly Prat, increase the heat and reduce by about half. Add the fish stock, then the crème fraîche, the saffron and a touch of piment doux. Thicken the sauce with some *beurre manier* (mix equal quantities of flour and butter together in a separate bowl – about 25 g of each should do) to make a paste. Increase the heat and add the paste, little by little, to your sauce and whisk briskly. The sauce will gradually thicken and produce a nice glaze which looks great when you serve up the fish. Check the sauce for seasoning and adjust to taste.

Remove the fillets from the cooking juices, drain them well, dress on hot plates and pour a little of the sauce over each (*nappé*).

Secret de Jean Marko: You can accompany this dish with fresh tagliatelle tossed in a little butter and olive oil with a knob of lemon butter on top.

WINE: Why not try a Petit Chablis or go for something totally different, a Pouilly Fumé from the upper Loire Valley near Sancerre.

Recipe supplied by Comité Départemental du Tourisme de la Corrèze.

AUBERGE DES GABARIERS
15 QUAI LESTOURGIE
19400 ARGENTAT

SANDRE AUX POIREAUX
perch on a bed of leeks

This recipe has been given to us by our dear friends Michel and Isabelle at the Gabariers (The Bargemen's) in Argentat. Although there are many fine eateries in the area, we have always been drawn to their restaurant because of the fine food, attentive service, excellent wine list, location and our hospitable hosts. They have recently employed two new chefs and have completely changed their menus with impressive results. Eating al fresco in the summer, sitting only yards from the Dordogne, letting the cares of the world drift by, draws us back there time after time.

The Gabariers is situated on the ancient Quai Lestourgie where, years ago, oak barges would be loaded with cheese, coal, nuts and oak and then skilfully guided down the Dordogne to Bergerac, Libourne and on to Bordeaux. The boatmen would sell their goods and their boats which were then used to make oak barrels for maturing fine wine and brandy, before *les gabariers* walked back to Argentat!

Recipe by Michel et Isabelle Roussanne
Auberge des Gabariers, 15 Quai Lestourgie, 19400 Argentat

Preparation time:	45 minutes
Cooking time:	50 minutes

Ingredients for 4 people

- *1 kg perch*
- *1 kg leek*
- *1 onion*
- *2 shallots*
- *1 bouquet garni (fresh)*
- *50 cl dry white wine*
- *50 cl water*
- *3 soup spoons of olive oil*
- *70 g butter*
- *salt and pepper*

For the sauce
- *20 cl court bouillon*
- *40 cl crème fraiche*

- *1 soup spoon of sugar*
- *salt and pepper*

Preparation

Get your fishmonger to remove the fillets and skin them for you -- try to buy them around 150 gr per portion.

Prepare a *court-bouillon* by cutting the onion, shallots and carrot into rounds. Put them into a pan with the wine, water, *bouquet garni*, a good pinch of salt and a few pepper corns. Bring to the boil, reduce the heat and simmer for 10 minutes.

Wash the leeks thoroughly, trim off most of the green part and then cut into half-inch discs. Melt the butter in a *sauteuse* over a medium to low flame, add the leek and cover with a lid and sweat down for around 10 minutes, stirring occasionally, remove the lid and cook for a further 5 minutes to remove any surplus liquid.

Prepare the sauce by adding 20 cl of the *court bouillon* to a saucepan then heat over a medium to high flame and reduce the liquid until nearly dry. Pour in the *crème fraiche* and mix well. Simmer over a low heat until the sauce reaches a creamy consistency. Add a little more *court bouillon* if necessary.

While the sauce is cooking, lightly season the fillets of perch and pan fry them in the olive oil on both sides for about 5 minutes in total, taking extra care when you turn the fillets over.

Present the fillets on a bed of melted leek and coat with the sauce. Serve very hot.

WINE: This exquisite fish deserves to be complimented by the finest wines. Try an Alsace Riesling Grand Cru or push the boat out and go for one of the quality white burgundies.

TOURTE AU SAUMON ET AUX CHAMPIGNONS
salmon and mushroom tart

This recipe was sent to me by Denise Mespoulet, one of our dear neighbours in France. She, like many others, rallied to the cause and sent me numerous wonderful recipes, unfortunately far too many for me to use. However, this has given me the opportunity to be more selective and hopefully produce a more diverse range of dishes for you to enjoy preparing – and of course eating.

We absolutely loved how this dish turned out when we tested it in our kitchen in the UK, in fact it was so good that we used it again a few days later when entertaining some friends for dinner. They were equally impressed and insisted that I wrote out the recipe for them before they left that evening!

Recipe by Denise Mespoulet

Preparation time:	25 minutes
Cooking time:	30 minutes

Ingredients for 6 persons

- *300 g puff pastry*
- *250 g skinned fresh salmon fillet*
- *150 g champignons de Paris (small button mushrooms)*
- *2 shallots – finely chopped*
- *1 small bunch of chives*
- *2 free range eggs*
- *25 cl crème fraîche*
- *50 g unsalted butter*
- *salt and pepper*

Preparation

Roll out the puff pastry to around 4mm thick and sufficiently large to line a 22cm flan mould. Butter the inside of the mould, using about half the amount of butter and line the mould with the rolled out pastry; you can trim the edges now or leave the pastry overlapping a little and trim it once the 'blind' flan is cooked. Prick the bottom of the pastry with a fork, cover with greaseproof paper or parchment and fill with some dried baking beans to weigh the pastry down while it cooks. Place into a pre-heated oven at 210°C for 10 minutes.

Melt the remaining butter in a frying pan over a medium flame and add the quartered mushrooms and shallots. Cook for a few moments, then cover with a lid and leave them to cook in their own liquid for a few minutes. Remove the lid and carry on cooking until all of the liquid has evaporated.

Remove the flan from the oven and carefully take out the baking beans and greaseproof paper. If you are going to trim the edges of the pastry at this stage (instead of earlier), do it now.

Cut the salmon into bite-size chunks and spread over the base of the pastry, then add the cooked mushroom mixture. Take a mixing bowl and add the eggs, *crème fraîche* and chopped chives and mix well. Lightly season and pour the mixture over the salmon and mushrooms.

Cook in your pre-heated oven at 210°C for 30 minutes.

Le secret de Denise: Serve luke-warm with a nice green salad and some crusty bread

WINE: To avoid 'pushing the boat out' too often, why not try a generic white Burgundy (Chardonnay) with this dish. You will find that some of the top growers produce real bargains from the environs of the Cote d'Or villages.

TRUITE AUX GIROLLES, BEURRE CITRONNÉ
trout with girolles and lemon butter

Twink and I discovered Les Voyageurs, a wonderful hotel-restaurant in 2001, the year when we brought our house in Monceaux-sur-Dordogne. My daughter Larnie and Ash (my youngest son) had driven down in my car with Twink, while I drove a hire van full of our furniture and possessions.

We wanted to show Larnie and Ash the Barrage du Chastang and so headed off into the hills on a bright sunny morning. After the barrage we carried on driving ever upwards until we reached the pretty village of St-Martin-la-Meanne. It was lunchtime, so we stopped for a drink and made our acquaintance with Catherine Chaumeil, who incidentally speaks perfect English, although we didn't find this out until just before we departed!

We promised to return for a meal and eventually got round to eating there in October 2002 when Twink's family joined us for a week's vacation. The food is of the highest standard and typifies everything I would hope to find in a Corrézienne restaurant: a warm welcome, rustic surroundings, oak beams and most of all food prepared and cooked with love and expertise by Jean Françoise.

Recipe by Jean-Françoise Chaumeil
Les Voyageurs
Place de la Mairie , 19320 St-Martin-la-Méanne

Preparation time: 25 minutes
Cooking time: 15 minutes

Ingredients for 1 person

- 1 trout (190/200 g portion)
- 100 g girolles
- 50 g bread crumbs
- 1 dl cream
- 1 dl of egg white

- salt and pepper
- 1 lemon
- knob of butter
- court bouillon
- 1 soup spoon of brandy

Preparation

Remove the dorsal from the trout. Season the inside with salt and pepper. Roughly chop the *girolles* and mix them with the breadcrumbs, cream, egg white and brandy. Season and mix well. Check the seasoning and add a little more if required. Stuff the trout with the mixture.

Cut a piece of tin-foil and butter it on one side. Place the trout in the middle of the foil, fold over the edges to make a bag shape and place the bag into a pan containing the simmering *court bouillon*. Cook the trout in the simmering liquid for 10 to 15 minutes. Remove the bag from the *court bouillon*, remove the skin from both sides of the trout and dress on a warm plate.

Take a small frying pan and melt the knob of butter. Once melted and bubbling, taking care not to let the butter colour too much, add the juice of one lemon and *nappé* over the fish. If you allow the butter to just start to colour, it will give off a wonderful nutty flavour.

Le secret de Jean-Françoise: Serve this fish with a *purée* of carrots, a *purée* of celery or curried rice.

WINE: You will find that a fairly delicate white wine will go well with this fish dish, so why not try one from Alsace, something like a Pinot Blanc.

Recipe supplied by Comité Départemental du Tourisme de la Corrèze.

HOTEL DES VOYAGEURS
PLACE DE LA MAIRIE
ST-MARTIN-LA-MÉANNE

TRUITE FARCIS AUX MIEL
Trout Stuffed with Mushrooms and Honey

Recipe by Malcolm Alder-Smith
La Maison aux Quat'Saisons, Laborie, 19400 Monceaux-sur-Dordogne

Preparation time: 30 minutes
Cooking time: 20 minutes

Ingredients for 4 people

- *4 fresh river trout*
- *2 medium onions*
- *250 g cèpes*
- *4 cloves of garlic*
- *4 bay leaves*
- *4 sprigs of thyme*
- *8 soup spoons of Corrézienne acacia honey*
- *flat leaf parsley*
- *white wine vinegar*
- *good quality olive oil*
- *unsalted butter*
- *salt and ground black pepper*

Preparation

Thinly slice the mushrooms, onions and garlic. Chop around a handful of the flat leaf parsley.

Place a heavy-bottomed frying pan over a medium flame, then add a small slug of olive oil and around 25 g of the butter. Fry the onions and garlic for around ten minutes until they are soft. Add the *cèpes* and cook for a further 5-10 minutes. Add the honey, herbs and vinegar and continue to cook until the onions and mushrooms are nicely browned. Remove from the heat, add the chopped parsley, season to taste, and allow to cool.

Turn each trout upside down, open the void, season with a little salt and pepper and add a knob of butter. Stuff each trout with the onion, mushroom, garlic and parsley mixture.

Take four pieces of tin foil, each large enough to hold a stuffed trout, brush with a mixture of melted butter and olive oil. Carefully place a trout onto each sheet of the tin foil. Pour a little olive oil over each fish and lightly season with salt and black pepper.

Fold the foil to make a bag and either place onto a hot barbecue or into a pre-heated oven at around 200°C for around 15 – 20 minutes depending on size.

Serve with a green salad of your choice and some boiled new potatoes finished with butter and chopped fresh chives.

TRUITE SAUMONÉ POCHÉ
poached salmon trout with a lime & dill mayonnaise

During a school half-term, a few short years back, we were staying with Jim and Fi at their riverside hotel and they had a couple of groups of *pêcheurs* staying for the weekend. One lot were from La Rochelle and the others from somewhere near Marseille.

The ones from La Rochelle had brought with them a 'mungus' box of *huîtres* (oysters). They asked Jim if they could prepare them in the kitchen, which they did, and generously shared them with us. So we cut some lemons, made up some shallot dressing and indulged ourselves with a nice bottle of Sancerre.

The ones from near Marseille came in on the Saturday evening with the most enormous salmon trout, which one of them had caught. They asked Fi if she would prepare the fish for them for their dinner, which she did in her usual efficient manner. She cooked the fish to perfection and I just had to include her recipe. I have added a couple of little extras, which I hope compliment this dish and do it justice.

You will need a salmon kettle with a trivet to cook this dish. It can be done other ways, but you will certainly find it easier in a kettle.

Recipe by Fiona Mallows
Au Pont de L'Hospital, 19400 Argentat

Preparation time: 15 minutes
Cooking time: 20 – 30 minutes

Ingredients for 6 – 8 persons

- *1 x 2 kg whole salmon-trout*
- *1 soup spoon whole peppercorns*
- *2 bay leaves*
- *1 lemon*
- *salt*

Lime and dill mayonnaise

- *200 ml mayonnaise de Dijon*
- *1 lime*
- *5 g dill*
- *Salt and pepper*

Gut and scale the salmon, alternatively, get your fishmonger to do it for you.

Pour around 3 litres of water in the fish kettle and add the peppercorns, bay leaf, juice from the lemon and a pinch of salt. Bring the water to the boil and gently add the salmon trout, ensuring that the fish is covered by the water. Bring the water back to a gentle simmer and leave it to poach for around 15 – 20 minutes.

Lift the fish out of the kettle, while still resting on its trivet. Drain off any excess liquid. Carefully remove the fish from the trivet, using two palette knives or two fish slices and place onto a warmed serving platter.

Remove the skin by taking a sharp knife and making a shallow cut through it along the backbone, paring the skin back as you go. Carefully remove the fins as you come to them.

You can now easily follow the line down the back of the fish to ease the flesh away from the bone. By using this method, you can judge the portion sizes without any problems. Cover the fish to keep warm.

To make the lime dressing, finely grate the zest from the lime, cut in half and squeeze the juice before adding to the mayonnaise. Chop the dill and add to the mixture and season to taste.

Serve this dish with a nice crisp salad and some boiled new potatoes with a good dollop of lime mayo on each plate.

VIANDES
Meat

Bienvenue au Pays du
VEAU FERMIER
ELEVE SOUS LA MERE

CAMPAGNE FINANCEE PAR LA
COMMUNAUTE EUROPEENNE

ici, un producteur de Veaux Fermiers : Bernard ULMET

Driving south down the N120 from Tulle to Argentat, we turn a bend in the road and see the first sign *"Veau fermier élevé sous la mère"*. It shows a baby cow suckling its mother. This is veal country and in France few people have any qualms about eating baby cows. The natural bringing up of *veau sous la mère* is an old tradition which is being pursued in the region with renewed vigour, as the breeds are popular in the kitchens of hotels and restaurants, much the same as the Aberdeen Angus beef is in the UK. *Veau sous la mère* is the *'Grand Cru'* of veal and the *Gris Argent, Roux, Froment* and *Gris Foncé* are recognised by gourmets as the very best.

The raising of livestock remains the main agricultural activity of the region of Limousin today. The breeds of Limousin cattle are given broad support for their power to adapt, their robustness, ability to reproduce and of course, and maybe most importantly, the quality of their meat.

The quality labels to watch out for are: *Blason Prestige, Veau Femier du Limousin, Le Veau des Connaisseurs* and *Le Veau Saveur Nature* – more about quality kite-marks later.

Pork is also popular and the *'Culs-noirs'* (Black Bottom) of the Arédien area have been around in the region since the 16th century in the part to the west of the Massif Central. Brought up in *'semi-liberté'* and fed on potatoes, chestnuts, acorns and roots, at an adult age of 18 months to two years the *cul-noir* weighs 250 to 300kg, and that, my friends, is some very large pork chops!!!

Tradition in the countryside meant that when ready, the household pig was killed as Christmas approached, providing a family with fat, and firm white meat which melts in the mouth, and I can assure you it really does. The *"Tuer de cochon"* (killing of the pigs), was a pagan feast which could last for up to three days and the custom still exists in certain areas. Some of the well-known products of Limousin are without doubt the famous *boudin aux châtaignes, confit de porc, le petit salé* and *l'andouille de viande.*

Limousin pork farmers, similar to their cousins the Limousin beef and veal farmers, bring up their livestock in a family environment, not an enclosed industrial one, as often happens elsewhere. Pork also carries its distinguished and deserved label of quality - *'Label Rouge'*. Each pig (*Label Rouge*) is individually identified as being bred from parents which carry the quality label.

Charcuterie – pork products, such as dried sausages, sausages of various shapes and sizes, salted and cured hams – can also carry the same quality mark, *Charcuteries Salaisons 'Label Rouge' du Limousin*. The pork farmers of Limousin try hard to work in collaboration with the artisan butcher *charcutièrs* to ensure top quality products of the hundreds of different *charcuterie* produced from the *'Label Rouge'*. So if you get the opportunity, sharpen your taste buds and try some.

As recently as 1984 *les Groupements de Producteurs d'Ovins du Limousin* (Lamb Producers' Trade Association of Limousin) selected the best breeds of lamb and created one marque of quality: *'Le Baronet'*, which identifies *"l'élite des agneaux"*. This is the *grand marque* and a sign of great quality. Since July 2000 it has been awarded an *"Indication Géographique Protégée"* (IGP), which is rather like the *Appellation Contrôlée* quality mark for wine.

Limousin lambs which carry the label have to be born, raised and slaughtered in the geographic region of Limousin and are individually identified by a unique number. They are fed by their mother's milk up to a minimum of 60 days, then with grass and cereals – no other methods of feeding are permitted.

At the end of the day, it is the customer who gets the best deal in the quality and taste of the end product, which is always popular at *Noël* (Christmas) and a treat at *Pâques* (Easter) and of course, a pleasure throughout the year. One of our favourites in the summer is to barbecue (roast) whole legs of lamb – delicious!

BLANQUETTE DE VEAU
FERMIER DU LIMOUSIN À L'ANCIENNE
veal stew in the traditional limousin style

This is one of those dishes which I really enjoyed cooking so much when I was a student at catering college, all those years back in the mid-Sixties. When we had reached the elevated position of being second or third year students we were allowed to prepare and cook the main course dishes for the college's public restaurant. I recall making a *cuisson* by poaching the mushrooms and onions separately before adding them to the sauce, then quickly reducing the cooking liquor right down to concentrate the flavours before adding that as well to enhance the natural flavours in the sauce. The method below is very slightly different, but the result, from one of the Limousin's brightest young star chefs, is outstanding.

I took the opportunity recently to cook this dish for Susie and Gillie Scott, two of our dear friends in France, the result was quite wonderful, especially as I had not cooked the dish for nearly 40 years!

Recipe by Gilles Dudognon

Preparation time: 60 minutes
Cooking time: 90 minutes

Ingredients for 4 people

- *1 kg diced veal, cut into 50 g chunks*
- *1 large carrot*
- *1 bouquet garni*
- *2 onions*
- *1 clove of garlic*

For the garnish

- *100 g small onions*
- *200 g small champignons de Paris (small closed button)*

For the sauce

- *1 lt white bouillon*
- *1 dl whipping cream*
- *lemon juice (according to taste)*
- *3 egg yolks*
- *salt and pepper*
- *1.5 dl double cream*

Preparation

Spread the pieces of veal out on a tray or large chopping board and lightly season with the salt and pepper. Put the veal into a large saucepan and cover with cold water, place over a high heat and bring up to the boil. Once the water has boiled, remove from the heat, remove the pieces of veal, rinse them well and drain.

Put the veal pieces into a saucepan, cover with the hot stock and cook over a medium to low heat for about 1 hour, allowing to gently simmer.

Cuisson des champignons: Wash the mushrooms, making sure you remove the stalks, put into a small saucepan and barely cover them with water, then add a knob of butter, a little salt and pepper, a little lemon juice and poach for 10 minutes.

Cuisson des oignons: Melt some butter in the bottom of a small saucepan, add the small onions, salt and pepper then half cover with cold water and cover with a buttered disc of greaseproof paper with a small hole cut in the middle. Cook over a medium heat and reduce the liquid by two thirds.

After you have removed the mushrooms, place them in the same pan as the onions and reduce the mushroom liquid by two thirds.

Preparation of the sauce: Pass half of the *cuisson* into a clean saucepan and reduce by two thirds. Add the remaining half of the *cuisson* and reduce again, then add the whipping cream and season with salt and pepper, if required. Whisk the egg yolks, and incorporate the double cream. Then quickly add a ladle of sauce to this mixture and mix well. Pour the egg mixture back into the reduced *cuisson* and carefully bring the sauce up to a gentle simmer – above all do not allow it to boil. Add a little lemon juice according to taste. If the sauce is too thick, add a little of the stock to reach the desired consistency.

Now dress the pieces of cooked veal in a large deep service bowl, and garnish with the onions and mushrooms. You can whisk or whiz-up the sauce with your hand blitzer to the consistency you desire, then mask the sauce over the meat.

Recipe supplied by Comité Départemental du Tourisme de la Corrèze.

BOEUF À LA BOURGUIGNONNE
beef bourguignonne

This is one of our favourites when we have friends or family arrive to stay at La Maison during the winter months. Most of our mates will have either flown in or driven down from the UK or driven up to 'ours' from Spain. Invariably when they arrive they are often a little jaded around the edges, just wanting to chill out around the kitchen table and chat endlessly over a traditional Corrézienne meal.

There are loads of recipes available for this dish and I am not going to tell you that this one is any better than the others – just that it works for us and has not failed me yet. I have seen some disasters in British pubs and restaurants over the years which have proclaimed a traditional Burgundy beef stew on their menu and then manage to produce a dish which is thin, unimaginative and bland.

When I visit my local supermarket in France, I tell the butcher that I want to prepare Boeuf Bourguignonne and he asks for how many people, I tell him and he trims and prepares large chunks of shoulder and neck of beef, not those dainty little bite-size pieces which 'we' tend to prefer *en Angleterre*.

I like to start preparing this dish the day before, so that the marinade has time to work its magic overnight.

Recipe by Malcolm Alder-Smith
La Maison aux Quat'Saisons, Laborie, 19400 Monceaux-sur-Dordogne

Preparation time: 30 minutes
Cooking time: 180 minutes

Ingredients for 4 people
- *1 kg well-hung neck or shoulder of beef (shin will do)*
- *1 calf's foot (not obligatory, but the flavour is great)*
- *3 medium sized onions*
- *3 medium sized carrots*
- *4 shallots*
- *2 cloves of garlic*
- *3 sprigs of thyme*
- *1 bay leaf*
- *flat leaf parsley, roughly chopped*

- *2 bottles of red Burgundy (we use the deep red Cahors)*
- *I pack of smoked lardons of bacon*
- *250 g champignons de Paris*
- *250 g shallots, peeled*
- *tomato purée*
- *olive oil, butter*
- *salt and pepper*

Preparation

Peel and roughly chop the onion, garlic, carrots, shallots and parsley and put them into a large saucepan with the prepared beef and herbs. Cover the lot with one of the bottles of wine – you may need to open the second bottle to make sure the ingredients are well covered. Place a lid or some cling-film over the pan and leave to one side overnight. The tendency is to put the saucepan in the fridge, but the marinade will work much better at a temperature between 8 and 14°C. However, if you don't have a cool spot in your kitchen, then go for the fridge option!

The aroma which hits you the following morning when you take off the lid is just fantastic. Remove the purple coloured chunks of beef and retain the marinade.

Take a large heavy-bottomed saucepan and fry off the smoked lardons in a little olive oil until they turn a light golden brown. Remove from the pan and keep to one side.

Add a little more olive oil to the saucepan and add the chunks of beef, a few at a time, until they are sealed on all sides. Remove the first pieces of browned beef and repeat the process until all of the beef is nicely coloured. Return the beef and the lardons to the pan, add a good couple of soup spoons of tomato *purée* and stir well before covering the meat with the reserved marinade, including the vegetables. Some folks strain the wine and dispose of the vegetables at this stage, but I prefer to extract as much flavour as possible from all the ingredients. Add the calf's foot and at this stage, bring to the boil and reduce to a gentle simmer, then cover the saucepan with a lid and allow to tick over gently for 120 minutes. You may need to top up with some of the spare wine, if not, take a good slurp yourself, you deserve it!

Remove the skins from the shallots, being careful not to take off too much stalk, or they will fall apart when you cook them. I like to top and tail them, by placing into a bowl and pouring over boiling water; allow them to cool sufficiently to handle and then hopefully you will be able to remove the skin without too much problem, this often reduces the tears as well – but not always!

Pan fry the shallots, in a little oil and butter, until they start to caramelise and turn golden brown. Place them to one side.

Remove the gritty stalks from the mushrooms, wash the mushrooms and pat them dry. Fry them off in the same pan as the shallots and place them to one side as well.

Strain the sauce through a good-sized sieve or colander set over another saucepan, pushing through some of the vegetables – this helps to enhance the flavour and thicken the sauce. Place the saucepan over a moderate heat, bring to the boil and reduce to a rolling simmer. I like to finish up with a sauce which is quite thick, so at this stage you can add a little arrowroot if required. If you want to cheat big-time and take the easy way out, use some beef gravy granules to attain the required consistency. Add a little salt and ground black pepper to taste.

Pick the chunks of beef out of the vegetable mixture and add them to the thickened sauce along with the browned shallots and mushrooms. Replace the lid and cook slowly over a very low flame for another hour. You may need to add some more wine as the sauce starts to reduce.

While the meat finishes off cooking, prepare some turned potatoes and either steam them or just plain boil. A *mélange* of root vegetables also works well with this dish.

We have some very large traditional white soup bowls which we tend to use for our one-pot dishes, these contrast beautifully with the deep rich colour of the sauce.

My secret: For the very best results, I will start to prepare this dish 36 hours in advance. Marinade overnight and most of the next day. The night before you plan to eat, cook for a couple of hours and allow to cool overnight. Finish off the dish the next day by re-heating an hour or so before your guests arrive – the flavour is fantastic.

WINE: A nice sturdy red will go well with this dish, so try a Pomerol or a St-Emilion.

CARRÉ DE PORC À LA LIMOUSINE
loin of pork limousin style

"In La Corrèze, we found the finest chestnuts in France. Eventually". *"It has often been said that there is no finer country cooking in France than in the south west, in the valleys of Perigord, Marche and Limousin. Here we find geese, truffles, hare, pork, red cabbage. And chestnuts. (The cele-brated carré de porc à la limousine is simply roast pork accompanied by braised red cabbage with chestnuts. Delicious.)"* - So say specialist food suppliers Merchant Gourmet in their magazine adverts for chestnut pieces, whole chestnuts and chestnut *purée*.

Reading a 'foodie' magazine recently, which had been posted out to us in France, I couldn't help but notice a pork dish which rather got the old grey cells working, so I thought I would play around with the recipe and give it a bash.

Recipe by Malcolm Alder-Smith
La Maison aux Quat'Saisons, Laborie, 19400 Monceaux-sur-Dordogne

Preparation time: 30 minutes
Cooking time: 180 minutes

Ingredients for 6 people

- *1.2 kg loin of pork – skin removed, boned and rolled*
- *sunflower oil*
- *1 carrot – peeled and chopped*
- *1 onion – peeled and chopped*
- *1 stick of celery – chopped*
- *salt and pepper*
- *25 cl cider or dry white wine*

For the red cabbage

- *1 small red cabbage*
- *1 medium onion – peeled and sliced*
- *2 oranges – zested and squeezed*
- *1–2 soup spoons of acacia honey*
- *2 cloves of garlic – peeled and sliced*
- *250 g prepared (cooked and chopped) chestnuts*
- *100 g caster sugar*

- *olive oil*
- *salt and pepper*

Preparation

Over a medium flame, heat a large roasting tray with some sunflower oil. Season the pork with the salt and pepper. Carefully place the joint into the hot fat and lightly colour on all sides to obtain a nice golden brown.

Remove the joint and put to one side for a moment. Add the chopped vegetables to the roasting tin and place the loin of pork on top. Pour a few slugs of oil over the seasoned joint then place into a pre-heated oven at 200°C and roast for around one hour. Make sure that you remove the joint after around 15 minutes and baste with some of the oil in the bottom of the roasting tray. Do this every 15 minutes or so to help keep the meat moist. After this time, continue to baste every 5 minutes or so.

While the pork is roasting, take the red cabbage and cut into four quarters. Trim off the heavy part of the stalk and cut across the quarters into thin strips. Prepare the onion and the garlic.

Take a heavy-bottomed frying pan and place over a medium to low flame then add a few slugs of olive oil. Throw in the cabbage, onion and garlic, sprinkle with the sugar and stir well. Cook for around five minutes to start the caramelisation of the sugar, then add the orange zest and the juice, stir well and reduce the heat. Cover and cook over a low flame for around 30 to 40 minutes until the cabbage is nearly cooked. At this point, add the acacia honey and stir well, then add the chopped chestnuts. If the vegetables become too dry, add a little more orange juice. Season with a little salt and black pepper; the dish is nearly ready and the flavour should be absolutely great.

Remove the pork from the roasting tray and set aside to rest. Pour off any surplus oil from the roasting tray and place the tray on your hob over a medium flame. Once the heat hits the vegetables and the juices start to bubble, add the cider or dry white wine and cook over a medium to high flame for five minutes or so. Lightly thicken with a little arrowroot, mixed to a cream with some water. Reduce to a simmer and allow the sauce to cook for a further five minutes or so. Strain the sauce through a sieve into a clean saucepan and leave to simmer gently for a few minutes.

My secret: Arrowroot will provide you with a clear sauce, whereas cornflour will make your sauce go cloudy!

CASSOULET DE PORC # 1
pork and sausage casserole

The Collins French Dictionary describes Cassoulet as a "Sausage and bean hot-pot", which makes it sound rather like a dish of sausages with a can of 'beanzzzz' chucked over the top and nuked for a few minutes in the microwave. I am not too sure what to make of this, but the description certainly does not do justice to a dish which has become a national treasure in France.

Cassoulet, originally *'Cassole d'Issel'*, literally meaning the glazed terra-cotta cooking pot from the small Languedoc town of Issel, has come a long way and there are many regional variations. This is a recipe which I put together when Twink's parents and Auntie Kit from Canada visited La Maison in October 2002. I cooked the whole lot in advance, so that when we got back home from picking them up from Blagnac airport at Toulouse (a six-hour round trip), we would have a tasty one-pot dish to warm us up. A navigational error of Biblical proportions on the way home created an unscheduled 60k detour to Figeac, which meant that we didn't get home until much later than anticipated. Unfortunately for most, the Cassoulet had to wait until the next day...

There are few rules to making this dish, the most important (to my mind) being that you use Toulouse sausages (10s if you can get them), but in general it is one of those dishes which you can play around with and after a few bashes, you will create a dish which is ideal for you and yours. You can definitely get hold of Toulouse sausages from your supermarket, which are bigger than the traditional UK – 8 to the pound, so twist them in the middle and cut each into two pieces before you start cooking.

I have taken the liberty of adding carrots and potatoes to this recipe, which you are unlikely to find in other Cassoulet recipes, but remember, my idea is for a one-pot dish to fill the family tummies in the depth of the winter months when the snow is lying on the ground and clearing the frost off your car windscreen takes laborious minutes of hard graft with your credit card.

Recipe by Malcolm Alder-Smith
La Maison aux Quat'Saisons, Laborie, 19400 Monceaux-sur-Dordogne

Preparation time: 30 minutes

Cooking time: 120 minutes

Ingredients for 8-10 people

- *500 g diced shoulder of pork*
- *500 g belly of pork*
- *12 Toulouse sausages (10 to the lb)*
- *500 g dried white kidney beans*
- *500 g chopped, de-seeded tomatoes*
- *150 g tomato purée*
- *500 g potatoes*
- *500 g large carrots*
- *1 lt vegetable stock*
- *2 medium onions chopped*
- *1 head of garlic chopped*
- *I bay leaf*
- *2 sprigs thyme*
- *4 soup spoons goose dripping*
- *salt and black pepper*

Preparation

Soak the beans overnight in cold water and drain them in a colander. Blanch them quickly in boiling water, drain and return to another pan of boiling water for an hour. Alternatively you can use tinned *flageolets* or similar.

Cut a cross in the bottom of each tomato and blanch them in a pan of boiling water until the skin starts to come away from the flesh. Drop them into a bowl of iced water to stop them from cooking and becoming mushy. Peel the skin off the tomatoes, cut them in half, remove the seeds and then roughly chop them. Place in a bowl and keep to one side.

I like to give the pork in this dish as much flavour as possible, so I start off by cooking the sausages off to a golden brown in either a heavy-bottomed casserole or saucepan. Remove them and put to one side. In the same pan, fry off the chopped onions in the goose dripping over a medium heat until soft and translucent and add to the sausages. Now fry off the pork in the same pan, a few pieces at a time, until lightly browned, using more dripping if necessary. The sausage and onion flavours in the bottom of the pan will be passed on to the diced pork

117

Take a clean casserole and add the cooked sausages, pork and onions. Peel the garlic, chop it roughly and add to the casserole, along with the tomato *purée* and chopped tomatoes. Add the drained beans and pour the hot stock over the ingredients, season well with black pepper and a pinch of salt, stir carefully and cook gently, covered with a lid, over a low heat for 90 minutes.

While the meat is cooking, peel the potatoes and carrots and cut into a rough dice of around 2.5 cm square. Blanch both in boiling salted water until nearly cooked. After the 90 minutes is up, add the blanched potatoes and carrots to the casserole and cook for a further 30 minutes. As the beans will absorb quite a bit of liquid, you may need to add more stock if necessary.

When ready, serve this dish in very large bowls with chunks of country bread.

WINE: For me this has to be a red Buzet from SW France or a generic Gaillac red – or alternatively a Fitou from the deep south would go well with this classic French dish.

CASSOULET DE PORC # 2
cassoulet with pork, duck and sausages

It seems that the stories surrounding Cassoulet abound and are often exaggerated to the extent of a whopping 'fisherman's tale'.

It appears that almost everyone in the South West of France makes 'the best Cassoulet' and different recipes abound from region to region, town to town and quite naturally, household to household.

This recipe is intended to follow more closely the expectations of one of the greatest country dishes of France. However, I am at a bit of a loss, because the more research I do into the dish, the more confused I become as to the 'correct' ingredients. The one clear and common ingredient is, of course, dried white kidney beans. The meat content, however, varies greatly and I have found recipes with chicken, confit of duck or goose (or both!), pork bones, bacon, pork knuckle, pig's trotters, loin and belly of pork, Toulouse sausages, lamb etc. Another great contention appears to be whether or not you top the whole lot with breadcrumbs before it goes into the oven.

There are three classical recipes:

Cassoulet de Castelnaudary, which is made up with pork meat.

Cassoulet de Toulouse is more rich than the Castelnaudary recipe as you add, in particular, lamb and Toulouse sausages.

Cassoulet de Carcassonne is made up with partridge.

Cassoulet is certainly a dish which can be prepared in advance and is one of those types of dishes where the flavour only improves if left for twenty-four hours before reheating and serving to your deserving family or friends. I only hope that my 'authentic' recipe meets with the approval of Cassoulet fans out there in gastro' land.

Recipe by Diane Alder-Smith
La Maison aux Quat'Saisons, Laborie, 19400 Monceaux-sur-Dordogne

Preparation time:	30 minutes
Cooking time:	150 minutes

Ingredients for 8 people

- *500 g diced shoulder of pork*
- *500 g belly of pork*
- *8 pieces of preserved duck*
- *750 g Toulouse sausages*
- *750 g dried white kidney beans*
- *100 g pork fat – cut into lardons*
- *1.5 lt water*

- *500 g tomatoes – skinned, de-seeded and chopped*
- *1.5 lt rich country stock*
- *2 medium onions chopped*
- *200 g white breadcrumbs*
- *1 head of garlic – peeled and chopped*
- *2 bay leaves*
- *2 sprigs of fresh thyme*

Preparation

Wash the beans, then soak them overnight in some cold water. Drain the beans in a colander the following day. Place the beans in a saucepan with some fresh water, bring the water to the boil and cook them for around 5 minutes in the rapidly boiling water. Drain and refresh the beans under cold running water.

Put the beans into a clean saucepan and cover with 1.5 lt of water. Add the pork fat lardons, bay leaves, sprigs of thyme and place over a high flame and bring to the boil. Reduce to a low flame, cover with a lid and simmer for around 90 minutes. Once cooked, most of the fat from the lardons will have been incorporated into the beans, so remove any remaining pieces, plus the bay leaves and sprigs of thyme. Put the beans to one side.

Lightly season the shoulder and belly of pork and fry this off to a golden brown in some goose dripping in a heavy-bottomed frying pan. Put the browned pork into a large casserole (if you are lucky enough to have an original style *'Cassole d'Issel'*, then you are one step ahead of almost everyone else!). Fry the onions and garlic to a golden brown and add to the pork.

Part-cook the Toulouse sausages to a golden brown in some goose fat. Place the sausages and preserved duck into the casserole with the pork mixture. Add the chopped tomatoes, tomato *purée* and the beans and stir well. Add the stock, and sprinkle the breadcrumbs over the top.

Cook in a pre-heated oven at 200°C for around 60 minutes to obtain your authentic Cassoulet.

CHOU FARCI
stuffed cabbage

This is one of those classic Corrézienne dishes which I just had to include in my book and I waited with eager anticipation for the right recipe to drop through the letter box onto my front door mat.

Although this dish is really well known in the Department, you may have to search around a bit to find it on *'le menu'*, however, I guess you are more likely to find it flagged up under *'le plat du jour'* or *'carte du jour'*. It is one of those recipes which does tend to take quite a while to prepare and cook, but the wait is totally worthwhile. So, whether you are eating this in a restaurant or trying out for the first time at home, I hope that you will enjoy the wonderful depth of flavour provided by the Aladdin's cave of protein ingredients, complemented by the pool of steaming 'gravy'.

Recipe supplied by Paulette Fruitiere

Preparation time: 40 minutes
Cooking time: 150 minutes

Ingredients for 6 people

- *100 g shoulder of veal*
- *200 g loin of pork*
- *120 g boiling bacon*
- *1 large Savoy cabbage*
- *1 veal bone, split in two*
- *1 onion*
- *2 cloves*
- *60 g rice*
- *8 basil leaves*
- *3 cloves of garlic*
- *1 bouquet garni*
- *1 soup spoon olive oil*
- *salt and pepper*

Preparation

Cut the root off the cabbage and remove any bad or marked leaves. Cook for 10 minutes in a large pan of boiling salted water. Drain the cabbage thoroughly, separate all of the leaves, carefully remove the heart and chop.

Cook the rice for 15 minutes in boiling salted water, refresh under cold running water and drain. Peel the onion and 'stick' with the 2 cloves. The French word for clove is *clous de girofle*, which literally translated means 'nail of clove', and if you think about it, the shape of a clove certainly resembles that of a nail. Crush the cloves of garlic with the basil leaves, finely mince the meat into one bowl and thoroughly mix together, then add the cooked rice and olive oil, stirring in a little salt and ground black pepper.

Arrange a piece of fine muslin in a bowl, place the blanched cabbage in the middle of the cloth and fill the centre with the meat and herb mixture. Pull over and gather together the four corners of the muslin to reform the shape of the cabbage. Tie a knot in the cloth or tie it up well with some butcher's string at the top.

Place the 'package' of stuffed cabbage into a large pan of boiling salted water in which you need to add a *bouquet garni*, the veal bones and onion stuck with cloves. Reduce to simmer and cook for approximately 120 minutes.

Remove the muslin bag from the stock and drain well. Place the bag into a hot round serving dish and take it to the table like this. Cut the string or open the bag and cut the cabbage into large slices or quarters, just as you like.

Le secret de Paulette: this dish can be eaten either hot or cold

CÔTELETTE DE PORC AUX MOUTARDES
pork chops with a grain mustard cream sauce

Not long before we moved to France, I got home from work quite late one evening and my darling wife produced the most fantastic dinner for us in no time at all.

All three of us, including our son Ashley, are quite keen pork fans and Twink had purchased some pork chops from Tesco or Sainsbury's, I am not quite sure which. Nice quality meat, cooked perfectly. She had used some Rosé de Loire in the recipe, which I know is quite unusual, but it really does work so incredibly well and doesn't intrude too much into the wonderful pork and mustard flavours.

Recipe by Diane Alder-Smith
La Maison aux Quat'Saisons, Laborie, 19400 Monceaux-sur-Dordogne

Preparation time: 5 minutes
Cooking time: 15 minutes

Ingredients for 4 people

- *4 regular pork chops (or bone out for quicker cooking)*
- *Maille Moutarde fins Gourmets (coarse grain mustard)*
- *125 ml Rosé de Loire*
- *salt and black pepper*
- *200 g champignons de Paris*
- *175 ml double cream*
- *unsalted butter*
- *olive oil*

Preparation

Place the four chops on your chopping board and lightly season with a salt and ground black pepper. Thinly 'butter' each chop on one side only with some coarse grain mustard.

Place a heavy-bottomed frying pan over a medium flame and when hot add a couple of slugs of good olive oil and a knob of butter. Once the butter has melted and the bubbles start to subside, place the chops into the pan, meat side down, and cook until well sealed and lightly browned.

Turn the chops over and cook the 'mustard side' for about another five minutes, adjusting the flame as necessary.

While the chops are cooking, clean the grit from the stems and underneath of the *champignons de Paris*, rinse in a colander and pat them dry before slicing them. Trim the bottom of the stalks.

Remove the chops from the frying pan, put onto a plate or a roasting tin and place into a pre-heated oven at around 180°C, for around 5 minutes.

Add the sliced mushrooms to the frying pan and cook over a medium to high flame until nearly cooked (the mushrooms should take up any surplus oil left in the pan). Add the rosé and allow to reduce down by around 50%, reduce to a medium to low flame and then add a half soup spoon of the coarse grain mustard, stir well then add the cream. Remove the chops from the oven then pour the juices into the sauce and stir well to incorporate all of the wonderful flavours.

Taste and adjust the seasoning and consistency to your liking.

Place one pork chop onto each of four hot plates and pour the sauce over the top of each.

Twink's secret: I like to start off cooking the chops in a ribbed skillet, just enough to mark both sides of the chops. Then transfer them to a frying pan to finish off the cooking.

WINE: As my darling husband, Malcy, is a red wine freak, I suppose I had better stick with something like a nice generic Montagne Saint-Emillion. Alternatively, we recently came across a fabulous bottle of Château Laffitte-Carcasset (Saint-Estèphe), which unfortunately you may find very difficult to get hold of in the UK.

ÉCHINE DE PORC EN MARINADE
marinaded loin of pork

This is a recipe which I used to use in my restaurant back in the early Eighties and although the outcome of the original was quite exceptional, I have tweaked it a bit since.

As I always like to include either some wine or citrus juice in my marinades I have added a little of both to assist in the tenderisation process.

As you will see from the marinade ingredients below, this dish is packed with bundles of flavour.

Recipe by Malcolm Alder-Smith
La Maison aux Quat'Saisons, Laborie, 19400 Monceaux-sur-Dordogne

Preparation time: 20 minutes
Cooking time: 100 minutes
Marinade: 24 hours

Ingredients for 8 people

- *1.5 kg loin of pork*
- *8 nice flat mushrooms*
- *2 shallots*
- *1 stick of celery*
- *25 g breadcrumbs*
- *50 g butter*
- *4 soup spoons of fresh cream*
- *salt and black pepper*

For the marinade

- *1 medium onion*
- *1 shallot*
- *1 stick of celery*
- *1 tsp freshly ground pepper*
- *1 soup spoon chopped fresh tarragon*
- *1 soup spoon chopped fresh flat leaf parsley*
- *1 soup spoon of fresh basil leaves (torn into small pieces)*
- *2 bay leaves*
- *2 fresh sage leaves*
- *1 sprig fresh rosemary*
- *1 tbsp grated fresh nutmeg*
- *half a glass of nut oil*
- *zest of one lemon*
- *juice of one lemon*
- *glass of nice dry white wine*
- *1 coffee spoon of salt*

Preparation

Get your butcher to skin, bone, roll and tie your loin of pork, alternatively select a nice joint off the shelf at your local supermarket.

Place the loin of pork into a heavy-bottomed casserole. Put all of the chopped marinade ingredients into a bowl and add the nut oil, lemon juice and dry white wine. Mix all the ingredients together well before pouring over the meat. Leave the joint to marinade for 24 hours, turning occasionally, in order to get all of those fabulous flavours on board.

Pre-heat your oven to around 200°C and roast the pork for 1 hour 45 minutes, turning the joint frequently. Retain the marinade to make the sauces.

While the joint is cooking, wash the mushrooms (do not soak) and pat them dry. Remove the mushroom stalks and finely chop them along with the stick of celery and the shallots. Place the finely chopped vegetables into a bowl then add the breadcrumbs and a little salt and ground black pepper. Trim the rounded top from each mushroom and place them 'hollow side up' on a baking sheet. Add a small knob of butter to each mushroom cup and lightly season.

Fill the mushrooms with the mixture and place small a knob of butter on the top of each mushroom. Put the mushrooms around the roast about 30 minutes before the end of cooking.

Remove the loin of pork and cut off the strings. Place onto a chopping board and carve into good slices, dressing neatly on a serving dish, surrounded by the mushrooms. Strain the marinade into a clean saucepan and make a liaison with the cream. Cover the slices with the sauce and serve immediately.

WINE: This dish deserves some serious treatment, so go for a Médoc. Alternatively try one of the reds from 'the other side of the river' to the east of the Gironde; Bourg, Blaye and Fronsac produce some stonkin' good red wines.

Fronsac is a picturesque area, producing increasingly fine red wines and so it should, it is situated just to the west of St Emilion!!!

EPAULE D'AGNEAU CONFITE À L'AIL
shoulder of lamb with a garlic compote

Recipe by Xavier Boutot
Le Saut de la Bergère, 19190 Aubazine

Preparation time: 15 minutes
Cooking time: 120 minutes

Ingredients for 8 people

- *1 shoulder of lamb boned and rolled*
- *3 large heads of garlic (around 200 g)*
- *400 g carrots*
- *1 dl olive oil*
- *salt and pepper*

Preparation

Place a large heavy-bottomed casserole over a medium to high heat, pour in the olive oil and brown the joint all sides. Peel the garlic. Peel the carrots and cut into chunky slices. Once the joint is golden brown, add the garlic and carrots to the casserole and lightly brown. Season with salt and pepper and cover the vegetables with water. Bring the liquid to the boil, then reduce to a low heat, cover with a lid and cook for a further 2 hours. During the course of cooking the joint, check out the level of the water every now and then to make sure that it is not drying out.

Once the meat is cooked, remove the shoulder joint and place in the bottom of a low oven to keep warm. Blitz or blend the vegetables until you have obtained a thick, smooth sauce. Check the sauce for seasoning and consistency and add a little more salt and pepper if necessary. If the sauce is too runny, thicken it up with a little cornflour or potato flour *(fécule)*.

Place the joint onto a chopping board and remove the strings. Cut the meat into slices and place an equal amount on each plate. Mask the meat with some sauce or on to the side of the plate depending on the consistency you have chosen.

Le secret de Xavier Boutot: Use *Le Baronet – Agneaux du Limousin,* which is the quality kitemark guarantee for lamb in the Limousin region. Serve this dish very hot and accompany it with rice or some fresh pasta.

WINE: Xavier Bouton suggests that you go for an oak-aged local red – Mille et Une Pierre (Corrèze).

FARCIDURE
potato cake

This recipe was kindly sent to me by André Saulle from Goûters à la Ferme de Pierrefiche at Albignac, which is featured in the Bienvenue à la Ferme, Corrèze 2003. His farm is on the RD 130, near to Auberzine to the east of Brive. They specialise in beef, veal, farm chickens and cereals. Their specialities are **fromages frais**, jams and patisseries.

Although I have included a similar recipe (Milhassou à la Corrézienne), this one is a real authentic *paysan* version of the potato cake which is prevalent to the north of the Department and in the Creuse.

I guess that because the original recipe was for 25 people, that this would be used for a large family gathering or celebration.

Recipe by André Saulle
Goûters à la Ferme de Pierrefiche, 19190 Albignac

Preparation time: 30 minutes
Cooking time: 205 minutes

Ingredients for 6 people

- *2 kg potatoes*
- *1 bunch of parsley*
- *2 free range eggs*
- *300 g lardons of bacon (petit salé)*
- *1 soup spoon of flour*
- *salt and pepper*
- *4 cloves of galic*

Preparation

Peel and grate the potatoes, wring them out in a clean tea towel without washing. Keep them covered or else they will turn brown very quickly.

Mix with the eggs, garlic, chopped parsley, flour, salt and pepper.

Cut the lardons into small dice and lightly fry them off in a little butter. Make balls of the potato mixture, placing in the middle of each a little of the cooked lardons. Squeeze each ball tightly to remove any remaining liquid (you can do this in a clean tea towel), and cook them for around one hour in a slowly simmering light vegetable broth.

FARCE
stuffing

Ingredients

- *garlic*
- *parsley*
- *swiss chard leaves*
- *lardons of bacon*
- *a little bread soaked in milk*
- *1 eggs*

To alter the previous recipe slightly, you can use the above ingredients to make a *farce* (stuffing), which offers an interesting alternative.

Preparation

Once you have finely chopped the garlic, parsley and chard leaves, knead them well together with the lardons, bread and egg.

Mould these into fairly small balls and form the *farcidure* mixture around them – scotch egg style!

GIGOT D'AGNEAU FERMIER
leg of lamb farmer's style

Recipe by Michel et Isabelle Roussanne
Auberge des Gabariers, 15 Quai Lestourgie, 19400 Argentat

Preparation time: 45 minutes
Cooking time: 55 minutes

Ingredients for 8 people

- *1 leg of lamb (Le Baronet) around 2.5 kg*
- *1 pain de campagne (flat round country bread)*
- *2 heads of garlic*
- *3 onions*
- *1 glass dry white wine*
- *goose or duck fat*
- *1 kg dried white kidney beans*
- *thyme*
- *bay leaf*
- *salt and white pepper*
- *200 g cured ham*
- *200 g larding pork, cut into cubes (lardons will do)*
- *100 g onions – chopped*
- *4 cloves of garlic*
- *3 peeled tomatoes*
- *1 bouquet garni*
- *2 lts vegetable stock*

Preparation

The day before you intend to prepare this dish, soak the beans thoroughly overnight.

Ask your butcher to de-bone the leg of lamb, tie it with butcher's string and break down the bones, which you will need. Peel some cloves of garlic then pierce the skin of the lamb with a narrow pointed knife in several places, and insert a peeled clove of garlic into each incision. Sprinkle the leg lamb with some salt and pepper and rub well into the skin.

Place the bones into a roasting tray and sit the leg of lamb on the top.

Lightly smear the skin with some goose or duck fat (oil will do the job just as well) and place into the middle of a pre-heated oven on 230°C for around 45 minutes. Half way through the cooking time, add the rest of the cloves of garlic in their skins and the chopped onions.

Drain the beans and cook them in some boiling salted water. Cut the ham, onions and tomatoes into dice. Finely chop the garlic. Take a heavy-based casserole and lightly brown the onion and garlic, add the chopped tomatoes and the blanched beans, the diced larding pork and the *bouquet garni*. Add around 12.5 cl of stock and simmer very gently for a long time until the beans reach the stage where they 'melt in the mouth'. Add a little more liquid if needed and check for seasoning and adjust if necessary.

Remove the leg of lamb from the oven, place into a clean dish and keep warm in the oven, after you have turned the heat down to around 125°C.

Drain the fat from the roasting tin and place the tin over a medium to high flame on your hob. Once the residue on the bottom starts to bubble, add the glass of wine and stir well with a wooden spoon, loosening the deposits from the bottom of the tin. Reduce the wine by two-thirds. Add the onions and the bones then moisten with around 1.5 litres of water (or vegetable stock) and bring to the boil. Transfer the ingredients to a saucepan, reduce the flame slightly to allow for a fast rolling simmer and reduce the stock by around 50% to take on board all of the flavours from the bones etc.

Serve a good portion of the beans onto each plate and top with some slices of the lamb.

Cut some slices of the country bread and squeeze each clove, so that the cooked pulp slides out, spread these onto the slices of bread and serve them on a separate plate.

Serve the *jus* (unthickened gravy) in a separate sauceboat.

NAVARIN D'AGNEAU PRINTANIER
Brown lamb stew – spring style

I just had to include this recipe for both personal and sentimental reasons, 'cause deep down I am the world's biggest softie and I get very emotional over old pop records, movies, certain recipes or meals I have eaten and other milestones in my life. Somewhere at La Maison aux Quat'Saisons, I still have my original cookery work book, which I wrote when I was sixteen while doing the pre-catering course at The Fairway Secondary Modern School, circa 1965.

In that book, I am sure I have a recipe for this dish. I have a very good reason for remembering this, because I distinctly recall burning the hell out of my lamb when I was doing an exam before venturing over to the big college on the mainland. I just hope that Eddie Burnett and my other 'old' lecturers, many of whom are now cooking in that great kitchen in the sky, are looking down and are proud of what I am creating here. I wouldn't have been writing this book if it weren't for their years of expertise, skill and perseverance.

Recipe by Michel et Isabelle Roussanne
Auberge des Gabariers, 15 Quai Lestourgie, 19400 Argentat

Preparation time: 30 minutes
Cooking time: 205 minutes

Ingredients for 4 people

- *1 kg shoulder of lamb cut into dice*
- *500 g young carrots*
- *500 g young turnips*
- *300 g haricots vert*
- *400 g shelled peas*
- *8 good young baby onions*
- *4 cloves of garlic*
- *4 tomatoes*
- *1 coffee spoon of concentrated tomato purée*
- *bouquet garni*
- *salt and pepper*
- *1 soup spoon of flour*
- *1 coffee spoon of sugar*

- *1 nut of butter*
- *4 spoons of olive oil*

Preparation

Season the pieces of lamb with the salt, pepper and sugar, then brown them quickly in two soup spoons of olive oil in a heavy duty casserole or saucepan until they are golden brown and lightly caramelized.

Sprinkle the flour over the meat and stir until it is blended in, gradually add some water, stirring all the time, until the meat is covered by the liquid. Skin the cloves of garlic and cut them into two before adding to the meat, cut each tomato into eight pieces and add along with the tomato puree and the *bouquet garni*. Bring to the boil, reduce the heat and simmer gently for one hour over a gentle flame.

After one hour peel the whole baby carrots, the baby turnips (cut in two) and along with the baby onions fry them in a little butter and olive oil and sprinkle with a pinch of sugar until they turn golden brown and just start to caramelise. Add the *mélange* to the simmering lamb with the shelled peas and cook for a further 30 minutes.

At the end of 30 minutes add the *haricots verts* and simmer until the beans are just cooked *al denté*. Adjust the sauce for seasoning and consistency and serve in a large round deep soup bowl.

WINE: I would tend to go for a full-flavoured red such as a young Côtes due Rhône or Corbières.

POÊLÉE DE RIS DE VEAU DE LAIT FERMIER AUX CÈPES DE LA RÉGION
veal sweetbreads with local cèpes

Recipe by Gilles Dudognon

Preparation time: 15 minutes
Cooking time: 20 minutes
Soaking time: 24 hours

Ingredients for 4 people

- *1 kg veal sweetbreads*
- *1 dl cream*
- *1 dl light veal stock*
- *2 shallots – finely chopped*
- *400 g cèpes (pan fried and drained)*
- *olive oil*
- *butter*
- *coarse salt*
- *salt and pepper*

Preparation

24 hours in advance, place the sweetbreads into a bowl of iced water with a handful of coarse salt and place into your refrigerator overnight.

The following day, fill a large saucepan with water and bring to the boil. Add the sweetbreads and when the water returns to the boil allow them to cook for 1 minute, remove from the water, then refresh immediately and drain. Cover with a linen cloth, put a light weight over the top and refrigerate.

After a time, cut the sweetbreads into cubes and lightly season. Place a heavy-bottomed frying pan over a medium heat and add a little oil, add a knob of butter and pan fry the sweetbreads a few at a time. Set aside to keep warm.

Add a little more oil and butter to the frying pan and fry the prepared *cèpes* over a medium to high heat, just before they are cooked, add the chopped shallots. Add to the sweetbreads, mix well and keep warm.

Make a reduction of the veal stock in the frying pan. Add the cream and a couple of soup spoons of the fried *cèpes*. Reduce by one third, mix well and pass into a clean saucepan. Blitz with your hand blender to make the sauce bubbly.

Arrange the sweetbreads and *cèpes* in a large soup bowl and pour the steaming sauce over – sprinkle with chopped flat-leaf parsley.

Accompany the dish with some fresh tagliatelle tossed in butter.

WINE: This is a rather grand dish, so equally you should go for a grand wine to accompany it.

This is a time to test out your wine supplier (or supermarket). See if you can get hold of a bottle of dry white Chateau-Grillet from the north of the Rhône. It's one of France's smallest A/C vineyards (only 9 acres) and uses only the Viognier grape which has an interesting flavour. This wine tends to be unquestionably over-expensive, so you may want to try an alternative.

My preference would be to go for a Condrieu, again from the northern Rhône, using the Viognier grape. This wine is soft and fragrant and has bags of character – it can be quite outstanding.

Recipe supplied by Comité Départemental du Tourisme de la Corrèze.

POT-AU-FEU CORRÉZIENNE OU "FARÇUN"
slow cooked beef stew

Our massive *cantou* fireplace, which dominates the salon at La Maison aux Quat'Saisons, has a great oak beam supporting the chimney breast which disappears ever-upwards towards the roof. When we 'opened up' the fireplace back in 2002, it had been blocked in for a couple of generations. We found dusty old hooks and chains, which apparently were used to suspend the large cast iron cooking pots in which this style of dish was traditionally cooked. I am giving you two similar style of recipes, this one and the other in the soup section called La Potée, which has a meat base of salt pork and sausages.

This is my version of one of 'the' classic French country dishes, which I tasted for the first time in a hotel called Le Lion d'Or in Montargis (south of Fontainebleau), back in the early Eighties. The sauce is thin, like a clear broth, rather than the sort of sauce you would expect to find with a beef stew in the UK.

The dish needs to be cooked very slowly over a very low flame, rather than in the oven. This is another one of those dishes which produces two courses. The cooking liquor can be eaten as a soup course, followed by the meat and vegetables as the main. Alternatively you can always leave one or the other until the next meal.

Recipe by Malcolm Alder-Smith
La Maison aux Quat'Saisons, Laborie, 19400 Monceaux-sur-Dordogne

Preparation time: 30 minutes
Cooking time: 250 minutes

Ingredients for 6 people

- *500 g diced beef (shin, neck, shoulder)*
- *6 carrots – peeled and cut in half*
- *6 turnips – peeled and cut in half*
- *4 leeks – split, cleaned, folded & tied with string*
- *4 sticks of celery*
- *6 potatoes*
- *2 onions, stuck with two cloves each*
- *2 cloves of garlic*
- *bouquet garni*

136

- *salt and pepper*

Le "Farçun"

  - *100 g butter*
  - *4 soup spoons of milk*
  - *2 eggs*

  - *10 g baker's yeast*
  - *flour*
  - *salt*

Preparation

Prepare the *farçun*: soften the butter in a bowl over a bain-marie. Add the salt, milk and the baker's yeast. Stir the mixture until thoroughly blended in together. Remove the bowl from the bain-marie and gently beat the eggs with a fork, add to the butter mixture, then add the flour, little by little, kneading until you have a clear paste which detaches from your hands, without the paste being too dry. Allow the paste to rise for 3 hours. The paste should double in volume.

Take a large *faitout* (cooking pot) or casserole, add around 2.5 litres of cold water and bring to the boil. Add the meat and leave to simmer rapidly for around 5 minutes until scum rises to the top of the liquid; remove the scum with a ladle and turn the heat right down so that the meat simmers slowly for around one hour.

Around this time, wash and blanch 4 – 6 good cabbage leaves. Cover a large sieve or colander with some of the cabbage leaves. Lay the enlarged paste on top of the leaves and fold them over to cover the paste. Cover the ball with another 2 cabbage leaves. Gently slide the paste wrapped in the cabbage into the gently simmering *pot-au-feu* and simmer for around 45 minutes to allow the paste to cook and swell without breaking-up on the surface of the *pot-au-feu*.

After this time, add the prepared vegetables, *bouquet garni* and seasoning and allow to continue to simmer for another couple of hours. Peel the potatoes and cut them into two or four depending on their size, add them to the broth and cook for a further 30 minutes or so until they are cooked.

Serve the *bouillon* in large bowls with the meat and surround with the vegetables and the *farçun* cut into portions, but still in the cabbage leaves.

WINE: A nice rustic red goes well with this dish, go for an oaked Cahors or Gaillac.

QUEUE DE BOEUF À LA MOELLE
oxtail with its beef marrow

This is another recipe supplied by our good friends Michel et Isabelle Roussanne at the Auberge des Gabariers, on the quay at Argentat.

Back in my old hotel and restaurant days, I always used to produce a wonderful braised oxtail which had the most incredible depth of flavour, after cooking for two or three hours. Unfortunately, in the UK, following massive health scares in the last five years, it has been virtually impossible to get hold of oxtail. It has only been recently that we have started to see it re-appear in our shops and supermarkets again, so this particular great British traditional dish will carry on.

Fortunately, we currently have no such problems, that I am aware of, in France and so I can experiment with this type of ingredient at leisure in my kitchen; however, I still have not managed to produce anything to beat my original recipe. So, my friends, I am going to give you two recipes to choose from; the first from the Gabariers and the second will be my 'old faithful', which I am yet to try out on our French friends.

Recipe by Michel et Isabelle Roussanne
Auberge des Gabariers, 15 Quai Lestourgie, 19400 Argentat

Preparation time: 40 minutes
Cooking time: 180 minutes

Ingredients for 4 people

- *2 kg oxtail – cut ready to cook*
- *1 marrow bone*
- *4 leeks*
- *400 g carrots*
- *400 g turnips*
- *400 g potatoes*
- *1 stick of celery*
- *3 onions*
- *thyme*
- *bay leaf*
- *parsley stalks*
- *coarse salt*

Preparation

Take a large cooking pot and add the oxtail, cover with cold water and place over a medium to high flame. Bring the water to the boil and skim off any impurities which rise to the surface, reduce the heat to a steady simmer.

Peel and wash the vegetables. Trim the root from one onion and cut it in half, without removing the skin. Place a heavy-bottomed frying pan over a medium flame, add a little oil, then the two halves of onion, skin side up. Allow to cook, flat side down, until the onion starts to caramelise and takes on a good deep, golden brown colour.

Make a *bouquet garni* using the green part of a leek, a sprig or two of fresh thyme, a couple of parsley stalks and a fresh bay leaf. Fold the leek over the herbs and tie with a piece of string.

Add the *bouquet garni* to the simmering stock, plus a little seasoning, the caramelised onion halves, the other two onions (skinned and left whole), the vegetables and the marrow bone. When they are cooked, remove the vegetables and the marrow bone.

To cook the oxtail perfectly (depending on the size of the pieces), allow for a little less than three hours' cooking over a low flame.

Once cooked, remove the oxtail from the cooking pot, drain and dress on a large serving dish and keep warm. Pass the *bouillon* through a sieve into a clean saucepan. Bring the *bouillon* back to the boil and reduce to a simmer. Correct the seasoning and consistency and ladle over the oxtail. Pour any surplus *bouillon* into a warmed *gras et maigre* (a special sauce-boat which allows you to pour 'neat' sauce/gravy over your meat, leaving the fat in the sauce-boat – clever stuff, eh?).

Serve with some crisp French green beans and some 'square chips'.

WINE: To compliment this dish, you are going to need to go for a rather rich red wine. Although in the UK, many people tend to look at oxtail as being rather a down-market dish, I would disagree big time, and suggest that you invest in a good quality red to do it justice. I am torn between different wines from different regions and so I am going to suggest a couple for Michel and Isabelle's recipe and a couple for my recipe which follows.

For this dish, I am going to suggest either a red burgundy, such as Nuits St Georges, or one of my favourites, Gevry Chambertin, alternatively try a good Châteauneuf-du-Pape.

QUEUE DE BOEUF BRAISÉE
braised oxtail

My version of this traditional Great British Classic has yet to be exposed to our neighbours and friends in France. The finished product, served in a large deep soup bowl, tantalises the taste buds and leaves you wanting more. I just love to take the odd slice or two of crusty country bread, spread it thickly with butter and dip each slice into the rich and unctuous gravy.

This recipe can easily be turned into a one-pot dish, if you like, by adding a variety of vegetables and/or potatoes to the simmering gravy at an appropriate time during the cooking process. Alternatively you can serve the tails with a fresh pea-mash (recipe to follow), or mashed potato with shredded leeks, cabbage or spring onions ('champ' style).

Recipe by Malcolm Alder-Smith
La Maison aux Quat'Saisons, Laborie, 19400 Monceaux-sur-Dordogne

Preparation time: 25 minutes
Cooking time: 180 minutes

Ingredients for 4 people

- *2 kg oxtail – cut ready to cook*
- *250 g carrots – peeled and chopped*
- *250 g onions – peeled and chopped*
- *250 g leeks – chopped*
- *250 g celery – chopped*
- *500 g tomatoes – skinned, de-seeded and chopped*
- *2 soup spoons of tomato purée*

- *75 cl of Cahors (red)*
- *1.5 lts veal stock (Maggi – Fond de Veau or similar)*
- *olive oil*
- *unsalted butter*
- *flour*
- *paprika pepper*
- *salt and black pepper*
- *bouquet garni*

Preparation

Pass the joints of oxtail through the seasoned flour, laced with paprika, salt and black pepper. Shake each piece well to remove any surplus flour. Place a heavy-bottomed frying pan over a medium to high flame and add a good couple of slugs of olive oil.

Fry the floured and seasoned pieces of oxtail on all sides until they turn brown. Remove the tails and drain in a colander.

In the same pan, fry the chopped vegetables over a medium flame until they turn a golden brown, adding a little extra oil if necessary. This will help to collect the deposits from the oxtail on the bottom of the frying pan and will help to give the dish the most wonderful flavour. Add the chopped tomatoes and tomato *purée*, stir well and cook for a couple of minutes.

Take a cast iron casserole dish and add the browned oxtail then cover with the vegetable and tomato mixture.

Add the red wine to the frying pan and reduce by two thirds. Add some of the veal stock and stir well. Pour the sauce over the oxtail and then add sufficient veal stock to barely cover the tails. Bring the gravy to the boil and reduce to a gentle simmer, cover with a lid and place into a pre-heated oven at around 175°C for 90 – 120 minutes until the meat comes away easily from the bone.

Remove the oxtail, place into another casserole (or large saucepan) and keep warm. Pass the gravy through a sieve into a clean pan and bring to the boil. Reduce the heat, add a few knobs of butter and stir well. You should finish up with a rich dark sauce which will taste absolutely wonderful.

Allow for three to four pieces of oxtail per person (depending on size) and place into the bottom of large soup bowls. Pour some of the hot gravy over the tails and sprinkle with a little chopped fresh flat leaf parsley.

My secret: This is another one of those wonderful dishes, a little like my Boeuf Bourguignonne recipe, which will taste even better the next day. Alternatively, use any oxtails and sauce that are left to turn into a fresh oxtail soup – divine!

Wine: For this one, go for a St Emillion or a Pomerol (Merlot), both producing some fantastic rich tasty wines. Pétrus is one of the most amazing wines you will ever taste, but get 'on-line' and increase your overdraft first before you buy, or be prepared to bend your plastic like never before on a bottle of wine.

RIS DE VEAU LIMOUSINE
Calves Sweet-breads Limousin Style

The kitchen at the Hôtel Fouillade is run under the expert direction of Michel Fouillade and the front of house by his wife Veronique. Both areas operate to the highest professional standards. The hotel has an excellent reputation with visitors and locals alike and is an absolute must on your 'places to dine' list, should you visit or wish to stay.

I think that out of all of the restaurants where we have eaten in La Corrèze over the last dozen or so years, the range of menus and à la carte, the preparation, cooking and quality of presentation of the food at the Fouillade has to be held up as one of the best. Do try it, I am sure you won't be disappointed.

I have been badgering Michel for nearly a year to get a recipe out of him to include in this book, but up to draft copy stage, I had been unsuccessful. In desperation, I wrote to my good friend Susie Scott, who has been eating at the Fouillade for more years than she cares to remember. Susie kindly put in a good word for me, and hey presto!

The Hôtel Fouillade is closed on Mondays out of season and usually closed for the annual vacation from around mid-November to mid-December.

Recipe by Michel Fouillade
11, place Gambetta – 19400 Argentat

Preparation time: 30 minutes
Cooking time: 20 minutes

Ingredients for 2 people

- *500 g prepared calves sweet-breads*
- *200 g cèpes*
- *½ onion – thinly sliced*
- *1 tomato (peeled, skinned and chopped)*
- *1/3 litre crème fraîche*
- *olive oil*
- *unsalted butter*
- *1 small branch of fresh thyme*

- *some chervil for garnishing*
- *salt and pepper*

Preparation

After you have blanched the sweet-breads and drained them thoroughly, heat a heavy-bottomed (metal handled) frying pan over a medium to high flame and add some oil and a knob of butter. Add the sweet-breads and brown them evenly. Once nicely coloured, add the *cêpes*, sliced onion and tomato. Lightly season with salt and pepper. Place the pan into a pre-heated oven at around 180°C for around 20 minutes.

When you remove the pan from the oven, skim off any fat which may have risen to the surface and then add the *crème fraîche*.

Wine: Michel Fouillade suggests that with this regional recipe you try a *vin de pays*, such as a local le Mille et Une Pierre (red).

HOTEL FOUILLADE
PLACE GAMBETTA
ARGENTAT

ROGNONS SAUTÉS AUX
MOUTARDE DE VIOLETTE DE BRIVE
Lamb's kidneys in a red wine and
Moutarde de Violette de Brive sauce

When we were on vacation at La Maison in October 2002, Twink's mum and dad, Roy and Ivy, and her Auntie Kit from Canada flew down to stay with us for a week. Somewhere between all of the shopping, sightseeing and visiting friends etc., we managed to fit in two or three of our favourite restaurants, one of them being Les Voyageurs set in the Place de la Mairie at St Martin le Meanne, run by Jean-Françoise and Catherine Chaumeil. Twink and her dad had this dish: I tried a little 'tastette' and was bowled over by the amazing flavour.

On a very recent trip to La Maison, we managed to buy some Moutarde Violette de Brive and brought some back home with us, purely to try to reconstruct the dish which Jean-Françoise had so lovingly created twelve months earlier. If I say that both Twink and I were happy with the way the dish turned out, this would be a slight understatement.

So thanks a million, Jean-Françoise for the inspiration for this dish, which can be served as a starter or main course, and long may your culinary skills bring joy to your many customers from near and far.

To make this dish really work 'my way', I will share with you my recipe for a rich red wine sauce, which Twink and I often use as a base recipe. You can cook this for a day or so topping it up with port, red wine etc., as it reduces and increases its intensity of flavour. Or you can knock it up in next to no time and let it cook while you are preparing the ingredients for the kidneys. Alternatively you are allowed to cheat a little bit and can get hold of some packets of veal gravy from your local supermarket and doctor it up, but the end result will not be quite the same.

Recipe by Malcolm Alder-Smith
La Maison aux Quat'Saisons, Laborie, 19400 Monceaux-sur-Dordogne

Preparation time:	45 minutes
Cooking time:	20 minutes (kidneys)

Ingredients for 4-6 people (main course, depending on your appetite!)

For the sauce
- *I medium onion – peeled and chopped (small dice)*
- *1 carrot – peeled and chopped (small dice)*
- *1 stick of celery – chopped (small dice)*
- *1 small leek – chopped (small dice)*
- *Mushrooms (champignons de Paris – stalks removed)*
- *1 large clove of garlic – crushed*
- *25 cl rich red wine*
- *tomato purée*
- *2 soup spoons of dark brown sugar*
- *2 soup spoons of red wine vinegar*
- *1 soup spoon of flour*
- *veal stock*
- *bouquet garni*
- *salt and ground pepper*

Preparation

Take a heavy-bottomed saucepan or *sauteuse*, place over a medium flame and add a little olive oil. Add the prepared vegetables and cook until they start to turn golden brown.

Add the dark brown sugar and when it starts to caramelise, add the red wine vinegar and stir well, allowing the sticky liquid to reduce just a little. Add the tomato *purée* and cook for a minute or so, then add the flour and stir well.

Little by little, add about half of the red wine and a little veal stock, stirring all the time so that your sauce doesn't go lumpy. Once you have added about half the amount of wine, add the *bouquet garni* and a little seasoning and bring to the boil for a moment, reduce to a slow simmer then cover with a lid and allow to tick along slowly for an hour or so. Stir occasionally and if the sauce reduces too much or starts to get a little thick, just add a little more red wine.

For the kidneys
- *1 kg lambs' kidneys*
- *250 g champignons de paris (chestnut mushrooms would do)*
- *Moutarde Violette de Brive*
- *tomato purée*

- *1 clove of garlic – finely chopped*
- *1 medium onion – finely chopped*
- *unsalted butter*
- *olive oil*

Preparation

The outer skin of the kidneys should be removed first, cutting away any gristle. If you buy your kidneys from a supermarket, you will not have to worry about this. Remove the kidneys from their packaging, place them into a large sieve or colander and allow to drain for a few minutes.

Cut each kidney into two, cutting from top to bottom (or vice-versa), then cut away the white core with a sharp knife. Place the prepared kidneys onto a tray and lightly season with salt and ground black pepper.

Place a heavy-bottomed frying pan over a medium to high flame and add around an ounce of butter and a little olive oil. Add the chopped onion and garlic and cook until they start to turn golden brown. Remove the onion and garlic and put to one side.

Turn the flame up a little and add the kidneys, a few at a time, cooking on both sides until they just start to take on some colour. Remove and place onto some kitchen paper, then add more kidneys and so on, until all the kidneys have been sealed and taken on a little colour.

Add a little more olive oil to the frying pan and sauté the mushrooms until they just start to take on some colour. Remove from the pan and add to the kidneys.

Pour off any excess oil that may be left in the pan and return to a medium flame. Add around 12.5 cl of red wine to deglaze the pan and reduce by around two thirds to concentrate the flavour. Return all of the kidneys, mushrooms and the onion and garlic mixture to a *sauteuse* or saucepan and place over a medium to low flame. Add one soup spoon of tomato *purée* and one soup spoon of Moutarde Violette de Brive and stir well.

Strain the red wine sauce through a sieve into a clean saucepan, bring to the boil, reduce to a simmer and correct the seasoning and consistency before adding sufficient of the sauce to barely cover the kidney mixture.

Cook the kidneys for a further 20 minutes or so, allowing them to take on the rich flavours from the *moutarde* and the red wine sauce.

My secret: There is, my friends, no substitute (nothing at all) for Moutarde Violette de Brive, which can be purchased from Denoix, 9, Boulevard Marechal Lyautey, 19100 Brive. Denoix is more or less directly opposite the Palais de Justice. Tel: 05 55 74 34 27, Fax: 05 55 84 41 69 or www.denoix.com. Alternatively you will usually be able to purchase a jar from one of the local supermarkets *en Corrèze*.

Denoix also produce the equally unique Quinqui Noix, a walnut aperitif which should be served lightly chilled to unsuspecting gastro's.

WINE: You have just got to go for something really fruity with a big punch to flatter the considerable flavour from this dish. Go for one of the good co-operative wines from St Emilion or a quality Fronsac from just around the corner.

RÔTI DE PORC À LA BOULANGÈRE
roast pork baker's style

This is not a traditional roast as we know it in England, so don't expect to have any crackling on your plate when you serve up this dish. It is more of a pot-roasted style dish which is cooked in a casserole in the oven, initially with a lid, half covered with water, stock, marinade or sauce. The difference between this and a traditional roast is that you will nearly always have a nice moist piece of meat at the end of cooking, rather than risk a dry, overcooked joint.

Although this recipe has been given to me by my good friends Michel and Isabelle at the Gabariers, I have tweaked it just a little by adding a tad extra carrot and leek. This is simple country food and the end result is a wonderfully moist piece of pork which will just melt in your mouth enhanced by the natural flavours of the herbs, leek and carrots – fabulous!

Recipe by Michel et Isabelle Roussanne
Auberge des Gabariers, 15 Quai Lestourgie, 19400 Argentat

Preparation time: 30 minutes
Cooking time: 90 minutes

Ingredients for 4 people

- *1 kg roasting pork (loin of pork is best)*
- *800 g medium sized potatoes*
- *20 g butter*
- *2 soup spoons of olive oil*
- *2 leaves of fresh sage*

- *fresh marjoram*
- *1 clove*
- *2 carrots*
- *2 small (thin) leeks*
- *salt*

Preparation

Get your butcher to remove the skin and then bone, roll and tie the loin of pork for you.

Wash and peel the potatoes and cut them into good ½ centimetre slices. Place into a bowl of cold water to prevent them from discolouring. Wash and peel the carrots and cut in two lengthways. Wash the leek and cut into 10 cm pieces.

Wipe the joint of pork dry with some kitchen paper, season and rub all over with the chopped marjoram. Pre-heat the oven to 200°C.

Heat the olive oil in a heavy-bottomed casserole and brown the joint of pork on all sides over medium flame, remove the joint and place to one side. The aroma of the pork and marjoram cooking together is just wonderful.

Take the sliced potatoes, drain and spread about a third of them over the bottom of the casserole. Season and sprinkle with a little marjoram. Place the joint of pork on top of the bed of potatoes and add the sage leaves, clove, carrot and the leek. Cover the joint with the rest of the sliced potatoes, season and sprinkle with marjoram.

Moisten with about 300/400 cl of hot water. Cut the butter into small pieces and dot over the top of the potatoes. Cover the casserole and cook in the oven for around 60 minutes. Remove the lid and brush the potatoes with a little melted butter and return to the oven, without the lid, turning the heat up to 250°C for the last 30 minutes to lightly brown off the potatoes.

Remove the pork and place onto your chopping board ready to carve. Take four heated plates and make a bed of the sliced potatoes on each, neatly adding a piece of carrot and some leek to garnish.

Using a sharp kitchen knife remove the butcher's string, carve the pork into approximately 1 cm thick slices and place overlapping on top of the potatoes. Take a ladle and pour a little of the *jus* (juice) over the pork.

Serve with some fine green beans cooked *al dente* and if you can get hold of some Aurelia Moutard de Dijon, this goes really well with the pork. Whatever you do – DO NOT serve apple sauce with this dish.

If you have any stock and potatoes left in the casserole, they can be easily turned into soup by adding a little more vegetable stock and whizzing it up in your food processor or by hand blender.

WINE: You should seriously think about a fairly light red, matured in oak for two or three years such as red Bordeaux or other Cabernet Sauvignon-based reds, or alternatively a rich white.

ROULADES DE VEAU FARCIES
DE POMMES ET MARRONS
Rolls of veal stuffed with apple and chestnut

Recipe by Doris Coppenrath
Auberge de Saint-Julien-aux-Bois
19220 Saint-Julien-aux-Bois

Preparation time: 60 minutes
Cooking time: 30 minutes

Ingredients for 4 people

For the stuffing:

- *2 shallots*
- *2 apples*
- *15 blanched chestnuts*
- *chopped marjoram*
- *50 g butter*
- *salt and pepper*

For the roulades

- *4 escalopes of veal*
- *4 soup spoons of "moutarde l'ancienne"*
- *0.5 lt dry cider*
- *2 cl Calvados*
- *2 soup spoons of crème fraîche*
- *salt and black pepper*
- *2 soup spoons olive oil*
- *1 soup spoon cornflour*

Preparation

For the stuffing, finely chop the shallots, the apples and the chestnuts. Brown the shallots in a frying pan then add the apples and chestnuts and leave to cook over a low heat for a few minutes. Season with the marjoram and the pepper.

Beat the escalopes of veal with a meat tenderiser and spread the mustard over each one, followed by the stuffing. Tuck in each end of the meat and roll the escalopes of veal into *roulades* (rolls) and tie each with three or four pieces of string; equally you could 'spike' each *roulade* a couple of times with cocktail sticks.

Heat a frying pan over a medium flame and add the olive oil, followed by the stuffed veal rolls and brown the meat on all sides. Add the Calvados and cider and leave to simmer for about half an hour.

To make the sauce: remove the *roulades* from the pan and place in a low oven to keep warm. Add the *crème fraîche* to the liquid in the pan and pass through a fine sieve into a clean pan and reheat to a low simmer. Dilute the cornflour with a little water and gently pour into the sauce, stirring or whisking well as you do to obtain a nice creamy consistency. Check the sauce for flavour then season to taste with a little salt and pepper and allow to simmer, while you get the roulades ready.

Le secret de Doris Coppenrath: Before service, cut each *roulade* diagonally across into slices and arrange neatly on each plate. Pour a little sauce over and around the meat and serve with *pommes parmentier* and fresh broccoli.

TÊTE DE VEAU
calf's head

Recipe by Didier Veron – Chef/Patron
Auberge du Lac, Le Bourg, 19170 Viam

Preparation time: 30 minutes
Cooking time: 4 hours

Ingredients for 4 people

- *1 boned head of veal with its tongue*
- *1 leek*
- *2 carrots*
- *½ swede*
- *1 stick of celery*
- *1 onion stuck with 5 cloves*
- *1 clove of garlic crushed with the back of a knife*
- *salt, pepper and a hint of five spice*

Sauce
- *yellow of one hard-boiled egg*
- *oil, a little vinegar, salt and pepper*
- *capers*

Preparation

Thinly slice the vegetables, cut into julienne (3.5cm strips) and make a stock.

While the stock is cooking, cut the head of veal and the tongue into 5cm x 5cm pieces.

Place the meat into a heavy-bottomed pan, pour over just enough of the stock to cover and leave to cook very slowly for 3½ to 4 hours.

To make the sauce, crush the cooked egg yolk and mix firmly with the mustard to obtain the consistency of cream.

Gradually add the oil a little at a time and whisk up to a creamy consistency, adding a little salt and pepper to taste.

Add a little alcohol vinegar to make the final consistency of cream.

Remove the cooked pieces of veal and tongue from the stock and drain. Remove the cooked vegetables from the stock and drain. Place the pieces of meat onto hot plates, garnish with a few capers and put a good spoon full of the sauce on the side of the plate. To finish off, add a little *mélange* of the cooked vegetables to each plate and some steamed turned potatoes.

If you are not keen on whole capers, then they can be chopped and mixed in with the sauce.

VOLAILLES
poultry

In Argentat, near *chez nous*, we have a large open-air market every first and third Thursday of the month. It is an experience, and we always indulge ourselves. The market sells something for everyone, from soap to farm equipment, vegetables, meat and fish – even beds. It is easy to see which are the stalls of great repute, as the locals queue and chat politely with each other while waiting to purchase some Cantal cheese or their favourite goats' cheese.

There is one section which sells baby livestock, of the feathered variety, ducks, chickens and geese. We always told our son Ashley that people brought them to take home as pets, but I think that he has sussed that one out now.

155

But, yes, your average rural household will often have ducks, geese or chickens tucked away somewhere in the garden, ready for when they are required for a family celebration or religious festival.

I guess that I had never given it much thought before, but when the general public refer to poultry in the UK, we tend to talk about chicken, turkey and maybe duck. Even the catering students' bible, *Practical Cookery* (Ceserani, Kinton and Fosket – Hodder & Stoughton), pays scant regard to recipes for duck and goose.

It is seldom that we see chicken on hotel menus *en Corrèze*, but we will always see duck breast, *confit* and *foie gras*.

The local *traiteur* will be able to supply you with *le poulet* (usually corn fed), *la pintade, le canard, les Cailles, la dinde noir, le chapon* and of course *foie gras*.

The main difference which we find in France is the quality of the product which we buy, be it from a supermarket or our local butcher. The birds to go for are *Label Rouge* free-range poultry, reared in grassy open air or open space buildings with low quantity flock sizes and access to open air environment.

The ultimate judgment, of course, is the taste. The taste of *Label Rouge* traditional free-range poultry is outstanding compared with standard poultry.

CASSOULET AU CONFIT DE CANARD
casserole of confit of duck

There are some recipes which I find quite 'orgasmic' – the ingredients may be few and simple, but the end result is a total delight – so, my friends, I am pleased to include this one. Just take a look at the ingredients and tell me that the end product will taste anything less than superb.

This recipe was inspired by a meal which Twink and I had at a restaurant a few years ago in Brive, which is an hour or so away from *chez nous*.

Preparation time: 30 minutes
Cooking time: 75 minutes
Soaking time: 12 hours

Ingredients for 4 people

- *400 g confit de canard (home made or can)*
- *400 g shoulder of lamb – bite sized chunks*
- *250 g loin of pork – bite sized chunks*
- *400 g Toulouse sausages (10's) twisted and cut in two*
- *400 g dried haricot beans*
- *2 carrots*
- *2 medium sized onions*
- *4 cloves of garlic*
- *2 bay leaves*
- *fresh flat leaf parsley*
- *2 sprigs of thyme*
- *salt and ground black pepper*

Preparation

Soak the dried haricot beans overnight in a bowl or pan or cold water. This should be done for a minimum of twelve hours.

Drain and place the beans in a pressure cooker with the peeled onions, the two bay leaves and the thyme. Re-cover the beans with some fresh water and cook for 20 minutes or so until the pressure valve starts to rotate.

Remove from the heat and release the pressure. Drain the beans in a colander and retain the liquid.

In the pressure cooker, melt two soup spoons of duck fat (from the *confit*) and brown-off the cubes of lamb and pork a few at a time. Add the peeled and sliced carrot and the peeled cloves of garlic, cover with the cooking liquor from the haricots, add a little salt and black pepper and close the lid of the pressure cooker; cook for around 20 minutes until the pressure valve starts to rotate.

In a separate casserole, heat the *confit de canard*, drain and add to the pressure cooker (making sure that you release the steam first), close the lid and cook for a further 10 minutes until the pressure valve starts to rotate.

Prick the Toulouse sausages so that they will not burst, put in the pressure cooker (making sure that you release the steam first), and cook for a further 20 minutes without covering with the lid. Add the chopped fresh herbs and simmer gently for another 15 minutes.

Using a hot, hollow service plate, arrange the meat and beans, pour over some of the cooking liquid and serve immediately.

WINE: I am going to suggest that you go for a local wine from the South West of France, such as a Minervois, Corbières or Fitou. However, my personal choice to go with this dish would be a nice Gaillac. Even a young Appellation Gaillac Contrôlée will usually produce a glass of deep red fruity wine to accompany your meal.

CONFIT DE CANARD AU CHOU ROUGE
preserved duck with red cabbage

This is one of the classic Corrézienne dishes: duck (or goose) cooked and preserved in its own fat.

In the UK we use a number of ways of preserving food: freezing, smoking, salting, vacuum packing, sterilising, pasteurising etc, etc... It is, however, unusual in the UK to find food which is preserved in this way.

The country folk of the Corrèze have been rearing poultry, pork and fattened geese and ducks for hundreds of years in order to conserve them in tall earthenware jars, ready to be eaten at any time of the year.

Nowadays, at certain times of the year, you can buy fabulous fattened duck legs from the local supermarkets, which, I am told, are specifically produced for making Confit.

Recipe by Malcolm Alder-Smith
La Maison aux Quat'Saisons, Laborie, 19400 Monceaux-sur-Dordogne

Preparation time: 30 minutes
Cooking time: 200 minutes

Ingredients for 4 people

- *4 fat duck legs*
- *1 can of duck or goose fat*
- *50 g coarsely ground salt*
- *1 soup spoon crushed black pepper corns*

- *1 soup spoon finely chopped fresh thyme leaves*
- *2 bay leaves finely chopped*

For the red cabbage

- *1 small red cabbage*
- *6 shallots*
- *2 oranges – squeezed*
- *100 g caster sugar*

- *4 soup spoons red wine vinegar*
- *olive oil*
- *salt and pepper*

Preparation

To prepare the duck legs in advance, trim and remove as much surplus fat as you can and retain the fat in your refrigerator.

159

A day or so before you need the duck, mix the dry marinade ingredients together and rub well into the skin of each duck leg. Cover with a clean tea towel and place in your refrigerator for a minimum of 24 hours.

The next day, take a heavy-bottomed saucepan and place over a low flame. Add the fat which you have trimmed from the duck legs and let it render down slowly until it turns to a clear liquid.

Wipe the marinade from the duck legs and place them tightly into the base of the saucepan. If the fat does not cover the duck legs, then pour over the duck or goose fat; you can always top this up with a little sunflower oil if necessary.

Cook very very slowly over a low flame for around 120 minutes. Test to see if the duck is cooked with the aid of a small sharp knife. Transfer the legs to a clean Kilner jar or jars and strain the duck fat over until covered. Sterilize for approximately 90 minutes in a pressure cooker.

If you don't want to keep the preserved duck for any period of time and intend using it within a day or so, then you can just place the legs in a bowl, cover them with the fat and refrigerate until needed.

To prepare the red cabbage, cut it into four quarters. Trim off the heavy part of the stalk and cut across the quarters into thin strips. Skin and slice the shallots.

Take a medium sized heavy-bottomed saucepan, place over a medium to low flame and add a few slugs of olive oil. Throw in the shallots and allow to cook slowly for a couple of minutes. Add the cabbage and sprinkle with the sugar, turn up the heat and cook for around five minutes to start the caramelisation of the sugar, then add the red wine vinegar and orange juice, stir well and reduce the heat. Cover and cook for around 30 minutes until the cabbage is nearly cooked. If the cabbage becomes too dry, then add a little more orange juice out of the fridge. Season with a little salt and black pepper and the dish is nearly ready to serve.

While the red cabbage is cooking, pre-heat your oven to 200°C. Remove the duck legs from the fat and wipe away any surplus. Place them onto a wire rack with a tray underneath to catch the fat which will run off the legs. Roast for around 40 minutes until the skin turns to a golden brown.

WINE: Go for a tannic young red Bordeaux or Cru Borgeois.

CONFIT DE CANARD OU D'OIE
preserved duck or goose

Recipe by Malcolm Alder-Smith
La Maison aux Quat'Saisons, Laborie, 19400 Monceaux-sur-Dordogne

Preparation time: 60 minutes (previous day)
Cooking time: 180 minutes

Ingredients for 4 people

- *4 fat duck legs*
- *50 g coarse salt*
- *10 g ground pepper*
- *1 soup spoon chopped fresh thyme*
- *2 bay leaves, finely chopped*
- *2 cloves of garlic – chopped*
- *duck or goose fat*

Preparation

Remove as much fat from the duck legs as you can and refrigerate.

Mix together the dry marinade ingredients together and rub them all over the prepared duck legs. Place the legs in a clean earthenware container, cover with a clean tea towel, weigh down lightly and cover with lid. To make the best confit, you will need to place the duck legs in the mixture of salt, herbs and garlic and refrigerate for 24 hours.

The following day, cut the surplus duck fat into small pieces and place into a heavy-bottomed saucepan over a medium to low flame on your hob. The fat will melt to a clear oily consistency.

Wipe the duck legs and carefully place into the duck fat. If there is insufficient fat to cover the legs then top up with some of the purchased duck or goose fat. Leave the legs to cook slowly for about 90 minutes. After this time, check to see if they are cooked by piercing with a small pointed knife alongside the bone. If no blood appears in the fat, the pieces are cooked. Remove from the fat and place one leg or more into each sterilized preserving jar, depending on the size of the legs and jar.
Boil, skim and filter the fat through a piece of muslin and pour over the

cooked duck legs. Using the rubber rings provided with the preserving jar, close the lids and sterilize for 90 minutes in a pressure cooker.

Remove the jars and allow to cool before storing away for a cold winter's night, when you can reheat and serve to the delight of those gathered around your table.

Although this recipe is fairly similar to the last one, the end result, I think is a little different.

Preserved goose legs are prepared in exactly the same way.

WINE: I am going to suggest a choice of either red or white, which should suit both camps. Either way you can't lose!

If you are going to go for a red, then consider a tannic Bordeaux Cru Borgeois. If white is your preference, try a Pinot Gris or a quality Gewürtztraminer, which is the most aromatic of Alsace wines – it has the fragrance of rose petals, with a hint of grapefruit and lychees to the taste. I think that this is one of the most distinctive wines on the market and good ones are really very, very good.

CONFIT DE CHÂTAIGNES
preserved chestnuts

This is not a dish, as are the others in this section, rather some info' on how to preserve chestnuts to keep them ready to use at a later date.

During one of our early visits to Corrèze, not too long after we had purchased La Maison aux Quat'Saisons, our dear friend and neighbour Georges Fruitiere arrived at our back door, bearing gifts (as he does on regular occasions).

He had, earlier that morning, taken our son Ashley to go and pick a couple of buckets full of chestnuts. At this time, we were unaware of the importance of chestnuts locally, and really weren't sure what to do with them, except bring them home for my sister who loves them. We insisted that Georges and his darling wife Paulette take some for themselves, however, he could see that we were a little flummoxed as to what we should do with 'our share' of the treasure. Georges insisted that he take our bucket and prepare them for us, which must have taken him the rest of the day.

Later that day Georges arrived with a very large Kilner jar full of chestnuts, which they had preserved previously and in the other hand he held a very heavy-looking black cauldron. He placed the cauldron onto our kitchen table, removed the lid and shared with us their secret for cooking chestnuts – very slowly over a bed of peeled potatoes.

This recipe is fairly simple, but chestnut preparation can be laboriously slow, frustrating and sometimes painful, should you get a piece of the inner skin behind your finger nail, so do take care.

Preparation

Make an incision in the skin of each chestnut. Place a pan of water over a medium to high flame then drop the chestnuts into boiling water to blanch for 5 minutes or so. Remove the chestnuts and place into a colander. Remove the outer and inner skin.

Place the chestnuts into an appropriate-sized Kilner Jar and add nothing else. Seal the jar and sterilise in boiling water for 90 minutes.

COQ AU VIN
chicken in red wine

This is one of those fabulous dishes which we often rely on as a 'safe bet' when we throw a lunch party in France. We prepare almost all of the ingredients the previous evening and throw the dish together in the morning, allowing the ingredients to cook slowly and take on all of those wonderful flavours, so that when our friends arrive we can spend much more time with them chatting and enjoying their company (and drinking wine of course), instead of rushing around the kitchen like a headless chicken – sorry about the pun!

Recipe provided by Denise Mespoulet

Preparation time: 15 minutes
Cooking time: 105 minutes

Ingredients for 4 people

- *1 large bird*
- *1 soup spoon of goose fat*
- *2 carrots – roughly chopped*
- *18 shallots*
- *2 soup spoons of flour*
- *1.5 lts good red wine*
- *bouquet garni*
- *2 sticks of celery – roughly chopped*
- *3 cloves of garlic – crushed*
- *200 g cèpe sliced (champignons de Paris will be OK)*
- *2 tomatoes – peeled, skinned and chopped*
- *150 g smoked lardons of bacon*
- *2 slices of bread*

Preparation

Cut the chicken into 8 sauté-sized pieces. To do this, remove the legs and the breasts and cut each into two. Place a large frying pan over a medium heat, add the goose fat and then carefully add the chicken pieces one at a time, starting with the four leg pieces, as they will take the longest to cook. Turn the legs as they brown and add the breast pieces after about five minutes. Cook all the pieces until golden brown and remove onto some kitchen paper, while you start to cook some of the other ingredients.

Add the chopped carrot and 6 of the shallots (roughly chopped) to the pan and cook until they start to turn brown. Reduce the heat to low, sprinkle with the flour and stir well; allow to cook for a couple of minutes, before gradually adding the wine a little at a time, stirring well to blend in with the flour. Add the chopped celery, the crushed garlic, slices of *cèpe*, chopped tomato and a little salt and pepper.

Cover the pan and cook over a gentle heat. While the dish is cooking, skin the shallots, making sure that you keep a little bit of the stalk in place. This will stop them falling apart when you add them to the sauce. There are a number of good ways to make this job a lot easier and far less tearful! I find the best is to trim the stalks to the required length, then place the shallots in a bowl or plastic measuring jug and pour very hot water over them. Leave to rest for about 15 minutes or so and the skins should come away quite easily.

Place a medium sized frying pan over a medium to high flame and add a little more goose fat. When the fat is nice and hot, add the drained and dried shallots, turning regularly to obtain a nice golden to dark brown colour. Remove the browned shallots and place them to one side. Add the smoked lardons to the same fat and cook quickly over a medium heat. Once coloured, add them to the shallots.

After about 30 minutes, take a ladle and skim away any fat which may have risen to the top of the sauce. It is easier to do this by tilting the bowl of the ladle on a slight angle and rotating it around the inside edge of the pan. You can now add the shallots and lardons and cook for a further 30 minutes or so.

While the dish is finishing off cooking you can cook your croutons. The French will often cut bread into triangles – I do like to improve the presentation of this dish by cutting heart shapes, but this can be a bit tricky for the uninitiated. Whichever you choose, once cut, take a clove of garlic and slice it in half, then rub both sides of your croutons with the garlic. Fry them quickly in the remaining goose fat, remove and place onto some kitchen paper.

The dish is ready to serve and you can either do this in individual dishes or a large casserole. Whichever, decorate the dish with one corner of the croutons dipped in chopped parsley.

Denise's secret: I add the shallots and smoked lardons as part of the garnish when I dish this up for friends – this always gives that extra little something to the presentation of the dish.

WINE: This is one of those dishes which you can drink either a wonderful red or fabulous white Burgundy – so go ahead and try something new.

CUISSES DE CANARDS FARCIES AUX CÈPES
legs of duck stuffed with cèpes

Recipe by L'Hostellerie de la Vallée
Rue des Cascades, 19800 Gimel-les-Cascades

Preparation time: 15 minutes
Cooking time: 120 minutes

Ingredients for 10 people

- *10 duck legs*
- *500 g minced pork*
- *125 g cèpes – finely chopped*
- *2 free range eggs*
- *3 cl madeira*
- *slightly stale bread, crusts removed*
- *milk*
- *olive oil*
- *salt and pepper*

Preparation

Take a sharp pointed knife and de-bone the legs, this is the hardest part of the recipe and the most time consuming. I don't advise that you try to tunnel bone the legs, just remove the bone by following the bone on the flesh side, gradually easing it away from the flesh as you go, taking care not to cut yourself.

Over a moderate heat, take a heavy-bottomed frying pan and *sauté* the mushrooms in a little olive oil. Take a bowl and soak the bread in a little milk before adding the eggs, the minced pork, the *sautéed* mushrooms, salt, pepper and Madeira. Blend this mixture thoroughly and divide into ten equal amounts before stuffing each leg. When each leg is stuffed, fold over the edges to seal in the stuffing and tie with pieces of butcher's string.

Place onto a baking-tray, season, add a little oil or melted butter and cook in a pre-heated oven at 180ºC for 90 minutes, basting every 20 minutes or so. When cooked remove the strings and set aside to keep warm while you make a light sauce from the juices in the bottom of the roasting tray.

I like to make a separate sauce for this sort of dish and often fry off some onion, carrot and celery over a medium heat, add a little dark brown sugar and some balsamic vinegar and allow to caramelise a little. Add a touch of tomato *purée*, some stock and some myrtille jam, salt and black pepper. I normally start this before I bone the legs, which gives the sauce time to cook out.

You can always add a touch of red wine or port and some sliced *cèpes* to finish off the sauce. Once the sauce is ready, cut the legs into four or five slices and arrange neatly on plates, pouring the sauce over and around the meat. The sugar and balsamic vinegar give the sauce a nice bite and also provide an attractive glaze.

Serve the dish with buttered carrots and turnips and some small turned roast potatoes.

Recipe supplied by Comité Départemental du Tourisme de la Corrèze.

DINDE DE NOËL
christmas turkey

Our good friends who live in La Corrèze have told me that the main meal at Christmas is usually celebrated on Christmas Eve and is called the *'reveillon'* (Christmas Eve Party). This often entails family and friends gathering around the dinner table to feast on delicacies, such as oysters, smoked salmon and *foie gras*. The 'bird' is either a turkey *(dinde)* or capon *(chapon)* and we are now looking forward to our first Noël experience *en Corrèze* in the not too distant future.

I felt that I should include a fairly straightforward turkey recipe, which can just as easily be produced in the UK as it can in France.

Recipe by Malcolm Alder-Smith
La Maison aux Quat'Saisons, Laborie, 19400 Monceaux-sur-Dordogne

Preparation time: 45 minutes
Cooking time: 180 – 200 minutes

Ingredients for 6 – 8 people

- *1 turkey (around 5 kg)*
- *650 g sausage meat*
- *250 g chestnuts*
- *2 medium sized onions*
- *100 g fresh white bread-crumbs*
- *grated zest of one lemon*
- *1 free range egg*
- *1 clove of garlic*

- *1 stick of celery*
- *50 ml dry Gaillac Perlé (light white wine)*
- *50 ml chicken stock*
- *50 g unsalted butter*
- *1 soup spoon chopped fresh thyme*
- *1 soup spoon chopped fresh sage*
- *1 soup spoon chopped flat leaf parsley*
- *salt and black pepper*

Preparation

Split the skin of each chestnut on the rounded sides. Place a large saucepan of water over a high flame and bring to the boil. Add the prepared chestnuts and cook for around 12 minutes. Turn out the flame under the saucepan.

Peel the chestnuts a few at a time, removing both the outer and inner skin, leaving the remainder in the water until you are ready to peel them. Preheat your oven to 210°C. Heat a saucepan of salted water over a medium flame. Add a little pepper and the stick of celery. When the water comes to the boil, add the peeled chestnuts and cook for about ½ hour.

While the chestnuts are cooking, peel and finely chop the onions and the clove of garlic. Place a small saucepan over a medium flame and add a little butter. When the bubbles subside, add the onion and garlic, cover with a lid and sweat without colour for around 5 minutes. Remove the pan from the flame and allow to cool.

Drain the chestnuts, roughly chop, and put into a large bowl. Add the sausage meat, onion, garlic, lemon zest, breadcrumbs, chopped fresh thyme, sage, flat leaf parsley and the egg and mix together well. If you have the turkey liver, then chop it finely and add it to the mixture; season and stir again. Season the inside of the bird with some salt and black pepper and then stuff with the sausage meat mixture and pack in firmly. Truss the bird with some butcher's string.

Sprinkle the skin with salt and pepper and rub in well with the flat of your hand. Divide up the butter, softened slightly, into small pieces and spread over the surface of the skin.

Place the turkey into a roasting tray, pop it into the hot oven and cook for around 2 hours, basting from time to time with the cooking juices to help prevent the bird from drying out, which is the most common mistake people make when cooking turkey.

Test the bird by inserting the point of a narrow sharp knife into the joint between the leg and breast, the juices should run clear.

Remove the turkey from the roasting tray and place onto a large serving dish or plate to keep warm. Just before you serve your turkey, pour off any residual fat from the cooking juices then deglaze the bottom of the roasting tray with white wine and the chicken stock. Bring to the boil and scrape the bottom of the roasting tin with a spoon to release the tasty deposits. Reduce by about half and pour into a *gras maigre* (special gravy boat).

Open up the turkey, remove the stuffing and cut it into slices. Carve the turkey and arrange neatly on a serving dish, surrounded by slices of the chestnut stuffing. Serve with the wine gravy separate.

My secret: Serve with a *purée* of celeriac and braised celery hearts.

WINE: Go for a classic Châteauneuf-du-Pape or a Gigondas.

MAGRETS DE CANARD AUX CERISES
breast of duck with cherry sauce

We are incredibly blessed, *en Corrèze*, to be able to get our hands on some of the most outstanding soft fruits, such as myrtilles, strawberries and some wonderful black cherries. We have a number of cherry trees in our garden and look forward to June when we can pick the bulging, dark skinned fruit from the trees to make *clafoutis* and we use our own cherries in this special dish.

Recipe by Malcolm Alder-Smith
La Maison aux Quat'Saisons, Laborie, 19400 Monceaux-sur-Dordogne

Preparation time: 10 minutes
Cooking time: 15 minutes

Ingredients for 4 people

- *4 duck breasts*
- *300 g dark, sweet cherries*
- *10 cl Mosel white wine (Riesling)*
- *3 soup spoons of white sugar*
- *3 soup spoons of Cognac or Armagnac*
- *2 small pinches of ground cinnamon*
- *olive oil*
- *flat leaf parsley*
- *salt and black pepper*

Preparation

Rinse and drain the cherries and de-stone them over a bowl to collect the juice.

With the help of a sharp knife, score the skin on the duck breasts diagonally, to make diamond shapes, taking care not to cut into the flesh of the meat.

Take a heavy-bottomed frying pan, brush lightly with oil and place the duck breasts skin-down into the hot pan to cook for five minutes. Turn the breasts over and cook for a further five minutes on the other side. Season with salt and pepper and place, skin side up, in a roasting tin in a pre-heated oven on around 175ºC to finish off cooking.

Drain off the fat from the frying pan and add the cherries and sugar. Pour over the cognac and carefully flame. If you don't have a gas hob, then allow the brandy to heat through, tilt the pan gently and light the spirit with a match or lighter. Alternatively you can heat the spirit in a ladle, set alight and pour over the ingredients. Allow to 'flame' for a short time then add the white wine and any juice which you got from the cherries. Add a couple of small pinches of cinnamon. Boil the liquid for between two and three minutes until the liquid starts to thicken lightly. The addition of a little more sugar will aid the thickening process, if required.

Remove the duck breasts from the oven and slice each with a sharp knife, on a chopping board, diagonally across the breast. Arrange the carved duck breast slices on hot plates and surround them with the cooked cherries. Spoon some sauce over the duck breasts and sprinkle with a little chopped parsley.

Serve immediately with some lightweight vegetables and some small turned roast potatoes.

WINE: This dish deserves a mature 'gamey' red wine such as Côte Rôtie, Morey-St-Denis or a nice Bordeaux or burgundy, you may even want to have a bash at a Hermitage from the Rhône or even a Bandol from way down south on the coastal region near Toulon, which produces Provence's best wines.

MAGRETS DE CANARD AUX MYRTILLES
breast of duck with a bilberry sauce

This is a dish which we have developed over the years and it all started off very much by accident one year not long after we had been married. Someone brought me a Rumtopf as a birthday present so we marinated a few pounds of loganberries in some vodka and sugar. Around nine months or so later, we were having a dinner party and knowing that our friends were ardent lovers of duck, we managed to get hold of some good sized duck breasts, at around 14 oz each. When it came to producing the sauce, we added some of the liquid and fruit from the Rumtopf and the end result was quite outstanding.

I love to 'cook out' meat sauces for some considerable time, which gives the sauce a great depth of flavour. The longest and best ever was for Millennium Eve, when I cooked a Port and Madeira sauce for nearly two days to serve with some fillet steak for a private dinner party – now that one was a real winner!

Recipe provided by Malcolm Alder-Smith
La Maison aux Quat'Saisons, Laborie, 19400 Monceaux-sur-Dordogne

Preparation time: 20 minutes
Cooking time: 90 minutes

Ingredients for 4 people

- *4 duck breasts*
- *550 g myrtilles (or myrtille jam)*
- *4 cl port*
- *1 large carrot*
- *2 sticks of celery*
- *1 medium onion*
- *2 cloves of garlic*
- *2 soup spoons of dark brown sugar*
- *4 soup spoons of balsamic vinegar*
- *duck fat*
- *tomato purée*
- *2 large tomatoes (skinned, deseeded and diced)*
- *chicken stock*
- *bouquet garni*

Preparation

As the sauce for this dish needs some time to cook-out, start with this first. Prepare your carrot, celery and onion and chop them into a *mirepoix* (0.5 cm dice). Take a heavy-bottomed *sauteuse* (shallow pan) and over a medium to high flame add the duck fat and cook the diced vegetables until a golden brown. Reduce the flame slightly, add the sugar and allow to lightly caramelise. Add the balsamic vinegar and cook for a minute or so before adding one soup spoon of tomato *purée*. Stir well and add the tomatoes, myrtilles (or jam), stock and the *bouquet garni*. Cover with a lid and cook the sauce slowly, over a low flame, for at least 90 minutes while you prepare the duck breasts.

I have worked with many chefs over the years, and they all have their own ideas of how you should cook a duck breast, but nowadays I normally always use the method which was originally shown to me by my mates Lee Hext and Kevin Early when we all worked together in the kitchens of a very busy country pub some years back.

Start to cook the duck breasts about 20 minutes before you are ready to eat.

Take the duck breasts and trim off the edges where you may have skin overlapping but no meat underneath it. Take a very sharp knife and carefully score the skin diagonally to make a diamond pattern on the top. Using a good frying pan over a medium/hot flame, add a little duck fat and when hot add the duck breasts skin side down. Cook for 5 minutes before turning and cooking the other side for around 3 minutes. Place the breasts onto an oven tray and put it into a medium oven to finish cooking. Drain any surplus fat from the frying pan and return to the heat. Pour over the port and deglaze the pan, reducing the liquid by half before adding it to the sauce.

The cooking time is dependant on three things – the size of the duck breasts, the heat of the oven and how you like your meat cooked. Personally I can see no other way of eating duck breast than having it cooked 'pink' - anything else would be sacrilege, however, the choice is yours.

When your sauce is cooked, it should have thickened naturally. Take a sieve or conical strainer and pass the sauce into a clean saucepan. If you push the sauce through you will find that you will also finish up with some *purée* of the vegetables as well, which will help to thicken the sauce. Check the sauce for seasoning and consistency.

Take a chopping board and using a sharp knife, trim off the ends and slice the duck breasts diagonally into about six or eight slices depending on size. Drizzle a little sauce over and around the breasts and serve immediately.

My secret: This dish is excellent served on a bed of braised pearl barley.

WINE: Try Cornas from the northern Rhône for a sturdy and very dark Syrah or alternatively and completely different go for a Chambolle-Musigny from the Cote de Nuits, which produces fabulously fragrant and complex wines.

OIE FARCIE AUX CHÂTAIGNES
goose stuffed with chestnuts

Just after Christmas 2003, I sent an e-mail to my buddy Malcolm Coutts, who lives just north of us near Forgès, to wish 'him and his' a happy new year. I had enquired if they had had a very *bon* Christmas and what they had eaten for their celebrations.

Malc replied quickly, as he does, and advised that they did the *'reveillon'*, the Christmas Eve dinner French style, and managed to demolish a meal of smoked salmon, *foie gras*, followed by a super *chapon* (capon) stuffed and cooked by his partner Maya, with all the usual trimmings. At the time of writing, I am awaiting a reply to my follow-up e-mail, begging for the full recipe. In the meantime, I have included a good alternative.

As mentioned previously, chestnuts were part of the staple diet in Corrèze and are still a traditional accompaniment for roasted chicken, turkey and goose.

Recipe by Malcolm Alder-Smith
La Maison aux Quat'Saisons, Laborie, 19400 Monceaux-sur-Dordogne

Preparation time: 30 minutes
Cooking time: 120 minutes

Ingredients for 4 people

- *3 kg goose (retain the liver and finely chop)*
- *150 g pork – minced*
- *150 g veal – minced*
- *1 kg Corrézienne chestnuts (cooked)*
- *Armagnac*
- *125 g lardons of bacon*
- *flat leaf parsley – chopped*
- *180 g fresh breadcrumbs*
- *30 cl milk*
- *2 medium sized onions – finely chopped*
- *1 medium sized onion*
- *1 carrot*
- *1 stick of celery*
- *unsalted butter*

- *15 cl white wine*
- *30 cl chicken stock*
- *bouquet garni*
- *salt and black pepper*

Preparation

To make the stuffing, place a heavy-based frying pan over a medium to high flame and once nice and hot, add a slug of sunflower oil and a large knob of butter. Just as the bubbles subside, add the chopped onion and the goose liver. Cook for a minute or two and add the minced pork and veal, reduce the flame a little, then add the lardons, chopped parsley, Armagnac, breadcrumbs and around 250 g of chopped chestnuts. Add the pre-heated milk little by little (do not allow the stuffing to become too moist), reduce the heat and stir well with a wooden spoon to incorporate all of the ingredients.

Turn the ingredients out onto a flat tray and allow to cool for a while. While the stuffing is cooling, season the inside of the bird with salt and pepper and drop in a couple of knobs of butter. Stuff the goose with the mixture and truss the legs with a heavy elastic band or some butcher's string, to help stop the stuffing from escaping while cooking.

Soften a little butter and carefully tuck under the skin of the goose, making sure that you don't tear the skin. Rub the outside with some butter and season with salt and black pepper. Peel and roughly chop the carrot, onion and celery then place into the bottom of a roasting tray and put the bird on top. Place into a pre-heated oven on 200°C, basting regularly until golden brown. After around one hour, reduce the heat to around 175°C and cover the bird with lightly buttered tin foil The goose will give off a lot of fat, so at this stage, you may wish to pour some off into a separate container part way through cooking and retain for cooking another time.

While the goose is cooking, place the wine, chicken stock and *bouquet garni* into a small saucepan, bring to the boil, reduce the heat and allow to simmer.

When the goose is cooked, remove the roasting tray from the oven. Remove the goose and place onto a large serving dish, surround with the remaining chestnuts and put back into a medium to low oven to keep hot. Drain off any remaining fat from the roasting tray and place over a medium to high flame. Add a few ladles of the stock and work the mixture with a wooden spoon to release all of the wonderful caramelised flavours from the bottom of the tray. Add the rest of the stock and allow to simmer gently for around 15 minutes. Strain the liquid into a clean saucepan and check for seasoning. If you prefer a thickened gravy, then you can add a little arrowroot or cornflour.

My secret: Goose is not the easiest of birds to dissect at the table, so you may want to portion it up on your chopping board in the kitchen and then dress it nicely on a serving dish with the chestnuts.

WINE: Try a mature gamey red such as Morey-St-Denis or a Côte Rôtie.

PAELLA

OK, OK, I know. I can hear you shouting at the top of your voice - *"Mad fool, thinks he's a chef, Paella's not a French dish!"*, however, I have two very good reasons for including this recipe. The first reason, and I guess the most legitimate, is that there are usually two vendors at our local outdoor market in Argentat, which is held every first and third Thursday of the month, who both serve the most fantastic concoction in the biggest paella pans you have ever seen. They start preparing their ingredients around 8.30am and by 10.30am or so people are already queuing up to buy some of the wonderful *mélange*. Customers arrive prepared with their own containers or are given a polystyrene one to take huge (or less huge) portions of steaming Paella home to their families for lunch.

The second reason is that I have been known to cook the meanest Paella and can honestly say that I have never used a recipe in my life. Paella can be the easiest of dishes to cook, if you follow a few simple rules and the end result is great for informal dinner parties or even better, when it's cooked over a barbecue in the summer. You should be able to access most all of the ingredients from your local supermarket, so here goes.

Not so long back, we visited our good buddies Dave and Jan, at their beautiful villa in Denia (Spain). We all mucked in together and prepared the most wonderful Paella, which we ate *al fresco* by the pool. I seem to recall in the alcoholic haze, that we consumed the odd bottle or three of nicely chilled Mâcon-Lugny.

Recipe by Malcolm Alder-Smith
La Maison aux Quat'Saisons, Laborie, 19400 Monceaux-sur-Dordogne

Preparation time:	30 minutes
Cooking time:	1 hour
Equipment:	Paella pan

Ingredients for 6 – 8 people (or 4 if you are really big eaters)

- *olive oil – extra virgin is best*
- *3 chicken breasts*
- *500 g diced pork (optional)*
- *8 langoustines*
- *500 g large prawns, shell on*
- *1 kg mussels – de-beard and discard any open shells*

- 250 g calamare cut into rings
- 500 g clams (optional)
- 2 medium sized onions
- 3 cloves of garlic
- 1 sweet red pepper
- 1 green pepper
- 4 large tomatoes (blanched, deseeded and chopped)
- 250 g paella rice
- chicken or vegetable stock (2½ x volume of rice)
- 1 sachet of SABATER paella seasoning (turmeric can be used)
- 2 large fresh lemons
- flat leaf parsley – chopped
- salt and black pepper

Preparation

Cut the chicken breasts in two and the pork into good bite-sized chunks. Coarsely chop the onion, peppers and garlic and lightly fry in the olive oil over a medium flame until they start to soften. Remove the ingredients, splash a little more oil into the pan and fry the chicken and pork until lightly coloured. Return the vegetables to the pan and mix the cooked ingredients together before adding the rice and paella seasoning, followed by the hot stock.

Cover the paella pan with some tin foil and cook over a low heat (or in the oven) until nearly all the stock has been absorbed by the rice. After about 20-30 minutes, check to see if the rice is cooked. If not, top up with a little more stock (if need be).

Mix in the mussels, calamares, clams, tomatoes and the prawns. Decorate the top of the Paella with the langoustines, by placing them on top of the other ingredients like the numbers on a clock face, replace the foil and finish cooking for a further five to ten minutes.

Cut the lemons into large wedges. Remove the pan from the heat and decorate with the lemon wedges then sprinkle liberally with the chopped parsley. Place the pan in the middle of the table with a ladle or very large spoon and just let everyone help themselves.

WINE: When I started writing this book I promised myself that I would only recommend French wines, so rather than go for the obvious young Spanish Rioja or dry white Penedès, why not try a dry white Bergerac or Buzet Rosé or of course Mâcon-Lugny as noted above and definitely tried and tested by yours truly!

SUPRÊME DE POULET AUX CROTTIN DE CHÈVRE
chicken breast stuffed with goat's cheese & spinach

This is a dish which Twink and I cook fairly regularly when we are entertaining at home. It really is simplicity personified and the beauty of this
dish is that you can prepare it in advance, cook it off just before your
guests arrive and finish it off while you are eating your 'starter'.

I got the idea from an old recipe which I used to use in my restaurant
back in the Eighties and it has just evolved over the years, with Twink giving it that final touch.

Recipe by Malcolm Alder-Smith
La Maison aux Quat'Saisons, Laborie, 19400 Monceaux-sur-Dordogne

Preparation time: 30 minutes
Cooking time: 35 minutes

Ingredients for 4 people

- *4 nice chicken breasts*
- *12 rashers of rindless streaky bacon*
- *1 bag of baby spinach leaves*
- *2 crottin de chèvre (goat's cheese)*
- *unsalted butter*
- *olive oil*
- *250 ml Maggi fond de volaille (chicken stock)*
- *250 ml Gaillac perlé (medium dry white wine)*
- *150 ml crème fraîche*
- *1/2 soup spoon moutarde fins gourmets (coarse grain mustard)*

Preparation

One at a time, place the chicken breasts between two pieces of cling film.
Using a meat tenderiser, flatten each piece until it increases in size by
around 50%. Do not get too enthusiastic or else you will finish up with
pieces of chicken with some rather large holes in them, so 'tease out' the
breasts to an even thickness. Once you have 'flattened' all four pieces of
chicken, remove them from the cling film and place them, 'skin' side down
onto a clean chopping board.

Season each breast with some salt and a little black pepper. Lay a few spinach leaves onto each breast. Chop the *crottins* into small dice and distribute them between the four breasts. Roll up each chicken breast into a torpedo shape, making sure that the filling is well encased.

Flatten each rasher of bacon with a rolling pin or the back of a kitchen knife, so that they become larger and thinner. Wrap two to three rashers around each chicken breast, ensuring that the ends finish up underneath (or as near as possible).

Place the chicken breasts onto a cold plate, cover in cling film and refrigerate.

Place a frying pan over a medium to high flame then add a slug of olive oil and a knob of butter. Place the chicken breasts into the frying pan and cook for around 4 minutes – reduce the heat if necessary. Check to make sure that the bacon is not colouring too much, and then turn them over and cook for a further 3 minutes. Remove the chicken breasts and place into a pre-heated oven on around 175°C to keep hot and finish off the cooking process.

Drain off any excess fat from the frying pan, add the dry white wine and stock, then over a medium to high heat reduce the liquid by around 50%. Add the mustard and *crème fraîche*, whisking or stirring briskly to create your sauce.

To finish off the dish, pop the rest of the spinach into a hot saucepan containing just a little olive oil. You only need to cook the spinach until it wilts and this will only take a matter of moments, so be attentive and tweak the spinach with a wooden spoon once or twice. Remove the pan from your hob and set to one side for a moment.

Remove the breasts from the oven, slice each diagonally into four pieces and arrange neatly on each plate. Ladle some of the hot sauce around each breast and pile up a little mound of the wilted spinach alongside each breast.

My secret: This dish works really well with a small portion of tagliatelle, tossed in some unsalted butter, Corrézienne style.

WINE: Try a nice old red burgundy or if your preference is for white, go for a medium to dry.

SUPRÊME DE POULET FARCIE EN PAPILOTTE
chicken breast stuffed
with spinach and asparagus

This is one of my more recently created dishes.

I got home from work early one evening and Twink was out with Ashley, so I raided the fridge to rustle up something special for when they got home. The end result was so good that they both begged for a repeat performance the following evening – unheard of in our house! Ash now loves both spinach and asparagus, previously being convinced that they would both do him some sort of everlasting detriment.

The concept of cooking food in a paper or tin-foil bag is not new; the advantage being that as it cooks, the moisture of what is being cooked and all of the flavours are retained and enhanced. Don't be put off having a go at this, although it may look a little complicated, you will find the end result is worthwhile, so roll up your sleeves and have a bash.

Recipe by Malcolm Alder-Smith
La Maison aux Quat'Saisons, Laborie, 19400 Monceaux-sur-Dordogne

Preparation time: 30 minutes
Cooking time: 30 minutes

Ingredients for 4 people

- *4 skinless boneless chicken breasts (preferably free range)*
- *125g washed baby spinach leaves*
- *1 small pack of baby asparagus*
- *100ml dry white wine*
- *50g butter*
- *2 tea spoons of Dijon mustard*
- *200ml double cream*
- *Salt and pepper*

Preparation

Take the chicken breasts, one at a time, and place smooth side down under a sheet of cling film. Using a rolling pin or meat tenderiser, flatten each breast evenly so that they reach about twice their original size. Use a fresh piece of cling-film for each one and then remove and discard.

Take half of the spinach and a quarter of the asparagus and blitz to a paste in a food processor. Place the four flattened chicken breasts onto a work surface, lightly season and then spread the spinach and asparagus paste evenly onto each one. Roll each breast diagonally to make a torpedo shape.

Tear off four pieces of tin-foil about 30cm square then fold in half and seal the two open sides by folding the foil over twice. This will leave you with an open ended 'paper bag'.

Gently place one chicken breast into each bag, adding a good knob of butter, a slush of white wine and just a little seasoning. Seal the top of the bags in the same way, place them on a baking tray and then into a pre-heated oven at 200°C for approximately 30 minutes.

Remove the baking tray from the oven and carefully open each bag, being wary of the steam from each. To prepare the sauce, gently drain the liquid from the bags into a small saucepan and reseal each bag to retain the heat. Reduce the liquid quickly, by a third, then add the mustard, cream and the remaining spinach and allow to cook briefly, seasoning to taste.

Remove the chicken breasts onto a chopping board and cut each one diagonally across the middle, putting two pieces onto pre-heated plates. Whizz the sauce with a hand blender until frothy and spoon the sauce over and around the chicken.

Serve with a *mélange* of fine green beans mixed with the remaining asparagus and some new potatoes.

WINE: You can drink virtually any wine with this dish, but I would tend to go for one of the more classy dry or medium dry whites or even a good quality old red burgundy. If you want to try something really local then go for Côteaux de Glanes, which you will definitely find more easily in the Corrèze than at your local Tesco store.

GIBIERS
game

LA CHASSE

Shootin' and fishin' epitomise the French rural way of life, where many of the menfolk appear to have a divine passion for killing anything that moves, within reason that is. To many people, hunting is not considered a pastime or a sport – it's an obsession. Hunting in France is, traditionally, to the French what cricket is to the English gentleman.

Partridge, thrush, pigeon, quail, hare, the rarely-seen woodcock and the pheasant are all fair game for *les chasseurs*. And in our neck of the woods, the Upper-Dordogne-Valley, with its densely forested hillsides provides excellent cover for deer and *sangliers*, the prized wild boars which are hunted with a passion.

The severed head of one of the massive beasts decorates the wall in Jim and Fi's *salle à manger*, and has, in the past, often inspired much heated breakfast conversation between *les chasseurs* when they come to stay for a weekend.

On Sunday mornings across France, they linger on the edge of woodland, dressed in full camouflage fatigues (their fluorescent waistcoats or hats rather defeat the object!). With their guns over their shoulders and a Gitanes hanging from one side of their mouths they discuss their morning's successes and of course near-misses; their dogs still scampering around the undergrowth sensing that there is still more work to be done before they head for home.

Hunting is generally seen as a team pursuit; some hunt individually or in pairs, but generally most get their pleasure from the shared occasion, empathy with fellow hunters and, of course, the joy of working effectively and efficiently with their favourite dogs.

The French hunting seasons vary according to what is being hunted, but in general walks in woodlands should be avoided, particularly on Sundays, between September and springtime. And as accidents do occasionally happen, take care, even if you are on your own land, as *les chasseurs* appear to have little respect for boundary fences, especially if they belong to someone else. Most accidents, fortunately or rather unfortunately, depending on your perspective, happen to the *chasseurs* themselves, rather than innocent passers-by.

We know where there are a couple of large fields which slope uphill away from one of the old winding roads heading south towards Beaulieu-sur-Dordogne, where we periodically see a pair of deer grazing close to the tree-line, ready to make a hasty retreat if the need arises. As our house is situated on the lower slopes of a hill on the other side of the valley, we often wonder on Sunday mornings whether the gun shots we hear across the valley have depleted the herd of these beautiful animals. There is, of course, no use me getting all sentimental, as I have been cooking commercially on and off since I left school, and have no inhibitions about eating almost anything that is put in front of me, or cooking it for that matter.

186

If you already hunt in the UK, and would like to pursue your sport when in France, you can obtain a short-term licence from the Préfecture, which you can renew more than one time in a twelve-month period. These can be obtained by providing the usual sort of proof of who you are i.e your passport, and you will also need to take along your UK licence and a couple of good quality passport photographs.

If you live in France and want to hunt, then you can obtain a licence for around 170€, but you'll have to pass written and practical examinations before you can obtain one.

For further information or organised hunting holidays through Club Faune in Paris, you can contact:

Hunting France
22, Rue Duban
75016 Paris
FRANCE

www.hunting-france.com
infos@hunting-france.com

This company will arrange hunting holidays

Hunting seasons:

Red Deer: from mid-September to the end of February.
Roe Deer: from the beginning of June to the end of November.
Fallow Deer: from mid-September to the end of February.
Mouflon: from mid-September to the end of February.
Chamois: from mid-September to the end of February.
Wild Boar: from the beginning of September to the end of February.

Shooting seasons:

Pheasant: from the beginning of October to the end of January.
Duck: from the beginning of September to the end of January.
Grey Partridge: from the beginning of October to the end of November.

CAILLES RÔTIES AUX ÉCHALOTES
roast quail with shallots

Recipe by Michel et Isabelle Roussanne
Auberge des Gabariers, 15 Quai Lestourgie, 19400 Argentat

Preparation time: 20 minutes
Cooking time: 25 minutes

Ingredients for 4 people

- *2 quail*
- *8 shallots*
- *2 soup spoons of goose fat*
- *15 juniper berries*
- *10 cl Chablis*
- *salt and pepper*
- *600 g shelled petits pois*
- *200 g lardons of bacon*
- *2 onions*
- *2 carrots*
- *5 g unsalted butter*
- *1 coffee spoon of caster sugar*
- *1 chicken stock cube*
- *fresh bay leaf*
- *fresh thyme*

Preparation

Blanch the shelled peas for 1 minute 30 seconds in boiling salted water, remove from the pan, refresh under cold water and drain. Using the same water, blanch the lardons of bacon for one minute or so, drain and pat dry with some kitchen paper then lightly brown them in a frying pan, using a little goose fat. Remove them from the pan and place onto some kitchen paper to remove any excess fat.

Peel the onion and carrots. Finely chop the onion and slice the carrots. Using the same frying pan in which you cooked the lardons, melt the butter and lightly brown the onions and carrots. Lightly season with the salt, pepper and sugar and then moisten with the stock, made up using 50 cl of boiling water. Add the peas, fresh thyme and bay leaf and cook over a low heat for around 25 minutes.

While the vegetable broth is cooking, season the inside of the birds. Peel the shallots, finely chop and then lightly brown them in some of the goose fat. When cooked, stuff the inside of the birds with the shallots and the juniper berries. Truss up the birds with some butcher's string and rub some salt and pepper into the skin.

Place the birds into a heavy-bottomed casserole and drizzle with a little olive oil. Cook them in a pre-heated oven at 210°C for around 12 minutes.

Remove the quails from the casserole and keep warm. Drain any excess fat from the pan and deglaze with the Chablis. Bring the liquid to the boil, reduce the flame slightly and thicken a tad with a little *beurre manier* (equal quantities of softened butter and flour, blended together), whisking vigorously with every addition.

Serve half a bird per person and pour a ladle of Chablis sauce over the top of each. Using a slotted spoon give everyone a good portion of the pea and vegetable broth, sprinkling each with the browned lardons.

WINE: This is a dish you can get a little adventurous with on the old wine front, and gives you the opportunity to push out the boat and spend more than maybe you normally would. The extra expense will be worth it.

Go for a fine white or red Burgundy. Spoil yourselves and try either a Montrachet (Puligny or Chassagne) or a Nuits St Georges or check out an Alsace Riesling Grand Cru from the foothills of the Vosges mountains – make sure you look for the word Riesling on the label.

If you want a safe bet go for a mature claret – at least eight years old.

CARRÉ DE CHEVREUIL AUX CÈPES
loin of venison with cèpes and pea mash

Yes, I know, my English interpretation sounds a little bit 'Gary Rhodes', but believe me this recipe really does work well and I hope that Mr Rhodes does not mind me using 'his' name in 'my book'.

Twink and I were first introduced to pea mash by our very good buddies, Dave and Jan Hill, who live in Denia, Spain. Dave and Jan had been in 'the industry' for nearly as many years as I have and ran two very well known pubs on the Isle of Wight, over a period of around 20 years, before they retired to Spain in 2001.

When they lived in the UK, we would often drop in to see them at their country cottage with only a few minutes' notice, and Jan was always totally expert at knocking up a gastro' treat with no effort and in no time at all. I think our first experience of her pea mash was when she served it up with some barbecued Cumberland sausages with onion gravy – totally orgasmic! These days, it is very seldom that Twink and I eat *pommes purée ordinaire*, it is usually enhanced with peas, a chiffonade of blanched leek or cabbage, sliced spring onion; the options, my friends, are endless.

I think that as I have already mentioned Gary Rhodes, I might as well milk it as much as I can and say that the best mashed potato I have ever tasted (apart from mine of course!), was when Gary Rhodes was head chef at The Greenhouse (London) in the mid-Nineties. Dave and Jan treated us to a day out and I had what I think was one of his signature dishes, Calves Liver with Mashed Potato, and I have to say that it was everything I expected or hoped it would be, having collected all of his books up to that point in time.

The knack, of course, is being able to produce the most wonderful, soft, creamy, buttery and tasty mashed potato, which I think we mastered a few years back following our visit to Gary's restaurant.

Everyone thinks that they can produce mashed potato, which may, or may not, be true. But, to produce a quality product that would stand the acid test on a City menu, takes dedication, time, skill and love of good food and quality ingredients. Just because the ingredient is inexpensive doesn't mean that it deserves any less attention than say, *foie gras* or truffle. Oh my God, I'm getting all 'celeb' and the book hasn't even been published yet!

We really want to dedicate this recipe to our mate Jan, for her inspirational cooking and endless friendship and support.

Recipe by Malcolm and Diane Alder-Smith
La Maison aux Quat'Saisons, Laborie, 19400 Monceaux-sur-Dordogne

Preparation time:	20 minutes
Cooking time:	30minutes
Marinade:	12 hours

Ingredients for 4 people

- *750 g loin of venison (trimmed)*
- *250 ml Maggi fond de veau (veal jus)*
- *250 g cèpes – sliced*
- *2 soup spoons of acacia honey*
- *250 ml banyuls (vin doux naturel)*
- *1 soup spoon fresh thyme leaves*
- *2 cloves of pink Lautrec garlic*
- *½ soup spoon raspberry vinegar*
- *1 onion*
- *1 branch of celery*
- *3 carrots*
- *1 small leek*
- *1 soup spoon of tomato purée*
- *olive oil*
- *500 g Maris Piper potatoes*
- *unsalted butter*
- *double cream*
- *250 g fresh peas*
- *salt and black pepper*

Preparation

To prepare the marinade, peel and finely chop the onion, 2 carrots, celery, garlic and leek and place into a bowl. Add the honey, Banyuls, thyme and raspberry vinegar and stir well.

Place the loin of venison into a small roasting tin or casserole and pour over the marinade. Cover and put to one side in a cool place and marinade for 12 hours.

The following day, remove the loin of venison and drain well. Place a heavy-bottomed frying pan over a medium flame and add a slug of olive oil. Season the loin with salt and pepper, place into the pan and cook until evenly browned on all sides.

While the loin is browning, pour the marinade into a saucepan with the tomato *purée* and the stock, stir well and place over a high flame then bring to the boil. Reduce the heat to a fast rolling simmer and reduce the liquid by around two thirds. Pass the liquid and marinade through a fine sieve into a clean saucepan and place over a low flame to simmer gently. Check for seasoning and consistency.

Remove the browned loin of venison and place into a small roasting tin over a finely diced carrot, pour over a little olive oil and place into the middle of a pre-heated oven at 200°C for around 30 – 40 minutes. This should leave the loin still slightly pink in the middle. To check this out, pierce with a small knife and if the liquid runs red, then cook for a little longer. Fry off the sliced *cèpes* and add them to the sauce.

While the loin is roasting, blanch the peas and refresh them under cold water. Boil the peeled and diced potatoes in salted water until cooked. Drain the potatoes in a colander and return them to the pan, cover with a lid and return to the hob. Holding firmly on to the lid and pan handle, shake the pan vigorously over the heat for a few moments. This will help to dry out the potatoes very quickly and they will take on a 'floury' appearance – but be careful that they don't stick and start to burn. Remove from the heat and mash thoroughly, adding some butter, cream, salt and pepper and stirring well until you have a light creamy consistency. Add the blanched peas, replace the lid and keep to one side to keep warm.

Place the loin on your chopping board and slice diagonally with a carving knife. The loin should be just pink in the middle.

Create a mound of pea mash in the middle of each plate. Place about three nice slices of venison over the top of the potato and pour some of the Banyuls gravy over the meat, ensuring that everyone gets some of the wonderful *cèpes* on their plate.

Our secret: Banyuls, a speciality of Rousillon, is our very favourite *'vin doux naturel'* which is (sweet wine fortified with alcohol, so the sweetness is 'natural'), usually made from a high percentage of Grenache or Muscat. The French often view it as a patriotic alternative to Port and we find that it helps to give a wonderful flavour to sauces for gamey meats. It is possible to get hold of it in the UK, but it's generally less expensive in comparison with Port when purchased in France.

WINE: Venison deserves to accompanied by a big red wine. Try a Bandol, made on the little coastal region near Toulon on the south coast, producing Provence's best wines and made predominately from the Mourvedre grape.

CHEVREUIL AU CHOU VERT
venison with green cabbage

Recipe by Diane Alder-Smith
La Maison aux Quat'Saisons, Laborie, 19400 Monceaux-sur-Dordogne

Preparation time: 20 minutes
Cooking time: 90 minutes
Marinade: 24 hours

Ingredients for 6 people

- *1.5 kg diced shoulder of venison*
- *500 g piece of smoked breast bacon (ask your butcher)*
- *2 onions*
- *2 carrots*
- *1 clove of garlic*
- *1 savoy cabbage*
- *1 bouquet garni*
- *100 g unsalted butter*

- *2 soup spoons of thick crème fraîche*
- *250 ml cream*
- *1 soup spoon moutarde de Dijon*
- *1 lt Reisling*
- *12 juniper berries*
- *salt and pepper*
- myrtille (bilberry) jelly

Preparation

Make the marinade the day before. Peel the carrots and cut into rounds. Peel one onion and the garlic and finely chop. Put the vegetables and half of the wine into a large bowl then add some salt and pepper and the juniper berries. Add the pieces of venison to the marinade and leave in a cool place over night.

The following day, remove the meat from the marinade and drain well in a colander. While the meat is draining, slice the side of bacon into 0.5 cm rashers and then cut again into 0.5 cm lardons.

Place a large heavy-bottomed casserole over a medium flame and add around half of the butter. When the bubbles start to subside, add half of the lardons and brown them evenly. Remove the lardons from the pan and keep to one side. Return the casserole to the hob over a high flame and add the pieces of venison a few at a time, sealing the pieces on all sides until they turn brown. Remove the browned pieces and add to the lardons. Cook the rest of the cubes of venison, adding a little more butter or oil if needed. When all the pieces are browned, return all the meat and the cooked lardons to the pan. Moisten little by little with the marinade, stirring well to deglaze the bottom of the casserole. Add the remainder of the wine. Cover the casserole and reduce the heat down to very low and allow to cook for around 90 minutes

While the venison is cooking, take off any damaged leaves from the outside of the cabbage. Remove any excess stalk and cut the cabbage into four, cutting through the remainder of the stalk. Trim any excess stalk away, so that the leaves become separated. Wash the leaves in salted water and drain.

Remove the venison when tender. Strain the stock through a fine sieve into a clean pan. Reduce the liquid by around two thirds. Add the mustard and cream and blend together with a wooden spoon, add the cubes of venison and stir well to coat the meat. Reduce the heat right down and allow the meat to simmer gently while you finish off the cabbage.

Place a large pan of water over a high flame, add some salt and when the water boils, add the cabbage leaves and blanch for around 5 minutes, then drain the leaves when they are just cooked. Peel and finely chop the second onion.

Melt the remaining butter in a saucepan and add the chopped onion and the blanched leaves, stirring all the time, then add the *crème fraîche* and season with the salt and pepper, stir again.

Dress each plate with some cabbage leaves, add equal portions of venison to one side and serve the myrtille jelly separately.

To finish off the dish, pan fry the remaining lardons in some hot oil and butter, until browned, drain and sprinkle over the dressed portions of venison.

Di's secret: I often add one or two soup spoons of myrtille jam to the sauce, which gives it quite a unique flavour. Unfortunately, this type of jam is not always easily available in the UK.

WINE: Try a nicely chilled bottle of Pinot Blanc from Alsace.

FRICASSÉE DE SANGLIER
fricassee of wild boar

Recipe by Malcolm Alder-Smith
La Maison aux Quat'Saisons, Laborie, 19400 Monceaux-sur-Dordogne

Ingredients for 6 people

Preparation time:	20 minutes
Cooking time:	60 minutes
Marinade:	24 hours

- *1.5 kg wild boar*
- *1 lt Bergerac (red)*
- *100 ml Armagnac*
- *125 ml cream*
- *unsalted butter*
- *125 g onions – chopped*
- *125 g carrots – finely chopped*
- *2 sticks of celery – finely chopped*
- *bouquet garni*
- *sprig of rosemary*
- *2 sage leaves*
- *salt and black pepper*
- *75 ml walnut oil*
- *50 ml red wine vinegar*
- *olive oil*

Preparation

Cut the meat into 2.5 cm chunks and place them into a large bowl. Cover with the chopped onion, carrot, celery, rosemary, sage, salt, pepper, red wine, 50 ml Armagnac, red wine vinegar and walnut oil, finishing off with the *bouquet garni*. Cover and allow to marinade for 24 hours, giving the occasional stir, so that the meat can take on board all of those wonderful flavours.

Remove the meat from the marinade and drain in a colander. Pat the meat dry and place a heavy-bottomed frying pan over a medium to high flame. Add a slug of olive oil and a good knob of butter. When the bubbles subside, add a few chunks of wild boar at a time and brown on all sides. Do not put too much meat into the pan at once or any residual moisture (in the meat) can mean that you finish up stewing your meat in liquid instead of frying it. Remove the first lot of meat and repeat the process until all of the chunks of meat have been turned to a nice golden brown. Turn the flame right up and return all of the meat to the pan, pour over the remaining Armagnac and flame.

Pour the meat and liquid into a heavy-bottomed casserole (or large saucepan), add the vegetables from the marinade, the *bouquet garni* and around 500 ml of the wine. Place the frying pan back over a medium to high flame and pour in a little of the remaining wine from the marinade to deglaze the bottom of the pan. Pour this liquid in with the other ingredients. Retain the rest of the wine, in case you need to top up the liquid. Place the casserole over a medium to high flame and bring to the boil. Reduce to a low flame and simmer gently for around one hour.

When the meat is cooked, remove and place onto a serving dish to keep warm. Discard the *bouquet garni*.

Strain off the vegetables into a sieve and push as much of the mixture through as you can, back into the liquid in a clean pan; this will help to thicken the sauce. Re-heat the sauce and stir to ensure the ingredients are thoroughly blended in together. Add the cream and bring back to a gentle simmer, test for seasoning and consistency and when you are happy, pour the sauce over the meat just before you serve. Sprinkle with a little chopped flat leaf parsley or dress with some sprigs of rosemary.

WINE: This dish needs a quality red wine. Try one of the good reds from Bourg, Blaye or Fronsac. There are some exceptional wines available from these areas.

LAPIN À LA MOUTARDE ANCIENNE
rabbit in a mustard cream sauce

This recipe uses the classic *champignons de Paris*, which can be found growing in the caves of the Mushroom Museum (Musée du Champignon) on the Loire at the beautiful town of Saumur – it is well worth a visit because just along the same road, caves dug out of Tuffeau rock are used to produce the fresh Champagne-style sparkling white wine at the Cave des Vignerons de Saumur, such as Gratien et Meyer. The rock from the caves was used to build many of the magnificent *châteaux* for which the Loire is famous.

Recipe provided by Paulette Fruitiere
Monceaux-sur-Dordogne

Preparation time: 20 minutes
Cooking time: 60 minutes

Ingredients for 4 people

- *1 rabbit (1.25 k) cut into 8 pieces*
- *50 g flour*
- *2 carrots*
- *2 medium onions*
- *2 sticks of celery*
- *4 soup spoons of sunflower oil*
- *200 g champignons de Paris*
- *20 cl dry white wine*
- *20 g butter*
- *20 cl crème fraîche*
- *4 soup spoons Moutarde de Meaux à l'ancienne*
- *salt and pepper*
- *1 bouquet garni*

Preparation

Season the flour with some salt and ground pepper and roll the prepared pieces of rabbit, coating well with the flour. Peel and wash the carrots, then cut them and the celery into thin rondelles. Peel and chop the onions and pre-heat your oven to 200°C.

Place a cast-iron casserole (Le Creuset-style) over a medium flame. Add some oil and lightly brown a few pieces of rabbit at a time, by cooking for around 2 minutes, more or less, on each side. Once all the pieces of rabbit are nicely browned, place them onto a dish with some kitchen paper and put to one side.

Using the same casserole, add the carrots, celery and chopped onion to the hot oil and lightly brown over a medium to low heat. Carefully drain any excess oil and return the pieces of rabbit to the pan, with the white wine and the *bouquet garni*. Add a little salt and pepper and stir gently. Bring to the boil, cover with a lid and place the casserole into the pre-heated oven for 40 minutes.

Remove the ends of the earthy stalks of the *champignons de Paris* and give the mushrooms a good wash. Wipe them with a damp cloth to make sure that you have removed all of the 'gritty' bits and pat them dry with a clean tea towel. Place a heavy-bottomed frying pan over a medium heat and add the butter. Allow the butter to melt and once the bubbles start to subside, add the prepared mushrooms and cook for around 5 minutes until nicely browned. Season with a little salt and black pepper.

Arrange the cooked pieces of rabbit on a hot plate or serving dish, surrounded by the onion, carrot and celery, and keep hot.

Pour the *crème fraîche*, as well as the mustard, into the casserole with the cooking liquor. Heat until the liquid starts to bubble lightly, then remove straightaway from the heat and using a fine sieve, pour over the mushrooms in the frying pan. Stir well and correct the seasoning if necessary. Pour the sauce over the rabbit and serve straight away – very hot.

WINE: This is another dish which you can drink with a quality red or why not chill down a nice bottle of Sparkling Saumur?

LAPIN AU CHOU CORRÉZIENNE
rabbit with cabbage Corrézienne style

Recipe by Malcolm Alder-Smith
La Maison aux Quat'Saisons, Laborie, 19400 Monceaux-sur-Dordogne

Preparation time: 20 minutes
Cooking time: 90 minutes

Ingredients for 4 people

- *1 rabbit (1.25 k) cut into 8 pieces*
- *100 g lardons of bacon*
- *sunflower oil*
- *4 carrots*
- *4 sticks of celery*
- *2 medium sized onions*
- *1 green cabbage*
- *Salt and pepper*
- *Stock*

Preparation

Place a large heavy-bottomed pan over a medium flame and fry the lardons in a little oil until golden brown. Remove the lardons and place to one side on some kitchen paper.

Prepare the celery, carrots and onions and cut into a rough dice.

Add a little more oil to the pan, if necessary, place the pieces of rabbit into the pan and cook until golden brown on all sides. Remove the pieces of rabbit and put to one side with the lardons, then fry off the celery, carrots and onions until they start to colour – remove and keep to one side.

Prepare the cabbage. Remove any low grade outer leaves and cut through the stalk into quarters. Remove any excess tough stalk by cutting diagonally from top to bottom. Place a pan of water onto a high heat and bring to the boil. Add some salt and then blanch the cabbage for 5 minutes. Drain the cooking liquid into a bowl or jug and refresh the cabbage under cold water.

Take a large heavy-bottomed casserole, layer the cabbage, onions, carrots, rabbit and bacon and season with a little salt and black pepper. Moisten with either some chicken stock or the stock from the cabbage; I prefer to use chicken stock, but the choice is yours. Cover with a lid and cook in a pre-heated oven at 200ºC for 90 minutes.

To serve, try to get hold of a large old-fashioned serving platter. Arrange the vegetables on the bottom and place the rabbit pieces on the top.

WINE: This dish has quite a delicate flavour and so wine selection is crucial. Try a bottle of medium dry Gaillac Perlé (white).

PAVÉ DE DAIM EN SAUCE XAINTRIÇOISE
venison steak with a xaintrie sauce

The Department is densely wooded and fleeting glimpses of deer can often be seen, although it is seldom that I have seen this dish on a menu.

Doris Coppenrath sent us this recipe from the Auberge de Saint-Julien-aux-Bois, which she runs with her partner Roland Pilger. The Auberge is located high up in the hills with extensive forests and pathways for walking, cycling and horse riding, not far from St Privat and only a short drive from Argentat.

Recipe by Doris Coppenrath
Auberge de Saint-Julien-aux-Bois
19220 Saint-Julien-aux-Bois

Preparation time: 45 minutes
Cooking time: 30 minutes

Ingredients for 4 people

- *4 venison steaks*
- *olive oil*
- *100 g of cooked chestnuts*
- *12 dried prunes*
- *25 cl red wine*
- *100 g coral lentils*
- *25 cl vegetable bouillon*
- *1 coffee spoon of powdered chocolate*
- *1 cinnamon stick*
- *2 bay leaves*
- *lemon juice*
- *salt and pepper*

Preparation

Soak the dried prunes in the red wine for 2 hours.

Add the lentils, vegetable stock, chestnuts, cinnamon stick and the bay leaves and cook for around half an hour on a medium heat. If necessary, add a little water or more stock. After this time, pour in the chocolate powder and mix in well. Season with the salt and pepper and lemon juice. If using a large lemon, pour in only half the juice to start and cook for a few minutes more and check the flavour. Add more juice if you wish.

Season the deer steaks with salt and black pepper. Heat the oil in a heavy-bottomed frying pan and fry the steaks for around 4 minutes on each side (depending on thickness and how you like your meat cooked).

Using a slotted spoon, place a mound of lentils onto each plate. Dress the steaks on top of each mound and then using a ladle or large spoon, divide the chestnuts and prunes between the four plates. Moisten the steaks with a little *jus*.

WINE: You need a big chunky red to go with this dish. So if you can get hold of some, why not try something really different and go for a single grape Bandol (Mourvèdre, alias Mataro). This produces an excellent dark aromatic grape from the little coastal region near Toulon near the south coast producing Provence's best wines. Alternatively go for a blended red Rhône or Bordeaux.

AUBERGE de SAINT-JULIEN-AUX-BOIS
SAINT-JULIEN-AUX-BOIS

PERDRIX AU CHOU
pot-roasted partridge with cabbage

This is a dish which I originally spotted in a book which I bought from a large wine warehouse just north of Cahors around 1992. I have played around with the recipe since then and this is what I have come up with – I hope you enjoy it.

Recipe by Malcolm Alder-Smith
La Maison aux Quat'Saisons, Laborie, 19400 Monceaux-sur-Dordogne

Preparation time: 30 minutes
Cooking time: 90 minutes

Ingredients for 4 people

- *2 oven ready partridges*
- *1 savoy cabbage*
- *4 Toulouse sausages (10's)*
- *1 medium sized onion*
- *2 carrots*
- *1 leek*
- *½ litre chicken stock*

- *bouquet garni*
- *salt, ground black pepper*
- *150 g bacon lardons*
- *4 slices of streaky bacon*
- *olive oil*
- *5 cl dry white wine*

Preparation

Prepare the cabbage and remove any damaged outer leaves. Cut into four and cut the stalk of each diagonally to trim, leaving sufficient to hold each quarter together. Take a large saucepan of boiling, salted water, place over a medium flame and blanch the cabbage for around 10 minutes, then refresh and drain well. Peel the carrot and onion and trim the leek, slice them and place to one side. Squeeze each sausage in the centre and then twist each end in the opposite direction and hopefully you will finish up with a couple of cocktail chipolatas when you cut them in half, giving you eight pieces of Toulouse sausage in total.

Season the inside of the partridges with the salt and pepper, add a knob of butter and truss them with some butcher's string (your butcher will be only too pleased to supply you with a length!).

Place a large heavy-bottomed frying pan over a medium flame, add a slug of olive oil and a knob of butter, and cook the birds until the skin turns to a golden brown. Remove them from the pan and place into the bottom of a good-sized casserole, then cover each with two slices of streaky to form a cross over the breasts of the birds.

Using the same frying pan add the carrot, onion, sausages and lardons and cook to a golden brown. Take care not to over-colour the vegetables or they can give the dish a bitter flavour. Add the leek for the last few minutes so it becomes soft.

Add the sausage and vegetable mixture to the casserole. Drain off any residual fat from the frying pan and return to the hob. Add the dry white wine and using a wooden spoon deglaze the bottom of the pan, reducing the wine by half. Add this to the casserole.

Finally add the four quarters of the blanched cabbage and season well; pour in the hot chicken *bouillon* and the *bouquet garni*. Cover with a lid and place into a pre-heated oven at around 180°C for 80 minutes. Turn the birds once or twice so that the breasts do not have the opportunity to dry out.

Find yourself a nice large serving platter and dress the partridges in the centre of the dish. Surround them with the vegetables and the sausages. Reduce the temperature of the oven and place the serving dish in the bottom to keep everything nice and warm.

Strain off the sauce into a clean saucepan and reduce down; adjust the seasoning, pour a little over the birds and serve immediately. Carve the partridges at the table and serve the remaining sauce in a *gras maigre*.

WINE: My old friend and former colleague at The Isle of Wight College, Dave Young (a wise and perceptive wine buff), always used to say to me: "Malc, when you go out for a special meal, just you and Di, always spend at least half the cost of the meal again on one really good quality bottle of wine." Dave's point being that you must never skimp on the quality of the wine you drink, unless of course you are just drinking socially (whatever that means!). Good on you 'Younger'!

So, my friends, if you really want to push the boat out with this dish, go for a quality Gevrey-Chambertin, Pommard or Grand Cru St Emilion. If you are not inclined to spend quite so much, try out a good Rhône red such as Gigondas or Côte-Rôtie.

PERDRIX AU POIVRE VERT
partridge in a green pepper sauce

A creamy green peppercorn sauce is quite often served in our Department with a crispy pan-fried duck breast, so Twink thought it would be fun to use it in a different way and we have found that it really works well with partridge.

Recipe by Diane Alder-Smith
La Maison aux Quat'Saisons, Laborie, 19400 Monceaux-sur-Dordogne

Ingredients for 4 people

- *2 oven ready partridges*
- *125 g unsalted butter*
- *500 g chanterelle mushrooms*
- *200 g smoked lardons of bacon*
- *2 carrots – 1 cm dice*
- *2 celery stalk – 1 cm dice*
- *sprigs fresh thyme*
- *1 lemon – cut into quarters*
- *2 soup spoons of walnut oil*
- *16 shallots*
- *100 ml Armagnac*
- *1 clove Lautrec garlic – finely chopped*
- *150 ml chicken stock*
- *400 ml cider*
- *bouquet garni*
- *salt and black pepper*
- *250 ml cream*
- *50 g green peppercorns in brine*
- *olive oil*

Preparation time:	30 minutes
Cooking time:	60 minutes

Preparation

Season the inside of the partridges with the salt and pepper, add a knob of butter and some of the mushrooms, lardons, sprig of thyme, flat leaf parsley and a lemon quarter to each bird and truss them with some butcher's string.

Place a large heavy-bottomed frying pan over a medium flame, add a slug of olive oil and a knob of the butter, and cook the birds, turning from time to time until the skin turns to a golden brown, pour over the Armagnac and flame (watch out for your eyebrows!).

Remove the birds and place them into a heavy-bottomed casserole dish with any residual liquid from the pan.

Add a little more olive oil and butter to the frying pan, add the lardons and the peeled shallots and cook for a few more minutes over medium to low flame. Increase the heat to a medium flame then add the remainder of the mushrooms, the carrots, celery, garlic, salt and pepper, and cook for around five minutes. Add these ingredients to the casserole, then pour over the cider and the chicken stock. Bring the liquid up to the simmer, cover with a lid and reduce the heat right down.

Cook the birds slowly for around 60 minutes, by which time they should be beautifully cooked and nice and moist. Remove the birds and the vegetables, place them into a roasting tin and pop into a low oven to keep hot.

Strain the remaining stock into a clean saucepan, add the peppercorns and reduce the liquid down by around one third. Add the cream, stir well and cook for another few minutes, then add the juice from the remaining two wedges of lemon and season the sauce to taste.

Twink's secret: Di usually dissects the birds in the kitchen and dresses them over a little mound of the vegetables on each plate. She then pours a good dose of peppercorn sauce over each portion and garnishes each plate with some crispy deep fried straw potatoes, a few fried lardons of bacon over each portion of partridge and sprinkles each with a little chopped flat leaf parsley.

WINE: Go for a similar choice of wine to those at the end of the previous recipe.

PIGEONNEAUX AUX PETITS POIS
pigeons with fresh garden peas

Getting hold of fresh dressed pigeons these days is usually not too difficult. I always tend to shop at my local butcher's and order the birds up to
a week in advance, so that they are prepared and in the best condition
for cooking. Make it quite clear that you won't accept anything that has
come out of the freezer – fresh is best!

During our formative years at La Maison we have been fortunate to have
my good friend and neighbour Georges Fruitiere, who has a plentiful supply of fresh garden peas, even in the middle of October! I would suggest
sitting around the fire the night before is the most therapeutic way of
'shucking' the peas. Place them into a bowl, cover with it cling-film and
refrigerate overnight.

Recipe by Malcolm Alder-Smith
La Maison aux Quat'Saisons, Laborie, 19400 Monceaux-sur-Dordogne

Preparation time: 40 minutes
Cooking time: 60 minutes

Ingredients for 4 people

- *4 dressed pigeons*
- *600 g shelled fresh garden peas*
- *250 g smoked lardons of bacon*
- *250 g small white onions (shallots will do)*
- *25 g unsalted butter*
- *sunflower oil*
- *2 soup spoons of flour*
- *12.5 cl chicken stock*
- *12.5 cl medium dry white wine*
- *10 cl double cream*
- *bouquet garni*
- *salt and ground pepper*

Preparation

Place a large heavy-bottomed frying pan over a medium flame and add
a little sunflower oil and the butter. Allow the butter to melt, then add the

pigeons, breast side down and cook until golden brown, turn onto the other breast and brown. Remove the birds and place into an oven-proof casserole.

Using the same frying pan, fry off the lardons until golden brown, remove and drain on kitchen paper, then add to the pigeons. Now add the small white onions and colour until they turn also turn golden brown, drain and add to the pigeons and lardons.

Add the flour to the remaining fat in the frying pan and make a roux. Gradually stir in the cold wine, a little at a time, then gradually add the hot chicken stock to make your sauce. Season to taste with the salt and black pepper.

Pour the sauce over the ingredients in the casserole. Add the fresh peas and the *bouquet garni* and pop the casserole into a pre-heated oven at 190°C for approximately 40 minutes.

When cooked, remove the pigeons and place to one side for a moment, strain the cooking liquor through a sieve into a clean pan, draining all the liquid from the peas, lardons and onions. Turn the pea, onion and smoked lardon mixture onto a serving plate and arrange the pigeons neatly on top, keep warm in the oven on about 120°C.

Bring the sauce up to the boil and reduce to a steady simmer. Add the double cream, stir well and adjust the seasoning and consistency to taste, before pouring the sauce over the pigeons which are now ready to be placed in the middle of the table for everyone to help themselves.

My secret: I like to add a good slug of Pineau des Charentes (white grape juice and Cognac) to the cooking liquor. This does tend to 'sweeten-up' the dish a tad, but I find it improves the flavour no end. This can be added instead of the wine; as well as the wine or just 50:50!

WINE: I would go for a Gaillac red every time with this dish. Alternatively, and by way of a complete contrast, try a lightly chilled Spätlese ("oops, just broke my 'all French' wine rule – sorry!").

RAGOÛT DE FAISAN AUX CÉLERI-RAVE
casserole of pheasant with celeriac and apple

Recipe by Malcolm Alder-Smith
La Maison aux Quat'Saisons, Laborie, 19400 Monceaux-sur-Dordogne

Preparation time: 30 minutes
Cooking time: 60 minutes

Ingredients for 4 people

- *4 plump pheasant breasts*
- *3 soup spoons sunflower oil*
- *25 g unsalted butter*
- *50 g flour*
- *125 g smoked lardons of bacon*
- *1 onion – chopped*
- *1 clove of pink garlic*
- *150 ml dry cider*
- *450 ml chicken stock*
- *2 soup spoons cider vinegar*
- *2 soup spoons apple brandy*
- *2 cooking apples*
- *3 sprigs of flat leaf parsley – chopped*
- *1 sprig fresh thyme*
- *1 bay leaf*
- *125 ml thick cream*
- *salt and black pepper*

Preparation

Season the pheasant breasts with a little salt and black pepper. Peel, core and chop the apples and place into a bowl of cold water with a little lemon juice to stop them discolouring.

Take a heavy-bottomed casserole and place over a medium flame then add 2 soup spoons of sunflower oil and the butter. When the bubbles start to subside, add the pheasant breasts, skin side down to start with and brown on both sides. Pour over the apple brandy and flame. As the alcohol burns off, the flames will subside, remove the pheasant breasts from the casserole and place to one side.

Add the onion, garlic and lardons and cook for around 3 minutes in the casserole, until the onion starts to go soft and translucent.

Stir in the flour and cook for a minute or two. Gradually add the cider, stock and cider vinegar, stirring all the time to ensure that you don't get a lumpy sauce. When all of the liquid has been incorporated, add the thyme and the bay leaf, increase the heat and bring to the boil, then add the pheasant breasts and chopped apple and turn the flame down to low so that the cooking liquor simmers gently. Cook for around 20 – 30 minutes.

Once the pheasant is cooked, remove it from the sauce and keep warm. Pass the sauce through a fine sieve into a clean saucepan. Place over a medium to high flame and reduce the sauce by around one third to help enhance all of those lovely flavours. Reduce the flame to low, stir in the cream and check for seasoning and consistency.

Place a pheasant breast on each plate and pour some of the sauce over and around. Serve with some lightly roasted turned potatoes and some green salad – an unusual combination, but it seems to work really well.

My secret: Garnish each plate with a couple of lightly caramelized apple rings, cut around 1.5 cm thick.

WINE: I would always go for something like a Gevrey-Chambertin, or if you want to push the boat out a little further, try a Chambertin-Clos de Bèze.

TRANCHES DE SANGLIER EN FARCE
braised leg of wild boar

Recipe by Michel et Isabelle Roussanne
Auberge des Gabariers, 15 Quai Lestourgie, 19400 Argentat

Preparation time: 45 minutes
Cooking time: 105 minutes

Ingredients for 4 people

- *1 kg leg of wild boar (jointed)*
- *2 large, ripe tomatoes*
- *1 carrot*
- *1 stick of celery*
- *1 onion*
- *2 bay leaves*
- *8 juniper berries*
- *salt and pepper*
- *½ bottle of red wine*
- *olive oil*

Preparation

The day before, prepare a marinade from the wine, carrot, celery, chopped onion, bay leaves and juniper berries. Place the joint into a suitable container, pour over the marinade and allow to infuse for 12 hours.

The next day, remove the joint from the marinade, drain well and pat dry with a clean cloth. Heat a little oil in a heavy-bottomed casserole and colour the joint on all sides.

Drain the vegetables, herbs and 'aromats' and add them to the casserole. Cook them for a few minutes until brown. Moisten with the red wine and add the blanched, seeded and chopped tomatoes, cover with a lid and allow to simmer over a very low heat for 90 minutes.

When the joint is cooked, remove from the liquid and allow to cool slightly. When sufficiently cool, carefully remove the bone and retain any small pieces of meat which may come away from the joint. Carve the rest of the joint into good slices, arrange neatly on a service dish and keep warm.

Remove the bay leaves and pass the sauce through a sieve into a clean saucepan. Return the pan to a medium flame and whisk in a few small knobs of butter to enrich and slightly thicken the sauce.

Finely chop the small pieces of meat, with the other vegetables from the marinade. Add these to the red wine sauce and mask the sauce and vegetables over the sliced meat.

Serve garnished with a stuffed tomato, turned carrots and some braised leeks.

WINE: This dish deserves a bit a serious treatment, so go for a nice red Fronsac from Bordeaux.

LÉGUMES
vegetables

I have deliberately kept this section on vegetables very short, because in general the majority of main course dishes *en Corrèze* are often only served with a delicate garnish which may be turned, steamed potatoes, *purée* of carrot, fresh peas, celeriac or celery or some lightly buttered home-made pasta.

BLETTE AU GRATIN
swiss chard in a white sauce

I have read so much about Swiss Chard in recent years, but have never seen it at Tesco, Sainsbury's or Safeway and have certainly never had the opportunity before to cook with it. So it was by a wonderful coincidence that on our autumn visit to La Maison in October 2003, Georges, our ever generous neighbour, arrived on our kitchen doorstep one morning bearing gifts (as he does on a regular basis), which included a generous offering of Swiss Chard. It took me a while to get Georges to confirm my original identification, that this was in deed, chard.

The problem was that when I asked how we should serve it, Georges gave me one of those, quizzical, sideways looks (which meant he didn't have a clue!) and said that I would have to ask Paulette, his wife, who would supply us with the perfect *recette*.

Some recipes, which we have seen, indicate that you only cook the stalk, but later conversations with Paulette, confirmed that there was only one way to prepare blette (Corrèze style) and that was with a white sauce. However, we were still left a little perplexed, because chard leaves are invariably quite massive, or at least the ones which Georges grows in his garden are, which would indicate to a chef that the leaves are going to cook a sight more quickly than the stalks. "Do we discard the stalks?" - "Oh no" exclaimed Paulette, "you must use it all."

I thought that this was the appropriate time to hand over the prep' and cooking to the boss, so *mes amis*, here goes – Twink's interpretation of Blette au Gratin.

We have since found that the green chard leaves, cooked on their own, have a unique flavour and just have to be tried, blanched, refreshed, drained and then re-heated quickly in some butter and nut oil, seasoned (salt, pepper and nutmeg) and served steaming hot – wonderful !!!

Recipe by Diane Alder-Smith
La Maison aux Quat'Saisons, Laborie, 19400 Monceaux-sur-Dordogne

Preparation time:	5 minutes
Cooking time:	30 minutes

Ingredients for 4 – 6 people

- *750 g Swiss chard*
- *75 g unsalted butter*
- *50 g flour*
- *0.5 lt milk – warmed*

- *grated gruyere cheese*
- *grated fresh nutmeg*
- *salt and pepper*

Preparation

Wash the chard leaves and drain. Cut the green leaf sections away from the white stalk. Take a couple of leaves at a time, roll them up together and cut them into 2.5 cm rolls. Take the stalk and slice from one end to the other, cutting into 1 cm strips.

Place a large saucepan of water over a high flame and bring to the boil. Add a good blast of salt and throw in the prepared stalk (which has a celery-like texture) and cook for around 15 minutes then add the prepared leaves and cook together for another 15 minutes.

While the chard is cooking, you can use this time to prepare the sauce. Melt 50 g of the butter over a medium to low flame and add the flour. Stir well to incorporate the ingredients. Bit by bit, add the warm milk, stirring as you go to obtain a smooth, clear mixture. The best way to test the consistency of the sauce is to dip a wooden spoon into it, remove the spoon and run your finger over the back of the spoon. The sauce should just cover the back of the spoon and leave a trail when you run your finger over it.

Pre-heat your oven to 200°C.

Melt the remainder of the butter and brush it over an oven-proof vegetable dish. Pour enough of the sauce into the dish to cover the base, drain the chard in a colander, arrange in the dish, pour over the white sauce and sprinkle with the grated cheese.

Place the dish into the pre-heated oven and cook until the top turns brown. Alternatively, heat it through in the oven and pop it under a medium grill for three or four minutes.

Twink's secret: This is one of those 'veggie' dishes which you can easily prepare in advance. If you are doing a dinner party, there is no problem getting this dish ready in the morning, pouring the sauce and cheese over the top and then finishing it off in the evening.

CHOU ROUGE BRAISÉE
braised red cabbage

You are getting spoilt, folks, as this is recipe number three for red cabbage and each is rather different from the previous one.

Recipe by Malcolm Alder-Smith
La Maison aux Quat'Saisons, Laborie, 19400 Monceaux-sur-Dordogne

Preparation time: 15 minutes
Cooking time: 120 minutes

Ingredients for 4 – 6 people

- *1 red cabbage*
- *1 onion*
- *3 shallots*
- *1 clove of garlic*
- *1 large apple*
- *125 g lardons of smoked bacon*
- *2 soup spoons of goose or duck fat*
- *250 ml red wine*
- *250 ml veal stock*
- *1 bay leaf*
- *1 sprig thyme*
- *salt and black pepper*

Preparation

Remove any damaged outer leaves and then cut the cabbage into quarters, remove most of the core and finely slice. Peel the onion, shallots and garlic, top and tail them and finely slice.

Place a pan of water on your hob over a high flame. Add around a tea spoon of salt to the boiling water and blanch the sliced cabbage for around 10 minutes or so. Strain the cabbage in a colander.

While the cabbage is blanching, prepare the apple. Simply peel, core and cut into quarters and roughly chop.

Take a heavy-bottomed casserole and place over a medium flame. When hot, add the goose or duck fat, onion, shallots and lardons, cover with a lid and sweat for 5 minutes or so until the onion is soft and translucent.

Add the cabbage, chopped apple, stock, red wine and herbs to the onion mixture, cover with the lid and place into a pre-heated oven at 200°C for around an hour and a half, or more if necessary, until most all of the liquid has disappeared.

CONFIT DE CHOU ROUGE AUX CHÂTAIGNES
braised red cabbage with chestnuts

Recipe by Malcolm Alder-Smith
La Maison aux Quat'Saisons, Laborie, 19400 Monceaux-sur-Dordogne

Preparation time: 15 minutes
Cooking time: 45 minutes

Ingredients for 4 people

- *1 red cabbage*
- *300 g shelled chestnuts*
- *4 slices of smoked streaky bacon*
- *3 soup spoons of cider vinegar*
- *2 soup spoons of olive oil*
- *4 shallots*
- *thyme*
- *salt and pepper*

Preparation

Remove any damaged outer leaves and then cut the cabbage into quarters, remove most of the core and slice. Top and tail the shallots (don't completely remove the stalk), peel and cut in half. Cut the slices of smoked bacon into narrow strips (lardons).

Take a heavy-bottomed frying pan and place over a medium flame, add a little olive oil and add the lardons. Add the red cabbage and the thyme.

Reduce to a low heat for around 30 minutes, stir from time to time so that the cabbage becomes impregnated with the flavour of the shallots and thyme.

Take a medium-sized saucepan and half fill with hot water. Place a *chinoise* (sieve) or small colander over the pan and add the peeled chestnuts. Cover with some tin foil or a lid and allow to cook for 12 – 15 minutes.

Once the cabbage is cooked, pour in the vinegar, salt and pepper and add the cooked chestnuts. Allow to cook for another 15 minutes, adding a little vegetable stock (or even water) if the mix becomes too dry.

My secret: You will, no doubt, have noticed that cabbage is quite popular *en Corrèze* and Twink and I have had great fun experimenting with a variety of recipes. We tend to leave the cabbage slightly underdone, so that it is a little on the crunchy side.

Serve this dish steaming hot with roast loin of pork or wild boar, it also goes well with some of the duck recipes which I have included. It has, however, a more delicate flavour than the recipes for red cabbage which I have included with Confit de Canard au Chou Rouge or the one for Carré de Porc à la Limousine. I guess it emerges as a good alternative if you tend to be less adventurous with your cooking, or prefer your food with less depth of flavour.

POMMES BOULANGÈRE
boulangère potatoes

This has been one of our favourite potato dishes for lunch parties when we entertain at La Maison. Although the Corréziennes use bread to fill themselves, we still prefer to offer this as an alternative, because it converts into the most wonderful soup for the evening or the following day.

When we are entertaining, I often look after the preparation and cooking of the main course dish, and Twink does the 'starters', veggies and desserts, so this is one of her recipes, which she appears to prepare effortlessly and always receives the appropriate accolades from our guests.

Recipe by Diane Alder-Smith
La Maison aux Quat'Saisons, Laborie, 19400 Monceaux-sur-Dordogne

Preparation time: 10 minutes
Cooking time: 60 minutes

Ingredients for 6 – 8 people

- *1 kg potatoes*
- *2 onions*
- *garlic*
- *flat leaf parsley*

- *1 lt chicken stock*
- *unsalted butter*
- *salt and black pepper*

Preparation

Peel and slice the onions and crush a couple of cloves of garlic. Chop the parsley and prepare the chicken stock. Wash and peel the potatoes. Wash again and slice into 0.5 cm discs.

Butter an earthenware oven dish. Arrange a layer of potatoes over the bottom of the dish. Add some of the sliced onions a little chopped parsley and lightly season. Continue to add a layer at a time.

For the final layer, overlap the potatoes neatly starting on the outside, working inwards. Pour over the stock until it nears the top of the potatoes. Melt a little butter and brush the potatoes to help the browning process.

Place into a pre-heated oven at around 200°C and cook for around one hour until the potatoes turn golden brown.

TOMATES FARCIES
stuffed tomatoes

One of my favourite vegetable dishes, when I used to cook in 'the industry', used to be tomatoes, top (lid) removed, the inside scooped out, add a little salt, black pepper and butter inside the tomato. Make a *duxelle* (finely chopped mushrooms, finely chopped onions or shallots, chopped parsley, breadcrumbs and seasoning) and cook in butter until the residual liquid has been reduced to nothing. Allow to cool and bind with an egg, then pipe the mixture into the tomatoes, brush with melted butter and place into a hot oven for 5 – 10 minutes. Replace the 'lid' at a jaunty angle, ready to garnish your favourite dish. This recipe really does bring back many happy memories of my days at college: *By the way – Whatever happened to my old mate, Dave Warwick?*

It seems such an innocent little menu item, but there are a few rules which you must consider when buying your tomatoes. The size of the tomato is important, as it must be of a reasonable size -- definitely not too small. Also the texture – don't use tomatoes which are over-ripe or too green. You have to think how the tomato is going to look on the plate, so colour is very important.

I guess if we took a general overview of the many hotel restaurants where we have eaten at *en Corrèze*, this garnish usually appears on someone's plate at some time during the evening. However, Twink has stuck to the traditional recipe, which is somewhat less complicated than the one above and you, my dear friends, have now got two recipes for the price of one!

Recipe provided by Diane Alder-Smith
La Maison aux Quat'Saisons, Laborie, 19400 Monceaux-sur-Dordogne

Preparation time:	15 minutes
Cooking time:	10 minutes

Ingredients for 4 people

- *2 medium to large tomatoes*
- *2 shallots*
- *1 clove of garlic*
- *flat leaf parsley*

- *2-3 sprigs of fresh thyme*
- *a handful of dried breadcrumbs*
- *unsalted butter*
- *salt and pepper*

Wash the tomatoes in cold water and pat dry. Cut the tomatoes in half (not through the stalk), brush with a little melted butter, lightly season with salt and ground black pepper and place onto a baking sheet.

Top and tail the shallots and finely chop. Peel the garlic, place onto your chopping board and coarsely chop. Remove the parsley from its stalks, strip the sprigs of thyme and add the leaves from both to the garlic. Finely chop the mélange and place into a small bowl, before adding the breadcrumbs and a little seasoning to taste.

Take a soup spoon of the mixture and place on top of each tomato. Sprinkle with melted butter and place into a hot oven for 5 -- 10 minutes and serve.

Twink's secret: Flash the tomatoes under a hot grill for a minute or so, to lightly brown the crumb mixture and serve immediately.

DESSERTS
Desserts

PATRICIA KELSALL

Call them sweets, puddings, desserts, 'afters' or whatever you like, most of us love them, and I guess that only a few of us hate them, and my waistline would certainly be better off without them, yet my dear friends, still we indulge ourselves.

When eating out *en France*, Twink and I religiously promise ourselves that we won't over-indulge. We enter the restaurant of our choice with every good intent and in the firm belief that we will just have a starter and main course, and of course a nice bottle of wine followed by a steaming cup of rich, black coffee and an Armagnac or three – that does it for me.

I guess the fact that our little boy, Ashley, always wants a dessert, is some sort of excuse for us weakening at the last minute. For him, even ice cream takes on a whole different meaning in France, when he samples some of the natural flavours on offer, so as he is generally a course ahead of us, we do often give in and go for it!

'Our' Department offers some interesting and wondrous dishes which are peculiar to the area using local fruit and nuts such as black cherries, strawberries, *fraises du bois* (wild strawberries), myrtilles (bilberry [UK], blueberry [USA]), walnuts and chestnuts. *Clafoutis*: black cherries cooked in an unusual sweet batter in a flan dish, or *Flognarde* served with apples or pears. One of my all time Corrézienne favourites from Hôtel Le Turenne, located at 1, boulevard Saint-Rodolphe-de-Turenne, Beaulieu-sur-Dordogne, is their superb Soufflé Glace aux Noix, served with a summer fruit coulis – totally, totally, totally orgasmic!

Back in the mid-Nineties when we were staying with Jim, I can recall one hot Whitsun afternoon having a very extended lunch out on his pontoon, which sits right alongside the river Maronne. There must have been at least 14 of us, plus Phillip and Gwyneth's boys. While we indulged ourselves in food and drink from the Department, the boys were climbing onto the roof of 'Bertha', Jim's aging blue Ford Transit, picking handfuls of dark red cherries from his two mature cherry trees. The adults, now slightly worse for wear from copious amounts of alcohol consumed over lunch, availed themselves of the sweet perfumed fruit, disposing of the stones directly into river. This was done either by squeezing the stones firmly between the fingers and projecting them river wise or for those more strategically seated, a deep intake of breath and a heavy exhale between puckered lips seemed to work a treat – as I recall!

Many of the traditional Corrézienne 'puddings' are made from a sweet batter and I have discovered so many different recipes with different names – Clafoutis, Flognard, Le Millassous – that I have found it quite confusing. However, I believe that I have found a couple which work really well, so you will have to try them for yourself.

WINE: Over the years, I have been told many reasons why the French follow their main course with cheese, which is traditionally followed by dessert. Only one explanation really makes any deal of sense to me. If you have just been drinking *un peu de rouge* with your main course, then surely the right and proper thing to do is to finish off that same wine with your cheese (savoury) rather than drinking it with sweet food (dessert) that will totally destroy the flavour on your palate. So my friends, if you want to drink a wine that will compliment your dessert, you might consider a nicely chilled sweet Sauternes from Bordeaux, or somewhat less expensive, from across the River Garonne from Sauternes are Loupiac, Ste-Croix-du-Mont and St Macaire – for budget buys, with good quality, try a Blanc Moelleux de Bordeaux.

Some of my readers will recall a generically labelled sweet white wine from the Sixties, simply known in this country at the time as Barsac. I can even remember in my early days 'in the industry' having customers drinking this buttery, sweet and sticky wine with a fillet steak – mistake, big time mistake!

Many people say that they don't like sweet white wines and this is often because they have not tried drinking them with the right food. My general advice would be only drink them with sweet desserts, that would be the safe bet.

The very best and, in these days of the global economy, most expensive sweet white wine is without a shadow of doubt Chateau d'Yquem (Bordeaux), which is the world's most famous sweet-white estate of some 250 acres. Most vintages improve in the bottle for 15 years, some have been known to 'live' for up to 100 years, with prices very much to match – WOW!!!

CLAFOUTIS AUX CERISES
black cherries cooked in a sweet batter

We have had an absolute ball trying out many of the recipes which we considered using in this book. However, we found that when we tried cooking one of the recipes for *Flognarde*, using a batter a few days earlier, it had been a tad of a disaster. So the first time Twink and I cooked this dish in the UK, we soon realised from the consistency of the batter (having followed the recipe precisely) that we would need to add a bit more flour. You need to make the batter so it is similar in consistency to a pancake or 'Yorkie Pud' batter. The end product is excellent, providing you with a golden brown sweet batter complimented by sweet fresh black cherries.

It is the presence of the 'nuts' (stones) in the cherries that helps to give *Clafoutis* its flavour, so don't de-stone them if you want to get the best results. Serve *Clafoutis* warm or at room temperature. It is not overly wise to try eating this dish straight out of the oven, as the cherries and stones could do irreparable damage to your mouth and throat if eaten too hot; nor is it at its best after it has been resting in a refrigerator overnight, as it tends to become rather 'lardy'. However, a quick 30-45 second 'nuke' in your micro will rejuvenate your *Clafoutis* to something like it was when you pulled it out of the oven the previous day!

If you can't get hold of fresh cherries, then you can buy some good quality tinned ones from your local supermarket. Drain them well and follow the recipe just the same. When you are nearly ready to eat your *Clafoutis*, put the cherry juice from the tin into a small saucepan on your hob over a medium flame and reduce the liquid by about a half. Add a couple of soup spoons of caster sugar and a knob of butter and stir in well, this will slightly thicken the liquid and give it a good shine, finish off with a good splash of Kirsch or *eau de vie* and pour over the *Clafoutis* just before you dish-up – *délicieuse*!

This recipe can be varied by using small red plums, such as Saint-Leonards. You prepare the dish using the same recipe, but the name changes to *"Flan aux Prunes rouges"* and you do need to de-stone the plums!

This particular recipe for *Clafoutis* was sent to me by Paulette, our neighbour in France. Her sister, Irène, had been staying over for a few days when my letter arrived, begging for traditional Corrézienne recipes. Irène, bless her, was determined to get involved and not miss out on the family involvement, so here goes, and thank you Irène for this wonderful recipe.

Recipe by Irène Mespoulet
Brive-la-Gaillard

Preparation time:	20 minutes
Cooking time:	25 – 30 minutes

Ingredients for 5-6 people

- *500 g small black cherries*
- *125 g flour*
- *25 cl milk*
- *75 g caster sugar*
- *3 whole eggs*
- *Pinch of salt*
- *1 soup spoon of Kirsch (cherry liqueur)*
- *butter*

Preparation

Remove the stalks, leave the stones in the cherries, wash them and wipe dry with some kitchen paper or a clean tea-towel. Arrange the cherries closely together in the bottom of a buttered oven proof flan dish and preheat your oven to 210ºC.

Mix together well all of the ingredients (except the butter) to obtain a clear, lump free batter. Pass the mixture through a sieve into a clean jug or bowl and then pour over the cherries.

Place in the oven and cook for 25 – 30 minutes. Sprinkle with a little caster sugar when the dish is removed from the oven.

Irène's secret: Garnish with a sprig of mint and serve with a quenelle of *crème fraîche*.

WINE: Sauternes, Loupiac, Blanc Moelleux or any of those mentioned above in the intro' to desserts.

CRÈME BRÛLÉE AUX POMMES DU LIMOUSIN
limousin apple crème brûlée

Preparation time: 15 minutes
Cooking time: 40 minutes

Ingredients for 4 people

- *2 apples – Golden du Limousin*
- *4 egg yolks*
- *45 cl whipping cream*
- *10 cl milk*
- *1 packet of vanilla sugar (or a few drops of vanilla essence)*
- *70 g soft brown sugar*
- *pinch of ground cinnamon*

Preparation

In a bowl, add 60 g of soft brown sugar, 4 egg yolks, 10 cl milk, 45 cl whipping cream, vanilla sugar or vanilla essence and a pinch of cinnamon. Whisk very well until the mixture is white.

Pre-heat an oven to around 150°C to 180°C.

Peel and core the apples and thinly slice over the bottom of four small dishes (suitable for the oven), then add the mixture on the top. Place in the oven to cook for 30 minutes then allow to cool and place into your fridge for 4 hours.

Before serving, sprinkle each dish with the rest of the brown sugar and place under a hot grill to caramelize. If you are lucky enough to own a chef's blow-torch, then one of these will do the job very well.

Chef's secret: Serve with a small piece of Corrézienne nut cake.

Recipe supplied by Comité Départemental du Tourisme de la Corrèze.

CROUSTADE AUX POMMES DU LIMOUSIN
limousin apple croustade

Preparation time: 15 minutes
Cooking time: 40 minutes

Ingredients for 6 people

- *300 g puff pastry*
- *5 apples – Golden du Limousin*
- *1 free range egg*
- *100 g butter*
- *100 g caster sugar*
- *10 g vanilla sugar*
- *icing sugar*

Preparation

Peel and core the apples and slice them around 1.5 cm thick. Put half of the butter in a non-stick frying pan, add the sugar and the slices of apple. Cook for 10 minutes over a medium flame, turning from time to time. Preheat your oven to 180ºC.

Separate the puff pastry into two pieces, one of which is bigger than the other. Thinly roll out the smaller piece of pastry and cut it into a circle the size of a tart mould. Roll out the second piece about 2 cm larger. Butter the inside of the mould and line it with the smaller piece of pastry and arrange the sliced apples on top of the pastry. Cut the butter up into small pieces and dot over the top of the apples then finish off by sprinkling the vanilla sugar over the apples and butter.

Cover the apples with the second piece of pastry and crimp all the way around the edge to seal. Separate the egg and mix the yolk with a little water or milk, mix well with a fork and paint the lid with a pastry brush. Place the croustade into the pre-heated oven and cook for around 40 minutes until golden brown. Remove from the oven and allow to cool a little before sprinkling with the icing sugar.

Serve warm with some home-made vanilla ice cream, alternatively the dish goes really well with *sauce anglaise*.

WINE: Why not go for a sweet white from the Loire, try a Vouvray or Anjou Moelleux. Alternatively a Monbazillac from the Bergerac region, for some of these wines can be like a fine Sauternes.

Recipe supplied by Comité Départemental du Tourisme de la Corrèze.

EAU-DE-VIE

Eau-de-vie literally means "Water of Life" and the term describes any colourless liquid which has been distilled into brandy or other spirit from fermented fruit juice or wine.

There are many names for *eau-de-vie* which is produced from wine, such as *eau-de-vie-de-marc, eau-de-vie-de-vin* etc. However, *en Corrèze* we normally associate *eau-de-vie* with having been produced from fermented fruit juice.

In the Corrèze, strawberry growing was a major industry until recently (Bonne Maman have a massive *confiture* factory at Biars), and strawberries have always been a popular base for production of this clear, fiery and very alcoholic liquid. Strawberry production has now been scaled down somewhat over the last ten years or so and the more popular flavours of *eau-de-vie* found these days tend to be *poire* (pear) and *prune* (plum).

It is considered by many to be a painkiller. This I can agree with, as the slightest over indulgence tends to leave you with no memory of the previous evening at all. My good buddy Jim wags his finger firmly and warns me that a couple of small sips only are within safe and sensible limits.

The distillation of 'home made' *eau-de-vie*, also known as *la goutte*, was until recently officially restricted to landowners (whatever that means) – although the world and his wife seemed to know someone who produced the odd bottle or two to keep out the winter chill.

Napoleonic laws dictated the rights of who could or couldn't produce the spirit and these rights were handed down from generation to generation. These days it is not always easy to find someone with a licence and the ability to "make magic" and turn fermented fruit juice into a quality high-octane spirit.

The art of distilling *eau-de-vie* (non-commercially) *en Corrèze* is still practised, but the menfolk who operate the stills are becoming a dying breed.

Only good quality fruit should be used to produce the fermented liquid (inferior fruit will have a negative effect on the end product), which then has to be taken to the local home-distiller, a *bouilleur de cru*. Some people will ferment the fruit on its own pulp, distilling the entire fermentation, others will separate some or all of the solids prior to distillation.

The fermented liquid is heated in a large "copper", traditionally over a direct flame using logs of oak or acacia. A "swan's neck" carries the vapours off the top of the "copper" through a condenser, which is a water-cooled coil of copper tubing and slowly, very slowly, the tiny droplets of clear liquid *eau-de-vie* appear.

The clear liquid is separated into three clearly identifiable groups of alcohol, these are globally known as the "heads", "middle" and "tails". The "heads" and "tails" are usually discarded as being unsuitable for drinking and only the "middle" is kept to produce the finest *eau-de-vie*.

The alcohol which is produced direct from the still is very strong indeed; it can be as high as 150 proof. To make the spirit drinkable it is often "cut" with distilled water to around 80 proof.

New laws have now decreed that the home-production of *eau-de-vie* will cease over a given period of time – "dream on!"

FIGUES GRAND-MÈRE
figs – grandmother style

Recipe by Michel et Isabelle Roussanne
Auberge des Gabariers, 15 Quai Lestourgie, 19400 Argentat

Preparation time: 15 minutes
Cooking time: 10 minutes

Ingredients for 4 people

- *20 figs*
- *50 g caster sugar*
- *½ lit of red wine*
- *4 roundels of orange*
- *4 roundels of lemon*
- *1 cinnamon stick*

Preparation

Place the red wine, sugar, slices of orange, lemon and cinnamon stick into a saucepan, bring to the boil and simmer for five minutes.

Remove the stalks from the figs and with a sharp knife score a criss-cross across the top of the fig. Alternatively, you can just cut them in half top-to-bottom. Add the figs to the simmering red wine. Cover for a few moments and remove from the heat when the liquid comes back to the boil.

Remove the fruit and place onto some ice cubes to allow them to cool quickly. Remove the cinnamon stick and reduce the liquid by three quarters.

Put the warm figs onto four plates and moisten with the reduced liquor. Decorate with the slices of orange and lemon.

WINE: My friend Michel, a wine buff with the most fantastic arched stone wine cellar at the back of his restaurant, suggests that a bottle of Clairette de Die (pronounced Dee) would go very well with this dish.

Clairette is not something that you will find that easily in the UK, but this unusual sparkling wine from the Rhône is worth a try. Go for the semi-sweet, Muscat flavoured version from the Eastern Rhône – definitely worth a bash.

FLAN AUX PRUNES ROUGES
small red plums cooked in a sweet batter

This is the final recipe supplied by our friends Michel and Isabelle from the Gabariers in Argentat. Although when they sent this recipe to me, it was flagged up as *Clafoutis aux Prunes*, I just felt that it was a natural follow-on to the *Clafoutis* recipe, so I took the liberty of changing the name. I trust that you will forgive the imposition, Isabelle. You will notice that the recipe for the batter is somewhat different to *Clafoutis aux Cerises* and I guess that you might even venture to play 'mix and match' and find the best between the two for use at home. Certainly any recipe that contains alcohol catches my attention, however, great care often needs to be taken, since with certain dishes you can burn off the alcohol and lose too much flavour too quickly. It's rather like pouring a few tots of brandy or *eau-de-vie* down the sink – you won't benefit from it all.

Recipe by Michel et Isabelle Roussanne
Auberge des Gabariers, 15 Quai Lestourgie, 19400 Argentat

Preparation time: 10 minutes
Cooking time: 20 minutes

Ingredients for 6 people

- *150 g flour*
- *250 g caster sugar*
- *6 free range eggs*
- *80 g butter*

- *50 cl milk*
- *1 soup spoon of eau-de-vie de prune (eau-de-vie will do fine)*
- *1 pinch of salt*

Preparation

Take a mixing bowl and mix together the flour, sugar and salt. Make a well in the flour mix then add the eggs, milk and the *eau-de-vie de prune* and mix thoroughly to a clear batter.

De-stone the plums. Over a gentle heat melt the butter and add the plums for just a few moments to start to soften. Butter a flan dish and add the plums skin side up. Pour the batter over the plums and cook in a pre-heated oven at 180ºC for 20 minutes.

Le secret d'Isabelle Roussanne: Try a glass of 'local' *eau-de-vie* with this dish.

FLOGNARDE
batter pudding served with apples or pears

Recipe by Pierrette Déjammes
(Mother of Roger, Giselle, Claudine et Jean-Pierre)

Preparation time: 20 minutes
Cooking time: 30 minutes

Ingredients for 6 people

- *120 gr plain flour*
- *100 gr caster sugar*
- *40 cl lukewarm milk*
- *3 free range eggs*
- *50 g butter*
- *icing sugar*
- *pinch of salt*

Preparation

Pour the flour, sugar and salt into a bowl. Carefully add the eggs one at a time, mixing thoroughly with a wooden spoon to avoid lumps. Little by little add the warm milk, mixing well.

Generously butter a flan dish, pour in the batter and cook in a pre-heated oven at 200ºC for approximately 40 minutes.

Serve warm dusted with icing sugar.

We often peel, core and chop apples or pears (or both) and cook them quickly in a small frying pan in some unsalted butter and sugar and finish them off with a little *eau-de-vie* or Calvados. We put a little (or a lot) of this mixture onto everyone's plate with a good helping of the pudding.

Pierrette Déjammes' secret: See the happiness in the sparkling eyes of the 'gourmandise' and his children.

"I think Pierrette is referring to my good friend, wine Négociant, Roger Déjammes when she refers to the 'gourmandise'. I am sure he would appreciate the 'label'".

GÂTEAU CHOCOLAT ET NOIX
chocolate gâteau with nuts

Recipe by David et Stéphane Lefevre
Hôtel Le Turenne, 1, boulevard Saint-Rodolphe-de-Turenne
19120 Beaulieu-sur Dordogne

Preparation time: 20 minutes
Cooking time: 25 minutes

Ingredients for 6 people

- *300 g plain chocolate*
- *1 pinch of salt*
- *1 glass of milk*
- *125 g flour*

- *250 g caster sugar*
- *260 g ground or chopped nuts*
- *8 free range eggs*
- *25 g butter*

Preparation

Place a bowl over a pan of lightly simmering water, chop the chocolate into small pieces and melt in the bowl, stirring regularly and making sure that the bottom of the bowl does not come into contact with the simmering water.

In a bowl, mix the flour, sugar, eggs, melted butter, glass of milk and salt. It is important that you whisk in the above ingredients in the order that I have noted. When the chocolate is completely melted, add it to the other ingredients and mix well. Lastly add the ground or chopped nuts.

Place the mix into an appropriately sized mould and cook in a pre-heated oven for 25 minutes.

You can serve this dish cold with a little chocolate sauce or warm served with a *crème anglaise*. I would tend to go for the latter, but would add a little spirit alcohol to the sauce. Fruit spirits would work very well and enhance the dish no end!

Le secret de David et Stéphane: Prick the gateau from time to time with a knife to test to see if it is cooked, if the knife comes out clean, it is cooked. If it comes out with mixture still on it – cook on!!

LE MILLASSOUS
sweet batter pudding

Recipe by Edwige Laage
Edwige Laage.
Quai de Lestourgie, 19400 Argentat

Preparation time: 15 minutes
Cooking time: 45 minutes

Ingredients for 6 people

- *50 cl milk*
- *150 g butter*
- *5 free range eggs*
- *100 g flour*
- *100 g caster sugar*
- *1 sachet of vanilla sugar*
- *1 coffee spoon of grated lemon zest*

Preparation

Boil the milk with the sugar and vanilla sugar. Take off the heat, add the flour and stir or whisk to blend. Add the butter and stir vigorously. Lightly whisk the eggs and flavour them with the grated lemon zest. Gradually add the eggs to the milk, sugar and flour mixture, whisking to a clear batter.

Pour this mixture into a buttered earthenware flan dish (a quiche dish should be fine) and cook for 45 minutes in a pre-heated oven at 180°C.

Sprinkle with icing sugar when you take the cooked pudding out of the oven.

Le secret de Edwige Laage: Serve the pudding warm with a *compôte* of fresh fruit.

SOUFFLÉ GLACÉ AUX NOIX
iced nut soufflé

During one of our early visits to the Corrèze, just before Ash was born, we decided to eat somewhere totally different and took the picturesque drive alongside the Dordogne down to Beaulieu-sur-Dordogne. Our good friend Jim had suggested that we should eat at the Central Hôtel Fournié in the Champs de Mars, as he said that the food there was excellent. We parked up in the tree-lined square and took a look at the menu outside, which was certainly impressive. A quick look through the windows indicated that the place was fairly empty and as we like a bit of atmosphere, we popped over the road to take a look at the Hôtel Turenne, an ancient Benedictine Abbey from the 12th century located in the heart of the village. The menu there looked every bit as good and there was a bit more life about the place so we took the plunge and asked for a table. The meal was fabulous which confirmed that we had made the right choice on that occasion. I finished my meal with a Soufflé Glacé aux Noix and I can honestly say that I had never tasted a dessert quite like it.

Twink and I have eaten at the Central Hôtel Fournié since and I would guess that their version of this classic dish is certainly on a par with the Hôtel Turenne. Both generally served it on a coulis of red summer fruits.

I now look out for this dish wherever we eat, but in a way I am pleased to say that there are only a few other places in the Department that I am aware of which reproduce the quality of these two superb hotel-restaurants in Beaulieu-sur-Dordogne.

Recipe by Central Hôtel Fourniê
4, place du Champ de Mars
19120 Beaulieu-sur-Dordogne

Preparation time: 15 minutes
"Cooking time":   18 hours

Ingredients for 10 people

- *8 eggs*
- *250 gr caster sugar*
- *25 cl cream*
- *10 cl eau de noix*
- *120 gr walnuts*

Preparation

Finely chop 100 g of the walnuts, place onto a tray and put in a pre-heated oven until lightly coloured. Remove and then macerate in the nut brandy. Keep a few nut kernels on one side for decoration.

Separate the egg white and the yolks (keeping the whites to one side) and whisk together with 150 g of the sugar up until they reach a ribbon stage; you will find it easiest to do this with an electric whisk. Pour the mixture over the macerating nuts. Whisk up the cream, not too firm, and blend in together with the previous ingredients.

Take the egg whites and the remaining 100 g of sugar and whisk until they 'peak' and reach a meringue consistency, then delicately incorporate into the nut mixture. Take a straight-sided mould, and line the sides with grease-proof paper so that the sides are raised. Empty the mixture into the lined mould.

Place into the freezer for about 18 hours. To serve, take off the grease-proof paper and decorate with the nut kernels.

Le secret du chef: Serve this dessert with a glass of *eau-de-vie de noix*.

Recipe supplied by Comité Départemental du Tourisme de la Corrèze.

TARTE À LA CITROUILLE
pumpkin tart

Recipe by Martine Ercole
Le Relais du Quercy
Avenue du Quercy – 19500 Meyssac

Preparation time: 15 minutes
Cooking time   30 minutes

Ingredients for 6/8 people

- *250 g pumpkin*
- *4 free range eggs*
- *6 soup spoons of caster sugar*
- *6 soup spoons of flour*

- *20 cl crème fraîche*
- *10 cl warm milk*
- *100 g butter*
- *3 or 4 eating apples (peeled, cored and cut into thick slices)*

Preparation

Cook the prepared pumpkin in a saucepan of boiling water for a few minutes and drain. Take a bowl and beat the eggs well, gradually add the flour a little at a time, mixing thoroughly, then add the *crème fraîche* and 10 cl of warm milk and mix well. Crush the blanched pumpkin with a fork and add to the batter, stir well to blend in.

Melt the butter and pour into a flan mould or equally you can mix the melted butter straight into the batter. If you do this, then brush the mould with some of the melted butter. Pour the batter into the mould.

Arrange the sliced apples on top of the batter and place into a pre-heated medium oven at around 180°C until lightly browned.

Remove from the oven and sprinkle with caster sugar.

WINE: Sweet white wines are often associated with famous vineyards of Bordeaux, so you could try a Barsac, such as a Chateau Climens or Chateau Coutet. Alternatively, and for something totally different, go for a Côteaux du Layon, a sweet white Chenin Blanc from the heart of Anjou on the Loire.

Recipe supplied by Comité Départemental du Tourisme de la Corrèze.

TARTE AUX FRUITS D'ÉTÉ
summer fruit crumble tart

Recipe by Diane Alder-Smith
La Maison aux Quat'Saisons, Laborie, 19400 Monceaux-sur-Dordogne

Preparation time: 40 minutes
Cooking time   30 minutes

Ingredients for 6/8 people

- *300 g sweet pastry*
- *250 g blackberries (washed and dried)*
- *250 g plums – stoned and halved or quartered*
- *100 g caster sugar*

For the crumble topping

- *200 g plain flour*
- *1 flat tsp ground cinnamon*
- *100 g caster sugar*
- *100 g butter – well chilled*

Preparation

Take the prepared sweet pastry out of your chiller for about 10 minutes before you roll it out thinly on a lightly-floured work surface to form a circle large enough to line a 23 cm fluted flan ring, with a removable base. Line the pastry with greaseproof paper or parchment and fill with dried baking beans.

Place onto a baking sheet and put into a pre-heated oven at 200ºC for 10 minutes. Remove the baking beans and the paper and return the flan to the oven for a further 10 minutes to dry out, reducing the temperature slightly.

Place the prepared plums and blackberries in a bowl, sprinkle with the caster sugar and toss the fruits gently together. Pour the fruit into the pastry case and smoothe down to an even level.

Now for the crumble topping. I like to make a really fine crumble mix to go onto the top of this lovely dish and find that the best results are obtained by spending the extra time crumbing the mix by hand.

Mix the flour, cinnamon and most of the sugar together. Cut the chilled butter into small pieces and drop them into the mixture. Gently rub the mix together until you obtain a really fine crumb.

Once you have obtained the right consistency, sprinkle the mixture over the top of the fruit, so that it is totally covered and lightly sprinkle the rest of the sugar over the top of the crumble mix. Place the prepared summer fruit crumble tart into the pre-heated oven, still at 200ºC, for approximately 25 minutes until the topping starts to turn to a wonderful golden brown.

Pre-heat your grill and 'flash' the tart for just a minute or so to obtain exactly the right finish to the topping.

Twink's secret: Serve hot or cold. I love this dish served with a large dollop of *crème fraiche* if we are serving it cold, or if hot, then it just has to be with some home made *sauce anglaise*. The vanilla flavour compliments this dish so well.

TARTE AU MIEL ET AUX NOIX
nut and honey tart

Recipe by Diane Alder-Smith
La Maison aux Quat'Saisons, Laborie, 19400 Monceaux-sur-Dordogne

Preparation time: 20 minutes
Cooking time   30 minutes

Ingredients for 6 people

- *225 g flour*
- *150 g butter – chopped*
- *75 g caster sugar*
- *1 free range egg yolk*

- *1 whole egg*
- *250 g walnuts*
- *500 g acacia honey (or similar)*
- *pinch of salt*

Preparation

Prepare the sweet pastry: Sift the flour with the salt and rub in the chopped butter until it resembles a crumb mixture. Stir the sugar into the flour and butter mixture, then add the egg and egg yolk. Work the mix together well to a clear paste. Wrap in cling film and put the ball of pastry to rest in your refrigerator for 2 hours.

Place the paste onto a lightly floured work surface and roll out into a circle, large enough to line a flan mould. Prick the base of the pastry with a fork, and refrigerate for 20 minutes before baking.

Line the pastry case with a circle of greaseproof paper, fill with dried baking beans. Bake blind in a pre-heated oven, set at 220ºC, and cook for 15 – 20 minutes. Remove from the oven, then take out the baking beans and the greaseproof paper.

Roughly chop the walnuts, mix them with the honey and pour the *mélange* into the flan case.

Return the flan to the oven and cook for a further 10 minutes.

Twink's secret: This is a dish which tastes equally good served hot or cold.

244

TARTE AUX MYRTILLES
bilberry tart

Recipe supplied by Paulette Fruitiere
Laborie, 19400 Monceaux-sur-Dordogne

Preparation time: 30 minutes
Cooking time   30 minutes

Ingredients for 4 people

- *300 g sweet pastry*
- *1 spoon of caster sugar*
- *300 g myrtilles*
- *100 g lump sugar*

Preparation

Take your prepared sweet pastry out of the chiller for about 10 minutes before you roll it out thinly on a lightly-floured work surface to form a circle large enough to line a 23 cm fluted flan ring, with a removable base. Line with greaseproof paper or parchment and fill with dried baking beans.

Place onto a baking sheet and place into a pre-heated oven at 200°C for 20 minutes. Remove the baking beans and the paper.

While the flan is cooking, wash and drain the myrtilles. Place a pan on a medium heat and using the lump sugar, add a little water at a time to make a syrup, cooking for a few minutes until you have a thick consistency. Take off the heat and add the myrtilles, infuse for a couple of minutes and put back over a very low heat for a further two minutes.

Pour the myrtille mixture into the cooked flan case and place on one side to cool.

TARTE AUX NOIX CORRÉZIENNE
walnut tart

Amongst all of the interesting information which I was sent from the Minoterie Daniel Farges (the old mill at Vimbelle), they kindly included around half a dozen 'nutty' recipes. As this dish is one of the specialities of the Department, I just felt that I just had to finish off my book with one last classic.

Recipe supplied by Minoterie Daniel Farges
Vimbelle 19800 BAR

Preparation time: 30 minutes
Cooking time   30 minutes

Ingredients for 5 people

Sugar Paste *(Pâté Sucrée)*

- *55 g butter*
- *20 g sugar*
- *1 g salt*
- *1 small egg*
- *125 g flour*

Nuts (noix)

- *1 egg*
- *35 g sugar*
- *40 g cane sugar*
- *50 g crème fraîche*
- *20 g butter*
- *60 g chopped walnuts*
- *8 g Grand Marnier*

Preparation

Mix together the butter, sugar and salt. Add the eggs, little by little, then the flour and mix to a clear paste. Place into the refrigerator.

Mix together the egg, sugar, cane sugar, chopped walnuts and the *crème fraîche*. Add the melted butter at 50°C and the alcohol.

Take the prepared sweet pastry out of your chiller for about 10 minutes before you roll it out thinly (around 2 mm) on a lightly-floured work surface to form a circle large enough to a line flan ring, with a removable base. Place the walnut mixture into the lined flan ring and decorate the top with half walnuts.

Cook the tart at 160°C for around 25 minutes. Refrigerate; then decorate the tart by sprinkling with icing sugar before you serve.

GASTRONOMIC EVENTS
Pays de Tulle

- Fête de la Myrtille
  Chaumeil
  End of July
  Tél: 05 55 21 34 11

- Fête du champignon
  Corrèze
  Beginning of October
  Tél: 05 55 21 21 00

- Marché des producteurs du pays
  Sainte-Fortunade
  Friday evenings from 17h00 to 20h00
  July / August
  Tél: 05 55 21 55 61

- Marché des producteurs du pays
  Treignac
  Friday evenings from 17h00 to 20h00
  July / August
  Tél: 05 55 21 55 61

Valée de la Dordogne

- Fête de la fraise
  Beaulieu-sur-Dordogne
  May
  http://www.conceze.com/economie/economie89.htm
  "Internationally famous strawberry fair"

- Marché de nuit
  Curemont
  1st Friday in August from 15h00 to midnight
  Tél: 05 55 84 05 27

- Marché de Noël
  Meyssac
  Mid-December
  Tél: 05 55 25 32 25   Fax: 05 55 84 07 28 (Marie)

- Marché des producteurs du pays
  Monceaux-sur-Dordogne
  Thursday evening from 17h00 to 20h00, from 5 July to 30 August
  Tél: 05 55 21 55 61

- Fête de la noix fraîche et des produits de la noix
  Saillac
  Biennial – beginning of October
  Tél: 05 55 25 41 37

- Pain cuit au feu de bois
  à l'ancienne, dans le four du village de Hautebrousse
  Saint Privat
  Thursday afternoon from 13h30 to 18h00
  Demonstration and sale of different varieties of bread,
  viennoiseries, pizzas, clafoutis...
  Tél: 05 55 28 21 22

- Marché de pays
  Servières-le-Château
  Regional products and arts and crafts
  On the morning of the 4th Sunday of July + 2nd Sunday in August
  Tél: 05 55 28 21 92

Vézère – Auvézère

- Fête de la prune
  Ayen
  End of July
  Tél: 05 55 25 16 67

- Fête de la framboise
  Concèze
  Mid-July
  Tél: 05 55 25 61 51
  Fax: 05 55 25 24 07
  http://www.conceze.com/economie/economie2003.htm

- Foire aux fruits d'automne
  Canton de Juillac
  End of September – beginning October
  Tél: 05 55 25 60 65

- Foire aux fruits d'autumne
  Canton de Juillac
  End of September – beginning October
  Tél: 05 55 25 60 65

- Fête de la pomme
  Objat
  Biennial – end of October
  Tél: 05 55 25 81 68

- Fête de la pêche
  Voutezac
  End of July
  Tél: 05 55 25 97 85 or 05 55 25 06 47
  Fax: 05 55 25 26 00

- Marché des producteurs du pays
  Voutezac / Le Saillant
  Tuesday evening from 17h00 to 20h00
  July 3rd to 28th August
  Tél: 05 55 21 55 61

Haute-Corrèze

- Marché des producteurs du pays
  Meymac
  Wednesday, from 17h00 to 20h00
  July and August
  Tél: 05 55 21 55 61

- Marché des producteurs du pays
  Ussel
  Friday, from 17h00 to 20h00
  July and August
  Tél: 05 55 21 55 61

- Journée Nationale de la tête de veau
  End of July
  Tél: 05 55 72 11 50
  Fax: 05 55 72 54 44

Les Specialités en Corrèze

André Ritou – Charcutier
Jambons secs Label Rouge, Saucissons secs, Label Rouges
Veau, Boeuf, Porc lable rouge du Limousin
05 55 27 80 71

Association Pommes du Limousin
www.pomme-limousin.org

Bureau Interprofessionel Fruits Rouges du Limousin
Agriculture Service, Z.I. Cana-Ouest, Rue Jules Bouchet, 19100 Brive
05 55 86 32 33

Comité Interprofessionnel
"Veau Sous La Mère"
1 Boulevard d'Estienne d'Orves
19100 Brive
05 55 87 09 01
vslm@veau-sous-la-mere.asso.fr

Corrèze Conserves
Z.I. du Verdier, 19210 Lubersac
05 55 73 53 80
Correze-Conserves@wanadoo.fr

Exidia
Truffes, Champignons
39, rue Beaumarchais, 19100 Brive
www.exidia.free.fr

Francep International
Cèpes, Girolles, Morilles, Truffes
25, avenue E. Duclaux, BP48, 19102 Brive
www.francep.com

La Charcuterie du Pays Vert
Porcs Châtaignou et Lable Rouge du Limousin
Ets Badefort et Fils
Z.A. 19700 SEILHAC
05 55 27 91 63

La Cuisine Corrézienne
Faure S.A. - Enval, 19100 Brive
05 55 24 24 50

La Production de Canards et d'Oies grasses en Corrèze
Emmanuel Carbonnieère
05 55 86 43 21

MONTEIL
Champignons des Bois
Z.I. Cana Est, 19100 Brive
05 55 88 00 73
www.monteil-sa.com

SALAISONS BOUTOT
Corrèze Gourmandes
19410 Perpezac-le-Noir
05 55 73 70 07

SOLAC
Saucisse, saucisson, charcuterie
Bellevue, 19140 Uzerche
05 55 73 24 53

Organisations de la Corrèze

Comité des Manifestations Agricoles
For information contact:
La Mairie de Brive-la-Gaillarde
BP 433, 19312 BRIVE-LA-GAILLARDE
05 55 92 39 39

Comité Départmental du Tourisme
Quai Baluze
19100 Tulle
05 55 29 98 78
cdt.correze@wanadoo.fr
www.cg19.fr

Comité Régional du Tourisme (CRT)
27, boulevard de la Corderie
87031 Limoges Cédex
05 55 45 18 80
tourisme@cr-limousin.fr
www.cr-limousin.fr

Office de Tourisme
2, Place Emile Zola
19000 Tulle
05 55 26 59 61
office-de-tourisme-de-tulle@wanadoo.fr
www.paysdetulle-developpement.org

Office de Toursime Cantonal d'Argentat
Place Da Maïa
19400 Argentat
05 55 28 16 05
office-tourisme-argentat@wanadoo.fr
www.tourisme-argentat.com

Promenades Gourmandes
EDIL communication
199 rue de Poussan
34370 Maraussan
www.promenades-gourmandes.com

Relais Agriculture et Tourisme
Chambre d'Agriculture de la Corrèze
Réseau Bienvenue à La Ferme
Le Puy Pinçon
Tulle est BP 30

Bienvenue à la Ferme
Le Puy Pinçon
Tulle est BP 30
19001 Tulle CEDEX
05 55 21 55 61
gites.de.france.correze@wanadoo.fr
www.bienvenue-a-la-ferme.com (key word : correze)

Les Confréries

Confrérie des "Entêtés de la tête de veau"
Monsieur Raymond Fraysse
Hôtel-Restaurant Les Gravades
St-Dézery
19200 Ussel
05 55 46 06 00

Confrérie des "Minjadours du chocolat fin"
Monsieur Daniel Borzeix
Le Loubanel
19260 Treignac
05 55 98 02 54

Confrérie des "Mangeurs de farcidures"
Monsieur Michel Simandoux
Le Bourg
19320 Champagnac-La-Noaille
05 55 27 87 06

Confrérie "Mycogastronomique Gaillarde"
Monsieur Jean-Pierre Faucher
Hôtel-Restaurant le Petit Clos
Le Pouret
19270 Ussac
05 55 86 12 65

Vins, apéritifs et liqueurs traditionnels

Bellet Distillerie à Brive-la-Gaillard
Liqueurs et apéritifs à base de châtaigne, Gentiane-Bellet (apéritif),
plantes aromatiques de montagne.
3, avenue du Maréchal Bugeaud
Brive-La-Gaillarde
05 55 24 18 07

DENOIX
Quinqui Noix and Moutarde Violette de Brive
Distillerie – Boutique – Cave
9, boulevard Maréchal Lyautey, 19100 Brive
05 55 74 34 27
www.denoix.com

Distillerie de la Salers
Salers gentiane, Salers (sirop tonic à la gentiane)
Montaignac Saint-Hippolyte, Egletons
05 55 27 61 01

Domaine des Volcans
Liqueur de Châtaigne, Liqueur de Myrtilles, Apéritif à la Gentiane "La
Planèze", Framboise des Orgues.
Des Volcans, Bort-les-Orgues

Elie-Arnaud Denoix
19500 Collonges-la-Rouge
05 55 25 44 72
Apéritifs, petites liqueurs et eaux de vie de fruits

Les Vignerons de Branceilles
Vin de Pays de la Corrèze
Cave Viticole de Branceilles, 19500 Branceilles

Rougerie et Fils
R.N. 89, Maussac
19250 Meymac
05 55 95 11 43
Fabrications de liqueurs de fruits et du pays

Vignoble des Mille et une Pierre
Monsieur Pierre Perrinet
Cave Viticole de Branceilles
19500 Branceilles
05 55 84 09 01

Les défenseurs du patrimoine culinaire
(The defenders of culinary heritage)

Monsieur Charlou Reynal, whose books include:
"Mes recettes du terroir" - Editions Olivier Orban
"Dictionnaire de la cuisine du Limousin" - Editions Bonneton

Monsieur Luc de Goustine
Le Crouzet
19300 Moustier Ventadour
05 55 93 04 84

Monsieur Daniel Borzeix (see confrérie)
Le Loubanel
19260 Treignac
05 55 98 02 54

A few more handy Websites

Bienvenue en Corrèze
www.correze.org

Corrèze Net
www.correze.net

Corrèze Office de Tourisme
www.tourisme.fr/office-de-tourisme/correze

Guide de l'Hebergement de Vacances en Corrèze
www.vacances-correze.com

Logis de France
www.logis-de-france.fr

Hôtels et Restaurants de la Corrèze

"My apologies to any hotels and restaurants which I may have not included in this fairly extensive list."

Name	Street	Town	Telephone	Fax
Auberge Limoussine	Les Quatre Routes	19380 Albussac	05 55 28 15 83	05 55 28 11 78
Roche de Vic	Les Quatre Routes	19380 Albussac	05 55 28 15 83	05 55 28 01 09
Chateau du Doux		19120 Altillac	05 55 91 94 00	05 55 91 94 10
Hotel Fouillade	Place Gambetta	19400 Argentat	05 55 28 10 17	05 55 28 90 52
L'Auberge des Gabariers	15 Quai de Lestourgie	19400 Argentat	05 55 28 05 87	
Le Gambetta	15, place Gambetta	19400 Argentat	05 55 28 16 08	
Le Sablier du Temps	13 avenue J. Vachal	19400 Argentat	05 55 28 94 90	05 55 28 94 99
La St Jaques	39, avenue Foch	19400 Argentat		
Auberge de la Mandrie	Route de Perigeaux-Lanouaille	19230 Arnac-Pompadour	05 55 73 37 14	05 55 73 67 13
Auberge de la Marquise	4, avenue des Ecuyers	19230 Arnac-Pompadour	05 55 73 33 98	05 55 73 69 30
Hotel du Parc	1, place du Vieux-Lavoir	19230 Arnac-Pompadour	05 55 73 30 54	05 55 73 39 79
Hotel de Coiroux		19190 Aubazine	05 55 25 75 22	05 55 25 75 70
Hotel Saint-Etienne	Le Bourg	19190 Aubazine	05 55 25 71 01	05 55 25 71 37
Hotel de la Tour	Place de l'Eglise	19190 Aubazine	05 55 25 71 17	05 55 84 61 83
L'Auvergnassou		19430 Bassignac-le-Bas	05 55 28 51 41	
Hotel Chateau de Chauvac		19430 Bassignac-le-Bas		
Central Hotel Fournie	4, place du Champ de Mars	19120 Beaulieu sur Dordogne	05 55 91 01 34	05 55 91 23 57
Les Charmilles		19120 Beaulieu sur Dordogne	05 55 91 29 29	05 55 91 29 30
Le Turenne	1, boulevarde Sainte Rodolphe	19120 Beaulieu sur Dordogne	05 55 91 10 16	05 55 91 22 42
Le La Fontaine	Lac de Miel	19190 Beynat	05 55 22 01 82	
Le Rider	701, avenue de la gare	19110 Bort-les-Orgues	05 55 96 00 47	05 55 96 73 07
Hotel Beausejour	33, avenue Abbe-Jean-Alvitre	19100 Brive-la-Gaillard	05 55 87 47 98	
La Chapon Fin	1, place de Lattre-de-Tassigny	19100 Brive-la-Gaillard	05 55 74 23 40	05 55 23 42 52

Name	Street	Town	Telephone	Fax
Le Chene Vert	Boulevard Jules-Ferry	19100 Brive-la-Gaillard	05 55 24 10 07	05 55 24 25 73
Le Collanges	3 – 5, place Winston Churchill	19100 Brive-la-Gaillard	05 55 74 09 58	05 55 74 11 25
Hotel Le Coq d'Or	16, boulevard Jules-Ferry	19100 Brive-la-Gaillard	05 55 17 12 92	
La Cremaillere	53, avenue de Paris	19100 Brive-la-Gaillard	05 55 86 97 97	05 55 86 85 02
Hotel Le Quercy	8 bis, quai Tourny	19100 Brive-la-Gaillard	05 55 74 09 26	05 55 74 06 24
Hotel Mercure	Z.I. Cana	19100 Brive-la-Gaillard	05 55 86 36 36	05 55 87 04 40
Hotel Le Montauban	6, avenue Edouard-Herriot	19100 Brive-la-Gaillard	05 55 24 00 38	05 55 84 80 30
Le Teinchurier	7, avenue du Treinchurier	19100 Brive-la-Gaillard	05 55 86 45 00	05 55 86 45 45
La Truffe Noire	22, boulevard Anatole France	19100 Brive-la-Gaillard	05 55 92 45 00	05 55 92 45 13
La Perigourdine	15, av' Alsace-Lorraine	19100 Brive-la-Gaillard	05 55 24 26 55	
Hotel Rerstaurant du Lac	Le Bourg	19430 Camps	05 55 28 51 83	05 55 28 53 71
Hotel du France	5, place du Marche	19370 Chamberet	05 55 98 30 14	05 55 73 47 15
Hotel Deshors-Foujanet	Le Bourg	19450 Chamboulive	05 55 21 62 05	05 55 21 68 80
Auberge des Bruyeres	Le Bourg	19390 Chaumeil	05 55 21 34 68	05 55 21 44 10
Hotel du Lac		19320 Clergoux	05 55 27 77 60	05 55 27 66 34
St-Jacques-de-Compastelle	Le Bourg	19500 Collanges La Rouge	05 55 25 41 02	05 55 84 08 51
Auberge de l'Etang	La Ville en Bois – RN 89	19250 Combressol	05 55 94 21 96	05 55 94 21 21
Le Pecheur de Lune	Place de la Mairie	19800 Correze	05 55 21 44 93	
La Seniorie de Correze	Le Bourg	19800 Correze	05 55 21 22 88	05 55 21 24 00
Lucette Conchon		19500 Curemont	05 55 25 43 29	
Auberge du Presbytere	Le Bourg	19300 Darnets	05 55 93 37 37	
Hotel La Gamade	Place Leon Madrias	19270 Donzenac	05 55 85 71 07	05 55 85 65 83
Hotel Borie	24, avenue Charles-de-Gaulle	19300 Egletons	05 55 93 12 00	
Le Jardin de Ventadour	1, place du Marchadial	19300 Egletons	05 55 93 10 57	
Le Vieux Puits	1, place de l'Eglise	19150 Espagnac		
Hostellerie de la Vallee	Rue des Cascades	19800 Gimel-Les-Cascades	05 55 21 40 60	05 55 21 38 74
Le Relais du Teulet	Le Teulet-Nationale 120	19430 Goulles	05 55 28 71 09	05 55 28 74 39

Name	Street	Town	Telephone	Fax
L'Auberge Limousine	Rue Saule	19320 La Roche Canillac	05 55 29 12 06	
Le Relais Saint-Jacques	RN 89	19800 La Bitarelle de Gimel	05 55 21 26 63	05 55 21 25 57
Le Central	Le Bourg	19150 Lagarde-Enval	05 55 27 16 12	05 55 27 31 85
Auberge du Rochefort	Rochefort"	19470 Le Lonzac	05 55 97 93 42	
Le Relais Lissacois	Le Bourg	19600 Lissac	05 55 85 39 15	
Hotel Le Souham	14, rue Souham	19120 Lubersac	05 55 73 56 51	05 55 73 95 01
Auberge Vieux Chenes	31, avenue Balzac	19360 Malemort	05 55 24 13 55	
Hotel de la Tour	Place Marcel-Champeix	19510 Masseret	05 55 73 40 12	05 55 73 49 41
Hotel Le Chavanon	Le Bourg	19340 Merlines	05 55 94 84 00	05 55 94 84 01
Hotel Le Limousine	78, avenue Limousine	19250 Meymac	05 55 46 12 11	05 55 46 12 12
Le Meymacoise	24, avenue Limousine	19250 Meymac	05 55 95 16 45	05 55 95 13 89
Le Relais du Quercy	Avenue du Quercy	19500 Meyssac	05 55 25 40 31	05 55 25 36 22
Chez Francoise	24, rue Fontaine du Rat	19250 Meymac	05 55 95 10 63	
Ferme Auberge de la Jonchere	La Jonchere	19400 Monceaux-sur-Dordogne	05 55 28 04 75	
Ferme-Auberge du Chastagne	Monceaux-sur-Dordogne	19400 Monceaux-sur-Dordogne	05 55 28 04 75	
La Maison aux Quat'Saisons	Laborie	19400 Monceaux-sur-Dordogne	05 55 91 28 09	
L'Oustal	Le Bourg	19460 Naves	05 55 26 62 42	05 55 26 06 06
Auberge de la Route SE	N20	19460 Naves		
Chateau de Mialaret	Route d'Egletons	19160 Neuvic	05 55 46 02 50	05 55 46 02 65
Hotel du Lac	La Plage	19160 Neuvic	05 55 95 81 43	05 55 95 05 15
Delage et Rey	53, av' Jean Lascaux	19130 Objat	05 55 84 12 50	
Hotel de France	12, av' Georges-Clemenceau	19130 Objat	05 55 25 80 38	05 55 25 91 87
Auberge de la Mandrie	Route de Perigueux	19230 Pompadour	05 55 73 37 14	05 55 73 67 13
Relais du Bas Limousin	R.N. 20 – Lafonsalade	19270 Sadroc	05 55 84 52 06	05 55 84 51 41
Hotel de la Maleyrie	Croix-Maleyrie – R.N. 20	19270 Sadroc	05 55 84 50 67	05 55 84 20 63
Relais des Monedieres	34, Montargis	19700 Seilhac	05 55 27 04 74	05 55 27 90 03

Name	Street	Town	Telephone	Fax
Auberge Bellevue	7, route de Bellevue	19130 Saint-Aulaire	05 55 25 81 39	05 55 84 12 01
Le Saint Hilaire	D 940	19170 Saint Hilaire les Courbes	05 55 95 68 34	05 55 95 43 68
Auberge de St-Julien-aux-Bois	Le Bourg	19220 Saint-Julien-aux-Bois	05 55 28 41 94	05 55 28 37 85
Les Voyageurs	Place de la Mairie	19320 St-Martin la Meanne	05 55 29 11 53	05 55 29 27 70
Rendez-Vous de Pecheurs	Pont du Chambon	19320 Saint Merd de Lapleau	05 55 27 88 39	05 55 27 83 19
Hotel Beau Site		19320 Marcillac-La-Croisille	05 55 27 79 44	05 55 27 69 52
Le Moulin de Lachaud		19490 Sainte-Forunade	05 55 27 30 95	
Soph'Motel	Le Croix-de-Fer – R.N. 20	19270 Saint-Pardoux-l'Ortigier	05 55 84 51 02	05 55 84 50 14
Auberge de la Xaintrie		19220 St-Privat	05 55 28 49 80	
La Ferme du Leondou	Le Bourg	19700 Saint-Salvadour	05 55 21 60 04	
Hotel de Rieux	Le Rieux	19240 Saint-Viance	05 55 85 01 49	05 55 84 26 33
Le Jardin de Saint-Viance	Le Bourg	19240 Saint-Viance	05 55 85 00 50	05 55 84 25 36
Auberge Saint Roch	Le Bourg	19140 Saint Ybard	05 55 73 09 71	05 55 73 09 71
Hotel des Voyageurs	Le Bourg	19170 Tarnac	05 55 95 53 12	05 55 95 40 07
Hotel du Lac	Les Bariousses	19260 Treignac	04 89 88 40 91	
La Brasserie		19260 Treignac	05 55 98 03 62	05 55 73 43 18
Hotel-Restaurant de la Gare	25, avenue Winston-Churchill	19000 Tulle	05 55 20 04 04	05 55 26 15 87
Restaurant Le Central	32, rue Jean Jaures	19000 Tulle		
Hotel Terminus	13, avenue Winston-Churchill	19000 Tulle	05 55 20 02 93	
La Toque Blance	30, rue Jean-Jaures	19000 Tulle	05 55 26 75 41	05 55 20 93 95
Hotel Le Dunant	136, avenue Victor-Hugo	19000 Tulle	05 55 20 15 42	05 55 26 70 50
Hotel Le Royal	70, avenue Victor-Hugo	19000 Tulle	05 55 20 04 52	05 55 20 93 63
Limouzi Ventadour	16, quai de la Republique	19000 Tulle	05 55 26 42 00	05 55 20 31 17
Le Central	12, 14 rue de la Barriere	19000 Tulle	05 55 26 24 46	05 55 26 53 16
L'entracte	1 bis, place Carnot	19000 Tulle	05 55 20 82 87	05 55 20 27 00
La Taverne du Sommelier	8 quai de la Republique	19000 Tulle	05 55 26 57 63	05 55 26 65 70
Le Petit Clos	Le Pouret	19270 Ussac	05 55 86 12 65	05 55 86 94 32

Name	Street	Town	Telephone	Fax
Auberge Saint-Jean	5, place de l'Eglise – Le Bourg	19270 Ussac	05 55 88 30 20	05 55 87 28 50
Grand Hotel de la Gare	Avenue Pierre-Semard	19200 Ussel	05 55 72 25 98	05 55 96 25 63
Hotel les Gravades	RN 89 – Saint Dezery	19200 Ussel	05 55 46 06 00	05 55 46 06 10
Hotel du Midi	24, avenue Thiers	19200 Ussel	05 55 72 17 99	
Hotel Ambroise	34, avenue de Paris	19140 Uzerche	05 55 73 28 60	
Hotel Moderne	Avenue Charles-de-Gaulle	19140 Uzerche	05 55 73 12 23	05 55 98 83 18
Hotel Telyssier	Rue du Pont-Turgot	19140 Uzerche	05 55 73 10 05	05 55 98 43 31
Domaine de Castel Novel	Route d'Objat	19240 Vartez	05 55 85 00 01	05 55 85 09 03
Le Relais Gourmand	10, av' du 11 Novembre	19240 Vartez	05 55 85 06 96	05 55 84 43 78
Hotel Roque	10, avenue de 11-Novembre	19240 Vartez	05 55 85 06 96	
L'Auberge du Lac	Le Bourg	19170 Viam	05 55 95 43 80	
Hotel du Midi	Place du Champ-de-Foire	19410 Vigeois	05 55 98 90 45	05 55 98 95 30

Some of the French-based books
published by the Léonie Press:

A BULL BY THE BACK
DOOR
by ANNE LOADER

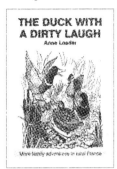

THE DUCK WITH A DIRTY
LAUGH by ANNE LOADER
ISBN 1 901253 0 90 £8.99

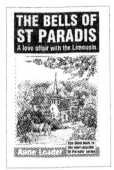

THE BELLS OF ST PARADIS
by ANNE LOADER
ISBN 1 901253 26 0 £9.99

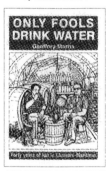

ONLY FOOLS DRINK WATER
by GEOFFREY MORRIS
ISBN 1 901253 10 4 £8.99

OU EST LE 'PING'?
by GRACE McKEE
ISBN 1 901253 11 2 £7.99

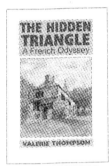

THE HIDDEN TRIANGLE
by VALERIE THOMPSON
ISBN 1 901253 32 5 £8.99

LILAC AND ROSES
by PEGGY ANDERSON
ISBN 1 901253 22 8 £8.99

BANANAS IN BORDEAUX
LOUISE FRANKLIN CASTANET
ISBN 1 901253 29 5 £10.99

POLLY TAKES THE SCENIC
ROUTE by GAY PYPER
ISBN 1 901253 33 3 £8.99

For more details visit our website: www.leoniepress.com